THE MIDDLE WESTERN FARM NOVEL
IN THE TWENTIETH CENTURY

The Middle Western Farm Novel in the Twentieth Century

by

Roy W. Meyer

UNIVERSITY OF NEBRASKA PRESS · LINCOLN

Some of the material in Chapter III appeared in somewhat different form in the September 1959 issue of *The American-Scandinavian Review* (Vol. XLVII, No. 3) and is here used with permission. Likewise, some of the material in Chapters II and IV appeared in slightly different form in the Spring 1961 issue of the *Journal of the Central Mississippi Valley American Studies Association* (Vol. II, No. 1), now published as the *Midcontinent American Studies Journal*, and is used here by permission.

Publishers on the Plains

UNP

813.09
M613m
10658 /

Manufactured in the United States of America

To my Father and Mother,
whose lifetime of farming has taught me both
the advantages and the limitations of farm life

Contents

THE MIDDLE WESTERN FARM NOVEL
IN THE TWENTIETH CENTURY

Introduction

IN THE YEARS between 1891 and 1962 at least 140 novels appeared dealing with farm life in the Middle West. Many of them, including some of the best, took as their theme the pioneer experience, often coupled with the parallel experience of the immigrant's adjustment to American conditions; others centered their attention on the philosophical question of whether the farm is a desirable or an undesirable place to live; some entered the realm of social and economic criticism, and a few approached proletarian fiction; still others treated the psychological and emotional problems of human beings in a rural setting. Taken together, this body of fiction constitutes a genre as distinctive as that analyzed by Blanche Housman Gelfant in *The American City Novel* and perhaps comparable to that treated by Walter B. Rideout in *The Radical Novel in America, 1900–1934*.

Considering the oft-repeated call for the use by American writers of native materials, a call answered as early as the eighteenth century by such men as Royall Tyler and Charles Brockden Brown, it was inevitable that agriculture, which until about 1890 engaged most of the nation's population, should sooner or later be treated in literature. For reasons which will be discussed later, however, the use of rural life as the substance of serious fiction was delayed until about the time when the United States changed from a predominantly rural to a predominantly urban country. But when such fiction began to be written, in the 1880's and 1890's, it became a vogue and eventually appeared in great quantity. From the initial efforts of Joseph Kirkland and Hamlin Garland, the number of farm novels published increased slowly until after World War I, when the genre burgeoned suddenly, perhaps, as John T. Frederick suggests, as the result of a "heightened cultural nationalism" in the 1920's.[1] From 1920 to 1945 the

[1] John T. Frederick, "The Farm in Iowa Fiction," *Palimpsest*, XXXII (March 1951), 127.

output of middle western farm fiction alone averaged four novels annually, with the greatest concentration coming in the 1930's. Although this fiction did not rank so high qualitatively as quantitatively, it did include some of the most popular fiction of the period and a number of prize-winning novels; Pulitzer prize awards went to Willa Cather in 1923, Margaret Wilson in 1924, Edna Ferber in 1925, Louis Bromfield in 1927, and Josephine Johnson in 1934.

Despite the unquestioned merit of a few farm novels, as well as the sheer bulk of farm fiction generally, not a great deal of scholarly criticism has been written on the subject. Several articles have appeared, notably those by John T. Flanagan, Caroline B. Sherman, and John T. Frederick, and some individual authors, such as Cather, Bromfield, and Rölvaag, have been studied in detail (though not specifically as writers of farm fiction), but there has thus far been no full-length examination of the whole genre in the region where it has chiefly flourished—the Middle West.

For purposes of convenience, the Middle West may be defined as that great central area of the nation, including the twelve states of Ohio, Indiana, Illinois, Michigan, Wisconsin, Minnesota, Iowa, Missouri, Kansas, Nebraska, South Dakota, and North Dakota. A few novels dealing with the adjacent prairie provinces of Canada have been included in this study, since the social and economic environment described in them is quite similar to that south of the international boundary. This vast region is one of immense diversity, and the Finn or Yugoslav grubbing out stumps in the cutover country of the western Great Lakes states may have little in common with the homesteader who combines ranching with a little wheat farming on the Dakota plains west of the Missouri River. Yet both are middle westerners, and the experiences of both are reflected in the literature of this region.

Restricting a survey of farm fiction largely to the Middle West and to the twentieth century does not constitute a serious limitation. Except for novels by Kirkland and Garland, there was in the nineteenth century virtually no real farm fiction, in the sense in which the term is here used. Furthermore, as Caroline B. Sherman noted in 1938, "Middle Western novels were far ahead in number and usually in quality," when the modern farm novel emerged.[2] Of 141 American novels of known locale listed in *Book Review Digest* under "Farm Life" between 1917 and 1962, more than half—77—were middle western. This compares with 26 from the northeastern states, 17 from the South, 14 from the Southwest, and 7 from the Northwest. Besides the 77 listed in *Book Review Digest* under the "Farm Life" heading, my annotated bibliography includes 59 other farm novels set in the Middle West, as well as 4 novels dealing with the adjacent Canadian area.[3] A sampling of farm novels from other regions indicates that novels dealing with other regions generally display the same characteristics that distinguish middle western farm fiction.

In this study I have repeatedly stressed the primary significance of farm fiction as social commentary rather than its secondary importance as artistic creation. Yet the two are by no means distinct. Novels on any subject are most valuable as social documents if they are also artistically satisfying. The primacy of the former is here insisted upon chiefly to justify the inclusion and sometimes detailed treatment of novels that admittedly have little esthetic merit. As Caroline Sherman observed in the article previously cited, farm fiction, to the extent that it represents a definite school, is characterized by material rather than by method. Consequently the novels discussed here are treated according to their subject or theme rather than according to their form. Some pigeonholing is inevitable with such a system of organization, but that would be true no matter what plan was adopted. A strictly chronological approach, while ideal to illustrate phases in the evolution of the farm novel, would entail rather forced comparisons between books alike only in that they deal with farm life and were published at about the same time.

[2] Caroline B. Sherman, "The Development of American Rural Fiction," *Agricultural History*, XII (January 1938), 70.

[3] The choice of locale within the Middle West may be of some interest. The 136 American novels listed in my annotated bibliography divide themselves as follows, on the basis of state treated: Iowa, 31; Minnesota, 19; South Dakota, 15; Nebraska, 12; Illinois, 11; Michigan, 9; Wisconsin, 9; Missouri, 8; Kansas, 7; Ohio, 6; North Dakota, 4; and Indiana, 3. Two are vaguely middle western, unidentifiable as to state.

I have, however, tried to secure the advantages of such an approach by maintaining a generally chronological order within each subject-matter division and by presenting in the last chapter some generalizations on technical developments in the farm novel since Garland's trailbreaking in the 1890's.

The pigeonholing is most evident in the case of novels or novelists that straddle the lines between these arbitrarily imposed categories. Common sense has been the guide in such instances. If a novel is concerned with more than one subject—for example, if it treats of both the pioneer experience and of the immigrant's struggle to adjust to conditions in a new land—it is discussed under the heading of what seems to me its dominant theme, with cross-references to the subsidiary themes. Since this is a study of the novel rather than of the novelist, if an author has written books which fall into different categories, the books are treated in separate chapters.

It should be noted also that the word "rural," used in reference to a population group, is here synonymous with "farm." The Census Bureau's policy of grouping all communities of less than 2500 inhabitants under the heading of "rural" is misleading, for the businessman in a town of 1500 feels that he has more in common with his business colleague in a city of 100,000 than with the farmer whose patronage he solicits. This urban orientation has not always been the case, but it has come to be increasingly prevalent in the twentieth century. As one study of the rural scene has noted, speaking of the period since 1900, "The time had been when the country town fronted toward the farm and was principally identified with rural life; now the town fronted rather toward the city, imitated the city, and, as fast as it could manage, moved to the city."[4]

With this point in mind, we can begin our examination of the middle western farm novel. Our first task will be to determine just what a farm novel is and how it differs from other types of fiction, including that which deals incidentally and peripherally with farm life.

[4] Theodore Saloutos and John D. Hicks, *Agricultural Discontent in the Middle West 1900–1939* (Madison: University of Wisconsin Press, 1951), pp. 26–27.

I.

What Is a Farm Novel?

By DEFINITION, a literary genre has characteristics that set it apart from other literary genres. These may be either of style or of content; frequently both are involved. Because the farm novel seems to possess no discernible uniqueness in point of style, it follows that its claim to genre status must rest upon the distinctiveness of its subject and its handling of that subject.

The first and most essential condition that a novel must meet in order to qualify as farm fiction is that it deal with farm life. Its setting must be the farm, at least through a large part of the action, and most of its important characters must be farm people. This requirement necessarily excludes novels, like some of those by Ruth Suckow, which concern chiefly village life and touch only tangentially on the affairs of the open country. Even Phil Stong's *Village Tale*, which takes place in a community of some twenty houses, is not properly a farm novel, for the chief characters are not farmers, and farm life is depicted only incidentally. Although the country town usually has a number of retired farmers in its population, they do not form a dominant element in the community, and often there is a sharp line of social demarcation between them and the people who run the affairs of the town.

Besides the obvious fact that a farm novel concerns incidents that take place on farms, there are several distinguishing features that should be present in such a novel if it reflects the realities of farm life with sufficient accuracy to be classified as genuine farm fiction. The criteria used in this evaluation are: accurate handling of the physical details of farm life; the use of the vernacular; and the reflection of certain attitudes, beliefs, or habits of mind often associated with farm people, of which the most important are conservatism, individualism, anti-intellectualism, hostility to the town, and a type of primitivism.

7

Accurate handling of the physical details of farm life, particularly activities peculiar to farming. This is a useful standard to employ in distinguishing between genuine farm novels and the work of city-bred authors who sought to capitalize on the popularity of farm fiction in the 1930's and early 1940's by writing on matters of which they really knew very little. Authentic farm fiction, the product of writers whose knowledge of rural life is sound and extensive, will reproduce with great fidelity the daily and seasonal tasks of the farmer and his family, their amusements and social activities, and the sights, sounds, and smells of the physical environment in which they live. Although the critic can —indeed must—rely to some extent on his own knowledge and experience in judging the accuracy of an author's treatment of this kind of detail, the circumstances of farm life vary so greatly from one section of the Middle West to another that no one could possibly be an authority on all of them. Thus the amount of detail often must be used as a criterion for determining the author's familiarity with his material. In general, one may assume that the more details an author uses, the more he knows about the kind of farm life he is describing, and the fewer details, the less he knows. Changing literary tastes must also be taken into account. For example, novels written before 1920 are likely to make less use of physical detail than novels written after 1930. The author's intention also figures in the matter. A writer attempting to give his novel a sociological significance will ordinarily use more details than one telling a conventional love story in a more or less incidental rural setting.

Use of the vernacular. Since the time of Edward Eggleston, if not earlier, writers have been concerned about reproducing the speech patterns of their characters in such a way as to give an authentic flavor to the dialogue. To be successful an author has had to possess a high degree of familiarity with the local vocabulary, idiom, and pronunciation, and hence his effectiveness has been limited largely to geographical regions with which he is well acquainted. In some cases he has depended upon a natural skill at hearing and reproducing everyday speech; in other cases he has relied upon deliberate and painstaking research. Some early writers, such as Edgar Watson Howe, paid little attention to dialogue, and their characters all sound much alike. Since 1900, however, the attempt to represent speech patterns has been almost universal. Furthermore, many authors have attempted to use a modification of the vernacular for expository passages, so that the contrast between the author's English and that of his characters, strongly evident in such an early novel as Kirkland's *Zury*, is scarcely noticeable. This technique tends to minimize the effect of the novel's having been written by an outsider and, by bringing the author nearer to his characters, lessens the distance between the reader and those characters.

Reflection, and perhaps acceptance by the author, of certain attitudes, beliefs, or habits of mind characteristic of farm people. This is an important criterion; and although any list of such traits may seem somewhat arbitrary, those following are indisputably taken from life and actually were typical of many farmers.

Despite many exceptions to the rule, farmers have long had a reputation for *conservatism*—political, economic, and cultural. They were portrayed in most of the farm novels as typically suspicious of innovation in any of these spheres, as shown by their tendency to vote for the political party their fathers voted for (a tendency not limited to farmers, of course), their resistance to technological change and new methods of farming, the persistence of the established religious bodies in rural areas, and their hostility or indifference to most forms of large-scale collective action.

The institutions to which the fictional farmer clung most tenaciously were the rural church, the rural school, and the family. Farmers were frequently pictured as more religious as a group than city people; although a good deal of unexpressed agnosticism might exist, the declared atheist usually had a rough time in the country. Sectarian rivalry of course existed in rural areas, sometimes between competing churches of one denomination, a situation occasionally mirrored in farm novels. The rural school also served as a center of community activity and local identity; and the farmer in fiction resisted school consolidation because he believed that by forming a school district in common with a town and sending his children there he would lose control both of the school and of his children. A common theme was the farmer's children attending school in town, losing contact with the farm and developing interests and associations that caused them to leave the farm permanently, and marrying outside the circle of the neighborhood known to their families. The farm family was also seen as emphasizing patriarchal authority, a clear-cut division of labor on the basis of sex and age, strictness and reticence in regard to sex, and a high sense of responsibility to the aged, the sick, and the handicapped. Economic conservatism has been portrayed particularly in such matters as the mechanization of farming operations, the conflict between land exploitation and conservation, and the transition from self-sufficiency to commercial agriculture.

Likewise, the farmer was customarily credited with being the supreme exponent of *individualism* in America. To his individualism was attributed his failure to achieve effective collective action, especially in the economic sphere. The farmer who was willing enough to extend aid to an injured neighbor or to participate in a barn-raising was extremely suspicious of action which involved his cooperation with hundreds or thousands of other farmers unknown to him personally toward a long-range objective. This characterization has been frequently used in farm fiction; and in the more perceptive studies of farm life, especially those written since 1930, the gradual weakening of the farmer's individualism in the face of modern collectivist trends is shown with skill and understanding.

Farm people were also pictured as displaying a conspicuous strain of *anti-intellectualism*, which often took the form of the notion that only physical labor deserved to be called labor. Businessmen (the much maligned "middlemen"), bankers, professional people, white-collar workers, government employees—all were relegated to an inferior position because, since they did not earn their living by manual labor, they did not really earn it at all. On its crudest level anti-intellectualism appeared in the contempt shown toward the youth who taught in the district school by his brothers who remained home and did the farm work; on a higher level it was manifested in the charges of parasitism hurled at the "unproductive middleman." More clearly identifiable as anti-intellectualism, however, was the widespread suspicion on the part of the fictional farmer of higher education and of recommendations made by agricultural colleges and experiment stations. A stock figure of scorn was the "book farmer," full of impractical ideas but devoid of common sense.

The farmer was also seen as *hostile to and suspicious of the town.* Despite the symbiotic relationship of farmers and town-dwellers, the farmer accused the town merchant of exploiting him, and the merchant dismissed the farmer as a hayseed. But the feeling extended beyond the economic and social sphere, into the deepest emotional stratum of man's being. The town—and the large city and the small village were seen as different only in degree—was the natural dwelling place of evil, just as the country was both the place of origin and the last refuge of good. The boy or girl who went to town to work was sure to be subjected to temptations he would never have encountered in the country and was very likely to fall victim to them.

Related to hostility toward the town is a kind of *primitivism* expressed in farm fiction that saw farm life, with its intimate association with the soil and the forces of nature, as intrinsically more wholesome and more natural than life in a largely man-made environment. Sometimes this idea appears on a simple biological level: fresh air and hard physical work exert a sanative influence on human beings; at other times it approaches a mystical concept of the essential unity of man with nature, a unity spiritual as well as physical. A good expression of both levels of thought, emphasizing the concomitant idea of urban life as fundamentally bad, is found in a paper entitled "Thoughts of Thinking People," by one of the leading farm novelists, Ole Edvart Rölvaag. He says, in part,

> The inhabitants of the large town do not envy the country man and would not change with him. But unknown to themselves, they are leading an unnatural life, cut off from the kindly and wholesome influence of nature, surrounded by vulgarity and ugliness, with no traditions, no loyalties, no culture, and no religion. . . . The life of the town artisan who works in a factory is a life to which the human organism has not adapted itself; it is an unwholesome and unnatural condition.[1]

[1] Quoted in Theodore Jorgensen and Nora O. Solum, *Ole Edvart Rölvaag: A Biography* (New York: Harper and Brothers, 1939), pp. 353–354.

Whether such a view was in fact ever consciously held by any appreciable number of farmers would be difficult to judge; it does, in any case, appear frequently in the novels under investigation in this study. Perhaps here is a situation in which literature defines rather than reflects a set of attitudes or beliefs. The greater sophistication of the novelist may enable him to detect and state an attitude of which the farmer himself is not entirely aware.

All these attitudes and beliefs are to be found repeated again and again in farm fiction. In fact, a novel displaying none of them would be difficult to justify as an authentic piece of farm fiction, for it would not be true to the realities of American rural life. On the other hand, a novel which gave no evidence of anti-intellectualism but instead showed a group of people deeply concerned about the education of their children, might be entirely acceptable. The opposite of any of these attitudes may be encountered in farm novels, as in real life, sometimes in surprising juxtapositions which the novelist is hard pressed to make credible.

The above criteria are intended to provide guidelines for our examination of middle western farm fiction. Although attention will be concentrated chiefly on those novels which possess the greatest artistic merit, some esthetically inferior works are treated because they display with unusual clarity certain of the characteristics just discussed and are therefore more representative of the middle western farm novel than the really distinguished productions. Since the origins of twentieth-century rural fiction are to be found in the last century, it will first be necessary to give some consideration to the treatment of farm life in the 1800's.

II.

The Farm in Nineteenth-Century Fiction

FICTION WHICH treats farm life seriously, realistically, and as the main subject is largely a phenomenon of the twentieth century. Paradoxically, during the nineteenth century, when the United States was a predominantly rural country, treatment of farmers and their lives was chiefly romantic or else occurred only incidentally, as background for a conventional love plot in which the principals were not farm people. Only when the transition had taken place late in the nineteenth century, and the urban population outnumbered the rural did authentic farm fiction appear in quantity and variety. One of the earliest writers to use a rural setting for her fiction, Alice Carey, suggested in the preface to *Clovernook* (1852) why farm life had been so long neglected:

> The pastoral life of our country has not been a favorite subject of illustration by painters, poets, or writers of romance. Perhaps it has been regarded as wanting in the elements of beauty; perhaps it has been thought too passionless and even; or it may have been deemed too immediate and familiar.[1]

This is not to say that the rural scene was totally neglected in nineteenth-century fiction; it was too much a part of the experience of a large body of readers and too familiar to the rest to be omitted altogether from the picture. But the portrayal of the farm was essentially romantic, unrealistic, and often patronizing. The picture of the farm that appears in the sentimental novel is probably characteristic. Herbert Ross Brown, in his study of this type of fiction, finds country life given a prominent place:

> The old homestead, aching with sentimental memories of lost sweetness, became a popular subject of panegyrics in domestic fiction.

[1] Alice Carey, *Clovernook, or Recollections of Our Neighborhood in the West* (First Series; New York: J. S. Redfield, 1852), p. v. The correct spelling of the author's name is Cary, but at the time the book was published both she and her sister Phoebe temporarily spelled it Carey.

13

> . . . There it stood in novel after novel: its broad barns bursting with
> yellow grain, its chimneys suggesting friendly hearthstones and long
> winter evenings. Cool parlors, clean dairies, cosy kitchens, graceful
> well-sweeps, sunny meadows, pleasant orchards—all these were heavily
> freighted with memories kept alive by widely scattered sons and
> daughters who were forced to live in dusty cities.

Among the characters in these novels he found "such familiar
figures as the venerable patriarch conducting family worship or
presiding proudly at family dinner, the stalwart sons and buxom
wives, their rosy children, and the faithful hired man."[2]

This nostalgic, idealized, saccharine interpretation of farm
life is so prevalent in nineteenth-century fiction as to require
mention here, but so stereotyped as to be adequately represented
by a few examples. Since only the older settled regions of the
country provided the stability necessary to this portrayal, such
novels concerned chiefly the East and the South. The eastern
fringe of the Middle West had been settled long enough, however, to lend it something of the same appearance of stability.
So we have in Miss Carey's *Clovernook, or Recollections of Our
Neighborhood in the West* (First Series, 1852; Second Series,
1853) precisely the kind of fiction just discussed. Not properly
novels but collections of short stories unified by locale, time, and
narrator, the two series of *Clovernook* sketches illustrate most if
not all of the sentimental stereotypes mentioned by Brown.
Among the characters who occur and recur in these pages are
the poor relative, usually badly treated; the forsaken damsel; the
Byronic young man, full of melancholy and self-pity; the heavy
drinker; and—though the locale is southwestern Ohio—the faithful darky who "knows her place." Honest poverty is repeatedly
contrasted with corrupt wealth, and the superiority of rural to
city life is stressed again and again. As in other sentimental fiction, death is used with extraordinary frequency as a solution to
difficult problems; more than half the stories either end with the
death of a major character or include the death of someone else.
The "Conclusion" to the Second Series of *Clovernook* stories
amounts to a defense of death and poverty as positive goods,

[2] Herbert Ross Brown, *The Sentimental Novel in America 1789–1860* (Durham: Duke University Press, 1940), pp. 283–284.

making explicit what is implicit in many of the stories. The physical details of farm life are rendered without too much idealization, but farm work is treated throughout as healthful, if hard.

Perhaps the best example of this sentimental kind of farm fiction is one with an eastern setting, Bayard Taylor's *The Story of Kennett* (1866). Taylor's novel is especially useful because it was written in a period of nascent realism and thus shows the persistence of the earlier romanticism in the post–Civil War period. Kennett is a rural township in the Brandywine district of eastern Pennsylvania. The action, which takes place in 1796 and 1797, centers about a group of landed gentry, most of whom do little or no actual labor in the fields. Their diversions consist of fox-hunting and organizing ineffective posses to bring to justice a Robin Hood type of highwayman who, on one occasion at least, joins their fox hunt in disguise. The novel has all the conventional claptrap: a love affair in the face of parental disapproval, a mortgaged farm, a weak villain, a rob-the-rich-to-help-the-poor outlaw, a lovable caricature of a spinster who serves as a *dea ex machina* when apparently insoluble problems arise, and a great deal of gothic mystery reminiscent of Charles Brockden Brown. That the action takes place in a farm environment is pretty much incidental. The hero labors to pay off the mortgage on his mother's farm, but he is not shown working, except in one scene where the spinster sees him walking behind a plow and notices the resemblance between his shoulders and those of the villain, who turns out to be his father. The countryside is described with loving detail, and some attempt is made to record the amusements of the local citizenry; but their everyday employments are not depicted, nor is there any suggestion of economic or other difficulties peculiar to agriculture. A class system is very much in evidence, with a good deal of talk about the importance of "birth" in determining whether one is a gentleman. If this novel may be taken as fairly typical, the interest in farm life shown by nineteenth-century fiction was not directed toward a realistic portrayal of the average farmer's actual existence but rather toward an idealistic depiction of farm life as someone familiar with it only at second hand supposed it to be. The authors themselves would, of course, resent this judgment of their work. Taylor's own interpretation of what he was doing is contained in his preface to *Kennett*:

> In these days, when Fiction prefers to deal with abnormal characters and psychological problems more or less exceptional or morbid, the attempt to represent the elements of life in a simple, healthy, pastoral community, has been to me a source of uninterrupted enjoyment.[3]

Taylor's statement is interesting for two reasons: first, it shows that he was aware that new trends in fiction were developing and was in conscious rebellion against these tendencies; and second, in the phrase "a simple, healthy, pastoral community," it reflects the widespread belief that country life is somehow more wholesome and more conducive to virtue than city life. Brown finds this idea prevalent in the sentimental novel. For example, a novel by A. E. B. N. Haven expresses the notion of the salutary effect exposure to the country has on even the hardened city-dweller and points out how quickly the scales of corruption that have accrued during years of life in the city are sloughed off in the country air. Brown remarks that a character in Haven's novel, "dissipated and bankrupt by urban luxuries, found blessings in barnyards, sermons in silos, and good in everything."[4]

The same contrast between farm and city life is found in *Clovernook*, where Miss Carey describes her characters as "plain and common-sense people . . . vexed with no indistinct yearnings for the far off and the unattained—weighed down with no false appreciation, blind to all good that is not the best—oppressed by no misanthropic fancies about the world. . . ." She remarks, "After all, the independent yeoman, with his simple rusticity and healthful habits, is the happiest man in the world." And one of her characters echoes this idea: "Yes, yes, they are the happiest, . . . it stands to reason that it hardens the heart to live in cities, and makes folks selfish too."[5] Our first glimpse of the city in these stories is of the slums and the slaughterhouses. Although there

---

[3] Bayard Taylor, *The Story of Kennett* (New York: G. P. Putnam's Sons, 1881), pp. iv–v.

[4] Brown, *The Sentimental Novel*, p. 313.

[5] Alice Carey, *Clovernook, or Recollections of Our Neighborhood in the West: Second Series* (New York: A. C. Armstrong and Son, 1884), pp. 15, 25.

are vicious people in country as well as city, and the farm environment is sometimes shown as narrow and stultifying, the cause is never the rural setting itself but the innate depravity of individual human beings.

Considering the frequency with which it has been attacked in the past century, the myth of the superiority of farm life to city life has shown remarkable persistence. As early as 1857, George Fitzhugh, a leading apologist for the slave system, tried to debunk it in *Cannibals All!*:

> Agricultural labor is the most arduous, least respectable, and worst paid of all labor. Nature and philosophy teach all who can to avoid and escape from it, and to pursue less laborious, more respectable, and more lucrative employments. None work in the field who can help it. Hence free society is in great measure dependent for its food and clothing on slave society.[6]

Later in the century the idealistic view of the country was again assaulted by Edgar Watson Howe, Joseph Kirkland, Harold Frederic, and Hamlin Garland, to mention only those whose writings fall most conspicuously within the scope of this study.

The glorification of country life may be seen as a survival of the cultural primitivism of Rousseau and the French physiocrats, evident also in such agrarians as Thomas Jefferson and John Taylor of Caroline. As such, it had a long and honorable history in American tradition, and there is no reason for surprise at the fact that it found its way into literature. Cultural primitivism was, however, in conflict with another belief held with equal tenacity: the theory of progress and civilization. According to Henry Nash Smith, this theory saw the course of human history as a gradual advance from savagery through barbarism to civilization, which itself developed in a series of stages, beginning with the first primitive cultivation of the soil and culminating in the formation of a society in which a leisure class, secure in its possession of status and wealth, could permit the "flowering of the higher graces of human nature."[7] An agrarian like James Feni-

---

[6] Quoted in Henry Nash Smith, *Virgin Land* (Cambridge: Harvard University Press, 1950), p. 144.

[7] *Ibid.*, p. 223. The two quotations in the following paragraph appear in the same source, p. 215.

more Cooper might see the culmination in a landed aristocracy (however much he might have avoided the word); others might see it in an urban leisure class whose wealth would be based on commercial, financial, or industrial achievement. But no one who endorsed the theory would be likely to see it in the small independent farmer, least of all in the frontier farmer, who was at or near the initial stage of "civilization," as the term was then used.

All this may help to explain why, when novelists came to deal with farm life, they chose either to treat it romantically, with emphasis on a cultured leisure class who did little actual work, or realistically but condescendingly and patronizingly. After discussing various early attempts to make the common farmer the subject of fiction, Smith concludes that he could not be made into an acceptable hero, because "his sedentary and laborious calling stripped him of the exotic glamor that could be exploited in hunters and scouts of the Wild West [while] at the same time his low social status made it impossible to elaborate his gentility." The writers of fiction revealed a fact that was obscured by the professions of social democracy made by politicians: "Whatever the orators might say in glittering abstractions about the virtues of the yeoman, the novelists found themselves unable to control the emotions aroused by the Western farmer's degraded rank in the class system." So Ishmael Bush, the backwoodsman and squatter in Cooper's *The Prairie*, is portrayed as a mere barbarian in whom the moral and intellectual virtues of civilized man are only latent. Cooper apparently intended that the love plot of Inez and Middleton, the upper-class hero and heroine, should command more of the reader's attention than the affairs of the Bush family. If the modern reader finds the depiction of the squatter and his family more interesting, his preference reflects a change in taste not without significance in a study of the farm novel in the twentieth century.

One of the earliest nineteenth-century authors to treat the pioneer farmer realistically was Mrs. Caroline Matilda Kirkland. A descendant of a Loyalist family and a woman of assured social standing in the East, she came to the Michigan frontier in the 1830's with her husband, who was attempting to establish a town northwest of Detroit. At first she found life in the West

well-nigh unendurable, not only because of the physical hardships but also because of the fiercely maintained social democracy
which prevailed on the frontier. In order to acquaint her eastern
friends with the life she was living, she wrote a book, *A New
Home—Who'll Follow?*, published in 1839 and later followed by
two other volumes on the same subject. *A New Home* is fictionalized autobiography, written in the first person in epistolary
form, and probably portrays with fair accuracy Mrs. Kirkland's
actual experiences. Her descriptions of the conditions she encountered are valuable historical documents and undoubtedly the
most useful parts of her writing. Shortly after her arrival, for
example, she wandered around the hills and reached a log cabin,
where she was hospitably received. The women of the house made
an effort to "dress up," combing their hair in their guest's presence, much to her disgust. A huge meal was prepared and a horn
was blown to call the men of the family to dinner. The following
passage describes what ensued and also provides a good example
of the author's style, except that it lacks her usual literary
allusions:

> After the "wash-dish" had been used in turn, and various hand-
> kerchiefs had performed, not for that occasion only, the part of
> towels, the lords of creation seated themselves at the table, and
> fairly demolished in grave silence every eatable thing on it. Then, as
> each one finished, he arose and walked off, till no one remained of
> this goodly company, but the red-faced heavy-eyed master of the
> house. This personage used his privilege by asking me five hundred
> questions, as to my birth, parentage, and education, my opinion of
> Michigan, my husband's plans and prospects, business and resources;
> and then said, "he guessed he must be off."[8]

Mrs. Kirkland was plagued by a variety of petty annoyances.
She objected to the frontier custom which required that those
who had lend to those who had not, only later (if at all) to be
paid back in inferior goods. "Mother wants your sifter, and she
says she guesses you can let her have some sugar and tea, 'cause
you've got plenty," demanded a child of her one day. The incident led Mrs. Kirkland to comment that "whoever comes to

[8] Caroline Matilda Kirkland, *A New Home, or Life in the Clearings* (New
York: G. P. Putnam's Sons, 1953), p. 34. Originally published as *A New
Home—Who'll Follow?* (New York: C. S. Francis, 1839).

Michigan with nothing, will be sure to better his condition; but wo [sic] to him that brings with him anything like an appearance of abundance, whether of money or mere household conveniences" (104). Such practices were, as Mrs. Kirkland undoubtedly realized, one evidence of the frontier leveling that she deplored, Another manifestation of the same phenomenon was the scarcity of household help; people who had no money and almost no food would not think of letting their daughters live out at service (66). Mrs. Kirkland was repelled by this attitude, in whatever form it manifested itself, and she stated her position emphatically:

> It would be in vain to pretend that this state of society can ever be agreeable to those who have been accustomed to the more rational arrangements of the older world. The social character of the meals, in particular, is quite destroyed, by the constant presence of strangers, whose manners, habits of thinking, and social connexions are quite different from your own, and often exceedingly repugnant to your taste. Granting the correctness of the opinion which may be read in their countenances that they are "as good as you are," I must insist, that a greasy cook-maid or a redolent stable-boy, can never be, to my thinking, an agreeable table companion . . . [85].

In fairness to Mrs. Kirkland, it must be added that she is not insensible to the real merits of the frontier people, and she cautions her eastern friends against showing condescension toward these people, should they ever find themselves in her situation. At best, however, her attitude is a patronizing one, and the little narratives she weaves into the central account are mostly about people, chiefly easterners, who scarcely fit into the scene but who she supposes will be of greater interest to her cultivated audience than the authentic frontier figures. Although she tries to reproduce the dialect of her characters, the resultant contrast between the uncouth frontier speech and her own highly polished, literary English gives the reader the impression that this effort at dialect writing is intended chiefly for comic effect.

Henry H. Riley's *Puddleford, and Its People* (1854), although concerned with village rather than farm life, deserves at least passing mention because it illustrates a somewhat different approach to the level of culture treated by Mrs. Kirkland. A series of sketches revolving about a half-dozen major characters and a multitude of lesser ones, *Puddleford* describes the frontier town at a period only slightly later than that of *A New Home*. The inhabitants of the community have to find solutions to new and old problems without the aid of exact precedents from an established society. Their solutions are imperfect and often ridiculous, but Riley wants the reader to understand that this is society in the making. Although he pays tribute to the ingenuity and homely wisdom of his characters, his portrayal of them amounts to caricature most of the time, with the result that they generate little more respect in the reader than Mrs. Kirkland's characters do. The only significant reference to farm life as such in the book is a statement indicating that Riley recognized the barrier between the farm and the small town. He remarks that "Puddleford village *had* a country, and village pride looked down upon it, just as it does in larger places." And he adds, placing himself with the sentimental writers, "The amusements and frolics of the country were more simple and hearty."[9] On the whole, however, Riley is not sentimental in his treatment of his subject. Unfortunately, in avoiding sentimentality, he leans too far in the opposite direction and, like Mrs. Kirkland, renders his characters amusing spectacles rather than sympathetically portrayed human beings.

None of the books just discussed can, properly speaking, be called middle western farm novels. Not until the farmer is handled more sympathetically than Mrs. Kirkland treats him—as a person of some consequence in his own right, and not merely as a curiosity exhibited for the amusement of an urban audience—and more realistically than Miss Carey treats him, can the farm novel be said to have begun to emerge. For evidences of this development, one must turn to the last three decades of the nineteenth century.

Caroline B. Sherman, writing in 1938, states flatly, "Only three novels published before 1900 are now considered to be genuine studies of rural life."[10] The novels she designates are Edward Eggleston's *The Hoosier Schoolmaster* (1871), Edgar

[9] Henry H. Riley, *Puddleford, and Its People* (New York: Samuel Hueston, 1854), p. 93.

[10] Caroline B. Sherman, "The Development of American Rural Fiction," *Agricultural History*, XII (January 1938), 67.

Watson Howe's *The Story of a Country Town* (1883), and Hamlin Garland's *Main-Travelled Roads* (1891), the last of which, of course, is not a novel at all. Garland himself listed the first two as worthy predecessors to his work and added Joseph Kirkland's *Zury: The Meanest Man in Spring County* (1887). Probably Harold Frederic's grim study of upper New York state farm life, *Seth's Brother's Wife* (1886) should also be added, and, if short-story collections are admissible, Maurice Thompson's *Hoosier Mosaics* (1875).

Because *Hoosier Mosaics* may be considered a milestone on the road from the romanticism of *Clovernook* to the realism of *Main-Travelled Roads*, it perhaps ought to be discussed first. A slender little volume of "sketches" published well before the full-blown romanticism of *Alice of Old Vincennes* (1900), it combines realistic description of the setting and realistic representation of speech with rather sentimental plot situations. There is an earthy realism about the description of the crude Indiana town of Colfax in the opening story, "Was She a Boy?," and of the coarse farmers who figure in several other stories, with their recurring "agues" and the primitive level on which they live. But Thompson seems inordinately fond of certain romantic stereotypes. Three of the nine stories revolve about mature men who fall in love with young girls; one dies, at least partly because of his disappointment in love, another vanishes, presumably also because of a broken heart, and the third lives to a sterile and bitter old age. Although certain other young lovers are treated humorously in the book, these three receive so much sympathy from the author as to leave him open to the charge of sentimentalism. Luke Plunkett's infatuation with the aptly named Hoiden Pearl strains the reader's credulity somewhat, as does Zach Jones's similar enchantment by the idealized Rose Turpin. But the contrast between Thompson's stories and those of Miss Carey, which they superficially resemble, clearly demonstrates a progress away from sentimentalism in the direction of realism. Thompson's characters at least talk like uneducated Hoosiers, whereas in *Clovernook* a character without education expresses her preference for farm over city life by saying, "Of course, my predelictions are all in favor of the habits to which I have been used."[11] Although some of Thompson's stories have a small-town setting, most of them take place in the open country and thus qualify as farm fiction.

As Caroline B. Sherman points out in the article cited earlier, the two major novels by Eggleston and Howe are not farm novels in the truest sense, since they deal only incidentally with farm life. Nevertheless, because they do mark something of a departure in the treatment of rural themes they deserve some attention here. Eggleston's reputation as a pioneer realist rests chiefly upon his conscientious and skillful reproduction of dialect and his authentic handling of folk customs and beliefs. His plots are melodramatic and sentimental, his minor characters are often crudely drawn and unconvincing, and his tendency to moralize is objectionable. For a western writer consciously committed to utilizing western life as the material of literature, he gives surprisingly little attention to farmers and farm life. The hero of *The Hoosier Schoolmaster* is a cultured young man with an ambition to teach in a rural school; the central figure in *The Mystery of Metropolisville* (1873) is an eastern idealist whose stepfather is a land speculator in Minnesota; in *The Circuit-Rider* (1874) the action centers about a peripatetic Methodist minister. Although farmers and farm life are introduced, the attention in each of these novels is concentrated on the main characters to almost the degree of the earlier romantic novels. Little is said about the actual farm work. In *The Hoosier Schoolmaster*, for example, Hannah Thomson, the "bound girl," is reported to be milking and doing other chores, but this is all the attention the subject receives. Eggleston's failure to write about the details of farm work is explainable by the fact that he was not a farmer and had no extensive first-hand acquaintance with farming.

Eggleston does, however, say a good deal about the amusements of these backwoods Hoosiers—coon hunts, spelling bees, revival meetings—and gives some attention to their external circumstances and to their dietary habits. His description of the Means's farmhouse is as realistic as some of Mrs. Kirkland's scenes:

[11] Carey, *Clovernook . . . Second Series*, p. 268.

the poplar table, adorned by no cloth, sat in the floor; the unwashed blue tea-cups sat in the unwashed blue saucers; the unwashed blue plates kept company with the begrimed blue pitcher. The dirty skillets by the fire were kept in countenance by the dirtier pots, and the ashes were drifted or strewn over the hearth-stones in a most picturesque way.[12]

Such descriptive passages are significant because they suggest the influence of Taine's *Philosophy of Art in the Netherlands*, which Eggleston had reviewed and which Henry Nash Smith thinks "had given him at least an inkling of a pure pictorial feeling for common and familiar scenes. . . ."[13]

While all this does not make Eggleston a farm novelist by any means, it does show that he saw in the backwoods rural environment of Indiana a subject for serious treatment in fiction. True, his attention is centered on the more cultured outsiders and his portrayal of the indigenous characters sometimes amounts to caricature, but Eggleston is not contemptuous or condescending toward farm people. Smith is no doubt correct in his observation that the more sensitive and ambitious of Eggleston's characters (like Bud Means) want to raise themselves above their environment (p. 233). But Eggleston, in introducing this theme, to be developed time and again by later farm novelists, also showed that he recognized that worthwhile individuals could appear in such unpromising surroundings.

Edgar Watson Howe's *The Story of a Country Town* is just what the title indicates and has even less to say about farm life than *The Hoosier Schoolmaster*. Although in the early portion of the novel the Reverend John Westlock and his family live in the country, where he combines farming with preaching, virtually nothing is said about their farm tasks, and the family soon moves to the village of Twin Mounds. The book is definitely an attack upon the bleakness of life in the rural West, but the attack is aimed primarily at the narrowness of village life rather than at farm life itself. Howe's *Story* is more the ancestor of Edgar Lee Masters' *Spoon River Anthology*, Sherwood Anderson's *Wines-*

---

[12] Edward Eggleston, *The Hoosier Schoolmaster* (New York: Orange, Judd & Co., 1871), p. 28.

[13] Smith, *Virgin Land*, p. 236.

burg, Ohio, and Sinclair Lewis' *Main Street* than it is the predecessor of the middle western farm novel. But *The Story of a Country Town* concerns us because the author, by implication at least, assaults the time-honored notion that the country is morally more wholesome than the town, and because he takes an extremely skeptical position with regard to the farm discontent of the late nineteenth century and the measures being advocated to relieve it, which were to be so heartily endorsed by Garland a few years later.

Ned Westlock, the son of the Reverend John Westlock, tells of two boys in the neighborhood who "seemed to have mastered all sorts of depravity by sheer force of native genius," for contrary to what might have been supposed, they were farm boys seldom allowed even to go to town, "and therefore could not have contracted the vices of civilization from the contagion of evil society."[14] When Ned and his father arrive in Twin Mounds to begin editing the local newspaper, a group of boys gather in front of the printing shop. Ned assumes that he will have to fight them, for "it was the understanding in the country that all town boys were knockers, and that every country boy who went there to live must fight his way to respectability" (156). These passages incidentally illustrate the town-country hostility which is often overlooked by urban critics who fail to distinguish between the village and the open country.

At the time *The Story of a Country Town* was written, the "agrarian crusade" was in full swing. The Granger movement had passed its peak, and the Greenback party was waning, but new organs of rural protest, the Farmers' Alliances, were springing up throughout the West. Eventually these separate forces were to coalesce and form the Populist party of the 1890's for which Garland wrote and campaigned so vigorously. In Howe's opinion, the Alliances were the creations of self-seeking politicians, eager to exploit the farmer's discontent by telling him he was more deserving of prosperity than he really was. His views

[14] Edgar Watson Howe, *The Story of a Country Town* (New York: Albert & Charles Boni, 1926), p. 41. It may be significant that when Howe came to revise his novel in 1927 he greatly altered or even omitted some of the passages quoted here.

are uttered through the outbursts of self-revelation of Lytle Biggs, a contemptible figure who pretends to be a man of the soil but devotes his time to organizing Alliances and otherwise seeking to defraud the farmer. Although Howe unquestionably means to portray Biggs as a fraud, in such moments of self-revelation he may safely be taken as the author's mouthpiece. Once he started a farmers' store, ostensibly to protect the farmer against grasping middlemen; the farmers agreed to patronize his store and did so until they discovered that he was charging them more than the merchants in town (91–92). Biggs suggests that all such organizers are frauds, in the business for what they can get out of it, and usually in the pay of the monopolists. The same goes for agricultural newspapers, to which he also contributes. He tells Ned that if he were to speak the truth, he would advise farmers "to take the papers which . . . censure the farmer when he deserves it, instead of pandering to his ignorance, and forever rubbing him on the back as an honest but oppressed fellow, through no fault of his own." He goes on to say that "the farmer follows the furrow because he can make more at that than at anything else; he is no more oppressed than other men. . . ." He insists that

> the pretence that a man cannot be honest except he plough or sow for a living is not warranted by the facts. Getting up very early in the morning, and going about agricultural work all day in rough clothes, does not particularly tend to clear the conscience, but because politicians who occasionally have use for them have said these things, the farmers go on accepting them, stubbornly refusing to be undeceived . . . [239–240].

Although put in the mouth of a young boy, the following remark may reflect Howe's fundamental conservatism:

> My father was at the country town a great deal of late, and the farm was being neglected in the hands of the renter and his two sons, who I often thought were shiftless men, or they would have owned a farm of their own, for land was cheap and plentiful [123].

Although no real farmers appear in Howe's novel, there is an evident concern with the social and physical conditions surrounding the western farmer and some interest in his welfare. In Howe's gloomy, unsparing realism there is a foreshadowing of

Main-Travelled Roads, despite the wide difference separating Howe and Garland in their economic and political outlooks.

Joseph Kirkland's *Zury: The Meanest Man in Spring County* more nearly approaches fulfilling the criteria of genuine farm fiction than any novel thus far discussed. In this tale of the settlement and development of the Illinois corn country there is the authentic ring of farm life as it was really lived. Kirkland's skillful use of dialect has much to do with his superiority to his predecessors. "Kirkland's ear for what people actually said was keener than that of any other writer who has dealt with the agricultural West, except Sinclair Lewis," says Henry Nash Smith.[15] But such fidelity to the actual speech of his characters could be a handicap rather than an aid, at least from the standpoint of the modern reader, both because it is sometimes difficult to understand what Kirkland's people are saying and because there is the possibility of a comic contrast, which would detract from the sympathy the reader might be expected to feel for the characters. More than accurate transcription of dialect, what makes for a feeling of genuineness in Kirkland's novel is the apparent familiarity with the everyday details of farm work: house-raising, rail-splitting and fence-building, "niggering-off" logs, corn planting and plowing (including the "new chronology," as he calls it, derived from the corn culture), banking up the house, and so forth. Furthermore, the farm is not merely incidental background for a conventional plot involving non-farm people; it is an integral part of the story, the environment that has made Zury what he is. The task of subduing the soil is a stern one, and only the hard men survive and conquer.

Two additional points are of interest in connection with this novel: one is the debunking of primitivism, the other the pronouncement of a theme and an attitude toward it that were to be prominent in many twentieth-century farm novels. Howe had done what he could to shatter the notion that virtue resided in the country and vice in the town; Kirkland attacks another aspect of primitivism. On her first morning in the Wayback district his somewhat improbable heroine, Anne Sparrow, awakens early to the disagreeable prospect of dawn in the malaria country. Her

[15] Smith, *Virgin Land,* p. 243.

reflections (which are practically indistinguishable from Kirkland's authorial comments) carry her far from the naturalism of *Walden*:

> And those naturalistic enthusiasts—how sublimely they talk about the charms of Nature! How sacred Nature's mysteries! How much more you adored her the nearer you got to her! How inalienable the rights of all her creatures, even the humblest and least attractive! Ugh! Did they know about bugs? Are malodorous parasites Nature's creatures with inalienable rights? Stuff! Mankind has been for twenty thousand years improving upon Nature, subduing her forces and killing her bugs—now the idea of going back![16]

This might almost have been written by Caroline Kirkland, the mother of the author of *Zury*, on the Michigan frontier. Such passages, although not in themselves proof of anything, agree well with the general tenor of the book and help to provide convincing evidence of a strain of anti-primitivism in the author.

The introductory chapter to *Zury* contains one of the clearest expressions in fiction of the widespread belief that the American continent was divinely intended for the white man's occupancy and, although the task of conquering it might be a demanding one, those who survived it would be richly rewarded. Because of the clarity of Kirkland's statement and the importance of this belief in later farm novels dealing with the pioneer experience, his remarks are worth quoting in their entirety:

> Great are the toils and terrible the hardships that go to the building up of a frontier farm; inconceivable to those who have not done the task or watched its doing. In the prairies, Nature has stored, and preserved thus far through the ages, more life-materials than she ever before amassed in the same space. It is all for man, but only for such men as can take it by courage and hold it by endurance. Many assailants are slain, many give up and fly, but he who is sufficiently brave, and strong, and faithful, and fortunate, to maintain the fight to the end, has his ample reward [1].

One of the most firmly held tenets of the American faith, this belief endured drought, dust storm, locust plague, Indian attack, blizzard, economic disaster, and even psychological attrition of the kind that finally drove Rölvaag's Beret to insanity.

[16] Joseph Kirkland, *Zury: The Meanest Man in Spring County* (Boston: Houghton Mifflin Co., 1887), p. 109.

Kirkland has his faults. The plot of *Zury* contains melodramatic features, like the flood which forces Zury and Anne to spend a night together in an old mine; the marriage of these two seems so implausible that it has been characterized as "one of the strangest matings in all literature"; and at times the stories about Zury's miserliness sound like a compilation of folk tales about stinginess.[17] But in its earlier chapters, especially those dealing with the settlement of the Illinois country and Zury's youth, it comes close to being a farm novel in the sense in which that term is being used in this book.

The year before Kirkland's *Zury* appeared saw the publication of *Seth's Brother's Wife* (1886), by Harold Frederic, a bleak, unlovely story of farm life in New York state. Frederic is chiefly remembered today as the author of *The Damnation of Theron Ware*, a realistic study of village narrowness and the effects of emancipation from that environment. *Seth's Brother's Wife* concerns the doings of the Fairchilds, a decadent rural family living on the memories of their past importance.[18] The chief value of this novel to the present study is its depiction of the bigotry, coarseness, dishonesty, and frustration which prevail in a supposedly idyllic rural community. As an attempt to debunk the myth of the farm as the repository of all virtues it is highly successful. All the characters can be classified as either fools or knaves or both, although Seth and one or two others have good qualities which at least do something to compensate for their frailties. The barrenness of the setting is well illustrated by a funeral scene near the beginning of the novel. Even nature has no charms in this decaying countryside, and the city to which Seth flees is not conspicuously superior to the country. City people, like the country people, are portrayed mostly as narrow-minded, selfish, and vicious, and apparently as much the products of their environment as the farmers. In this novel Frederic did

[17] Smith, *Virgin Land*, p. 243.

[18] There are indications that the British writer Stella Gibbons had this novel, among others, in mind when she wrote her comic parody, *Cold Comfort Farm* (1932), whose cast of grotesques includes a young sensualist named Seth and an embittered dowager who saw "something nasty in the woodshed" at age two and lived in seclusion ever afterward.

for eastern farm life what Howe had done for village life in the
West.

In the middle and late 1880's a middle western farm boy,
Hamlin Garland, was studying and teaching in a Boston school
of oratory and giving occasional lectures on literary subjects.
Garland read all of the novels just discussed, reviewed some of
them, and concluded that it was time for the Middle West to be
represented in literature as New England had been. Writing
about this period much later, he reconstructed his feelings of the
eighties:

> The Farm Life of New England has been fully celebrated by means
> of innumerable stories and poems. . . . its husking bees, its dances,
> its winter scenes are all on record; is it not time that we of the west
> should depict our own distinctive life? The middle border has its
> poetry, its beauty, if we can only see it.[19]

"The Western Corn Husking" was his first story to be published.
That he did not intend this new literature to be romantic or
unrealistic in tone is indicated by the fact that he included in
his story an "insistence on the painful as well as the pleasant
truth . . ." (351). And when the editors called for "charming love
stories," Garland stated his position in unequivocal terms:

> No, we've had enough of lies. . . . Other writers are telling the
> truth about the city,—the artisan's narrow, grimy, dangerous job is
> being pictured, and it appears to me that the time has come to tell
> the truth about the barn-yard's daily grind. I have lived the life and
> I know that farming is not entirely made up of berrying, tossing the
> new-mown hay and singing *The Old Oaken Bucket* on the porch
> by moonlight [376].

Despite the suggestion of heroics and self-idealization in Garland's manifesto, there is no reason to doubt his sincerity in his
determination to show western farm life as he knew it. He wrote
many stories in the following years, and in 1891 six of the best
were collected and published under the title *Main-Travelled
Roads* by his friend, B. O. Flower, who had earlier printed his
stories in the *Arena*. During this time he had the encouragement
of Kirkland, among others. It was Kirkland who called him "the

[19] Hamlin Garland, *A Son of the Middle Border* (New York: Macmillan
Co., 1944), p. 351.

first actual farmer in American fiction" and who told him, "You can go far if you'll only work. I began too late. I can't emotionalize present day western life—you can, but you must bend to your desk like a man. You must grind!"[20]

So much has been written of the psychological causes underlying Garland's stories—guilt feelings over what seemed to him a desertion of his mother, an acute awareness of the contrast between his own material success and his family's failure—that this point need only be touched upon here. It is enough to say that his fiction was motivated by a mixture of nostalgia and indignation. The ambivalence of Garland's attitude toward the farm is clearly marked, and it shows up frequently in his writing. Although he fled the farm at almost his earliest opportunity, he felt a profound sympathy for those who stayed behind and experienced a nagging desire to help them. Because he was able to generalize his own experience and that of his family, his indignation had a breadth and scope that made it possible for him to produce literature. In a later autobiography he represented in these terms his feeling just before he began writing:

> The essential tragedy and hopelessness of most human life under the conditions into which our society was swiftly hardening embittered me, called for expression, but even then I did not know that I had found my theme. I had no intention at the moment of putting it into fiction.[21]

Main-Travelled Roads is supposed to have aroused the wrath

[20] *Ibid.*, pp. 355, 371. The associations of these writers with one another are worth noting. Garland was influenced by or in touch with all of them. He considered *The Hoosier Schoolmaster* a milestone in his own literary progress as well as in the development of western fiction, and he felt once when in Faribault, Minnesota, that he was on sacred ground, for the scene of *The Mystery of Metropolisville* was Cannon City, near Faribault. He corresponded with Howe, and the somber tone of *Main-Travelled Roads* probably owes something to *The Story of a Country Town*. Kirkland was a personal friend of his, as a result of a review of *Zury* that he wrote for the Boston *Transcript* in 1887. He reviewed *Seth's Brother's Wife* the same year, also for the *Transcript*. Kirkland told Garland that he wrote with Eggleston's and Howe's novels in mind but with the hope of improving upon his predecessors.

[21] *Ibid.*, pp. 366–367.

of some conservative critics, but William Dean Howells, whose opinion Garland valued highly, gave it a favorable review in his "Editor's Study" section of *Harper's*. Howells admired the realism of the stories but wondered if they were altogether true to fact: "If anyone is still at a loss to account for that uprising of the farmers in the West . . . let him read *Main-Travelled Roads* and he will begin to understand, unless, indeed, Mr. Garland is painting the exceptional rather than the average." In keeping with the convictions of a man who believed that literature should deal with the more smiling aspects of life, Howells added a word of caution: "He has a certain harshness and bluntness, an indifference to the more delicate charms of style; and he has still to learn that though the thistle is full of an unrecognized poetry, the rose has a poetry, too, that even over-praise cannot spoil."[22] Garland later liked to emphasize the furor the book aroused among the conservatives:

> Statistics were employed to show that pianos and Brussels carpets adorned almost every Iowa farmhouse. Tilling the prairie soil was declared to be "the noblest vocation in the world, not in the least like the pictures this eastern author has drawn of it."[23]

The sort of thing Garland was up against is illustrated by a letter he received from Richard Watson Gilder, then editor of the *Century*, in 1892. Commenting on a story, Gilder cautioned,

> I must tell you what embarrasses me in stories of this sort. As you know, the newspaper press nowadays is vulgarizing. . . . Now if

[22] William Dean Howells, "The Editor's Study," *Harper's New Monthly Magazine*, LXXXIII (September 1891), 639–640. The relationship between Garland and Howells is treated in Everett Carter, *Howells and the Age of Realism* (Philadelphia: J. B. Lippincott Co., 1950), especially pp. 111–112 and 120–121. Just as Howells was to some extent the victim of his time, so his critical judgments were influenced by the tastes of this period. In general, his praise of *Main-Travelled Roads* was high, and he regretted Garland's later shift to the writing of western romances.

[23] Garland, *A Son of the Middle Border*, p. 415. Garland's reasons for wishing to correct current notions about the Middle West are also expressed in *Crumbling Idols* (1894), where he characterizes most middle western writing of the day as conventional, short stories "absolutely colorless, when they are not pirated exotics." *Crumbling Idols* (Cambridge: Harvard University Press, 1960), p. 14.

we print too many stories which are full of the kind of language which should not be used, we seem to many persons to be continuing the work of vulgarization. . . . People who are trying to bring up their children with refinement, and to keep their own and their children's language pure and clean, very naturally are jealous of the influence of a magazine—especially of the *Century Magazine*—in this respect.

Years later Garland said that this letter was a "wholesome lesson" to him.[24]

The significance of *Main-Travelled Roads* in the history of the farm novel is that here for the first time was the real thing—genuine farm fiction written by a man who knew farm life at first hand, who understood and sympathized with the rural population, and who handled his materials in a thoroughly realistic fashion. In other stories written about the same time (and later) Garland romanticized his material, but the six original stories of *Main-Travelled Roads* were as realistic as anything written up to that time. *Main-Travelled Roads* was not a novel, and when Garland came to write novels he ran into difficulties he had not encountered with shorter fiction. Nevertheless, Garland may rightly be considered the first authentic farm novelist and *Main-Travelled Roads* the first authentic piece of farm fiction. Kirkland, despite an auspicious beginning in the early chapters of *Zury*, where he described the harsh side of farm life realistically, allowed himself to be sidetracked into the romantic plot of Anne Sparrow's improbable reformation of Zury; it remained for Garland to finish what Kirkland had only started.

Because Garland can be considered either the culmination of one movement or the pioneer of another,[25] he will be dealt with in both this chapter and the next. *Rose of Dutcher's Coolly* (1895) will be discussed later as the first of a series of "success stories" in which the hero or heroine escapes from the farm and achieves fame and material success in the city. It is important at this point, however, to note that Garland's first published book marked the climax of a process that began early in the nineteenth century

---

[24] Hamlin Garland, *Roadside Meetings* (New York: Macmillan Co., 1930), pp. 182–183.

[25] Smith, *Virgin Land*, p. 224.

with a romantic treatment of farm life or the relegation of the farmer to a minor role, sometimes comic, in a novel about people of quite another social class, and progressed through a series of increasingly realistic stages to the point where finally farmers and farm life were considered legitimate material for serious fiction and could be sympathetically portrayed.

III.

The Pioneering Venture
The Farm Novelist as Historian

FARM FICTION developed slowly after the initial impetus given it by Garland's trail blazing. Only a few novels appeared in the first decade of the twentieth century and not many more in the decade from 1910 to 1920. For nearly thirty years after the end of World War I, however, there was a continuing interest in this type of fiction and a correspondingly increased output.

Most of the early farm novels took for their subject matter the settlement of the West—the conquest of the soil. This historical process was, of course, no innovation in American fiction, for the frontier and frontier life had been the topic of innumerable novels in the nineteenth century, ranging from Cooper's Leatherstocking series through the books of Mayne Reid to the dime-novel thrillers about Deadwood Dick and Calamity Jane. In one respect at least the early farm novels were closer to the Wild West thriller than to the present-day farm novel: they provided the reader with vicarious experiences by dealing with the exciting, the remote, the exotic. By contrast, many farm novels of the 1940's chose to deal with the commonplace, everyday experiences that were familiar to large numbers of their readers. Furthermore, the early farm novels treated of a period of history that was past, whereas the later farm novels have shown a preference for the present or recent past. The phase of the westward movement that most appealed to farm novelists was the occupation of the Great Plains region of Dakota and Nebraska. A few, such as Herbert Quick, wrote about a slightly earlier period of settlement farther east, but these were exceptions to the general rule.

Although the greater number of novels about pioneering restrict themselves to the settlement process, a few take up simultaneously another type of pioneering—the adaptation of European immigrants to the American environment. Many of the settlers who took up new lands in the West faced a twofold problem: subduing the land and adjusting to a human environment that was alien to them. The tide of immigration swelled year by year in the decades following the Civil War, and much of it overflowed into the western states and territories, where the land-hungry newcomers took advantage of liberal laws and established themselves on the prairies. The story of their trials and achievements eventually made its way into the national literature, first as seen by the descendants of earlier immigrants, who proudly called themselves "native Americans," later in the writings of the immigrants themselves. Since a number of the best farm novels are concerned with this experience, it is necessary to give some attention to at least the most significant.

Garland himself experimented with fiction about pioneering, both in such romantic short stories as "Drifting Crane" and more significantly in the brief novelette called *Moccasin Ranch* (1909). Based on Garland's own experiences in "proving up a claim" on the Dakota prairie, *Moccasin Ranch* has as its setting the unoccupied country of present-day eastern South Dakota during the land rush of the early 1880's. The plot centers about a domestic triangle involving Will Burke and his wife Blanche, who have taken up a claim on the prairie, and Jim Rivers, who, with his partner, Bailey, runs a store and post office in the nearby settlement. Blanche, discontented with life in this wilderness and with her husband's ineffectuality, takes up with Rivers and eventually becomes pregnant by him. Convinced that she is now by rights his wife, Rivers runs off with her at the end of the novel. Bailey tries to stop them at first, but when he comes to realize that the matter is more complex than he imagined, he withdraws his resistance and gives the couple his blessing.

This plot, unconventional for 1909 but not otherwise striking, is less important for our purposes than the backdrop against which the drama is played. Garland gives a memorable picture of the Dakota prairie in the early years of white occupancy—the wildlife of the open country, natural phenomena such as blizzards and tornadoes, the types of people who took up land, the customs of the settlers, and the psychological effects of life on the prairie. Everyone from eastern lady schoolteachers to western outlaws can be found in the "land of the straddle-bug" (the triangular structure of boards set up to indicate possession), living in an easy camaraderie that is perhaps somewhat idealized by Garland. Such was the state of affairs in the summer; when winter came, many of the landseekers left, temporarily or permanently, and those who remained found life a hard struggle for survival. In his analysis of the psychological effects of a Dakota winter on the settlers, especially the women, Garland anticipated Rölvaag, although with less penetration—and less experience—he failed to pursue the subject as far as Rölvaag was to do. Speaking of winter on the prairie he says:

> The land of the straddle-bug had become a menacing desert, hard as iron, pitiless as ice.
> Now the wind had dominion over the lonely women, wearing out their souls with its melancholy moanings and its vast and wordless sighs. Its voices seemed to enter Blanche Burke's soul, filling it with hunger never felt before. Day after day it moaned in her ears and wailed about the little cabin, rousing within her formless desires and bitter despairs.[1]

Because there is no actual breaking of the soil in *Moccasin Ranch*, it can be called a farm novel only by courtesy; but it portrays the initial stage of a process which was to be shown in its entirety by later writers. Although by its concern with the strange and remote this story is more akin to the typical Wild West thriller than to the earlier *Main-Travelled Roads*, the characters are at least planning to become farmers, as Garland's father did, by taking up land in one of the few places where it was still to be had cheaply.

Although Garland as a boy living near Hesper, Iowa, played with the Norwegian children from just across the Minnesota line in Newburg township, Fillmore County,[2] he has comparatively little to say about the immigrant groups, and what he does say suggests no great degree of understanding. In "Up the Coulé,"

---

[1] Hamlin Garland, *Moccasin Ranch* (New York: Harper and Brothers, 1909), pp. 70–71.

[2] Garland, *A Son of the Middle Border*, pp. 77–78.

when a young woman is asked if she is being pursued by the local young men, she replies, "Oh, a young Dutchman or Norwegian once in a while. Nobody that counts."[3] Other references to immigrants are only slightly less contemptuous, as in the treatment of Julia Peterson's family in "Among the Corn Rows." There is no real effort to analyze the peculiar problems of the immigrant; he is just part of the setting Garland uses.

The Plow Woman (1906), by Eleanor Gates, and *The Homesteaders* (1909), by Kate and Virgil D. Boyles, both roughly contemporary with *Moccasin Ranch*, are entitled to be considered farm novels by the standards applied to that novel. Because of general inferiority in style and plot, however, neither merits extended treatment here. Both involve attempts at farming along the Missouri River in Dakota Territory. In both cases these attempts are frustrated by local hostility, rather than by the physical obstacles of climate and geography which are given more attention by later novelists. The characters are largely stock figures, the dialogue is stiff, and the plots are filled with improbabilities and an excess of violence, calculated chiefly to afford the hero or heroine an opportunity to display his courage or fortitude. In neither novel is much attention given to the actual details of farm life, and there is little sense that the central characters are even potentially farmers.

Garland had dealt with the pioneer experience tentatively, experimentally; the minor writers just discussed had used it as background for conventional stories of western romance. It remained for Willa Cather to embrace this theme wholeheartedly and, by the touch of her genius, make it the material of real literature. She deals with it chiefly in the two early novels *O Pioneers!* (1913) and *My Ántonia* (1918), the only two of her novels that properly fit into this study. Both deal with Nebraska in the pioneering and post-pioneering periods, and both are based on Miss Cather's observations during her first years in Nebraska. Although her stay in the open country was brief, it apparently made a deep impression on her. After her family moved to the town of Red Cloud, she was subjected to a new

[3] Hamlin Garland, *Main-Travelled Roads* (Boston: Arena Publishing Co., 1891), p. 82.

set of impressions, concerned more with social stratification and attitudes than with the natural environment. Both novels reflect her experiences in the country; *My Antonia* also owes much to the years she spent in the microcosm of Red Cloud.

O Pioneers!, Miss Cather's first important novel, centers about the personality of Alexandra Bergson, the eldest child and only daughter of the John Bergsons, Swedish immigrants to the Nebraska prairie. When the novel begins, Alexandra is in her early twenties and the Bergson farm has been occupied for eleven years. John Bergson dies early in the story, one of the casualties of pioneering, and leaves Alexandra in charge of the family, both because she is the oldest of the children and because she is clearly more competent in practical matters than her stolid, unimaginative brothers, Lou and Oscar. Another brother, Emil, is only a small child at this time. Three years of prosperity follow, then three years of drought and failure. Many of the settlers leave the country, and Alexandra's brothers wish to follow them; but Alexandra insists, with a mixture of mysticism and practical shrewdness, that the good years will come again and that the sound policy is to buy up land in expectation of better times. Ten years later, when the story is resumed in Part II, her faith has been rewarded, and the Bergsons are prosperous landowners, with Alexandra the acknowledged head of the family, although Lou and Oscar are now married and farming for themselves.

Meanwhile, Emil, the youngest brother, has grown up and graduated from the state university. The rest of the novel is concerned chiefly with his growing attachment to Marie Shabata, the unhappy wife of the temperamental and unstable Frank Shabata. Emil goes to Mexico for a time to forget Marie, but when he returns the affair continues, ending in the murder of both Emil and Marie by Frank when he finds them together in his orchard. Frank is sent to prison, and Alexandra, forgiving him for his act, vows to help him to gain his release. At the end of the novel she decides to marry Carl Linstrum, the artist son of one of the families who left the prairie during the bad years. Carl has been conducting a rather chilly courtship for several years, and now, when they are both about forty, his suit is finally successful.

Since *O Pioneers!* and *My Antonia* can most profitably be

considered together, it seems desirable to outline the plot of the latter book before going on to discuss their treatment of the pioneering theme. The chief figure in *My Ántonia* is Ántonia Shimerda, the daughter of a Bohemian family who settle on the prairie near Black Hawk, Nebraska. Her story is told by a first-person narrator, Jim Burden, who comes as a boy of ten from Virginia to live with his grandparents on the farm next to that of the Shimerdas. Jim and Ántonia arrive the same day, so their careers are parallel from the start. Anton Shimerda, Ántonia's father, is a melancholy, sensitive man, with no farming experience, who longs for his native Bohemia and finally commits suicide because of his desperate loneliness on the prairie. His wife and a son, Ambrosch, are by contrast earthy, crafty, and somewhat arrogant, and they fail to enlist the sympathies of the Burdens, who nevertheless feel obligated to help them in their need. Ántonia combines the best qualities of her parents; she has her father's sensitivity and her mother's robustness and seems ideally suited to the task of pioneering. Presumably because most of Miss Cather's experience was with town life, she moves both the Burdens and Ántonia to Black Hawk and there introduces a number of other characters, of whom only Lena Lingard, the daughter of Norwegian immigrants, is important to the plot.

Although Jim Burden confesses that Ántonia has the qualities he most admires, his interest in her appears never to go beyond simple friendship. He goes away to the university, has a brief and innocuous affair with Lena Lingard, and upon graduation (from Harvard, where he has gone to escape the fascination of Lena) returns to Black Hawk. Upon inquiring about Ántonia, he learns that she has fallen in love with a railway conductor and gone away to marry him, only to return home a few months later unmarried, deserted, and pregnant. When Jim visits her, she proudly displays her daughter. Twenty years later he again visits the Black Hawk country and finds Ántonia married to Anton Cuzak and the mother of a dozen children. The Cuzaks are moderately prosperous; and although Ántonia has necessarily aged, she has fulfilled her destiny and has not lost the qualities of personality and character that Jim admired when they were children.

Both of these novels begin in the period familiar to Miss Cather from her early experience. In *My Ántonia* the newer settlers, like the Shimerdas, live in sod huts, and the road winds around "like a wild thing, avoiding the deep draws, crossing them where they were wide and shallow."[4] Old Ivar, the half-crazy Norwegian in *O Pioneers!* who lives alone and sees visions, lives in rough country inhabited only by some dozen families of Russians, "who dwelt together in one long house, divided off like barracks."[5] But the original occupation of the land has already taken place, the Burdens have had time to build a white frame house, and the towns of Hanover and Black Hawk (in *O Pioneers!* and *My Ántonia* respectively) have attained some stability, amounting almost to stagnation in Black Hawk.

The country is new, however, in the sense that it is untried, or at least unproven. This is most evident in *O Pioneers!*, where at the very beginning of the novel, the settlers have been discouraged by several years of drought. A respite follows, but when the three bad years come (to be followed by many more), Alexandra's brother Lou expresses the general feeling when he says, "The fellows that settled up here just made a mistake. Now they're beginning to see this high land wasn't never meant to grow nothing on, and everybody who ain't fixed to graze cattle is trying to crawl out (50–51). Miss Cather here introduces the theme enunciated by Kirkland: this country is "all for man" and will amply reward those who survive the ordeal of conquering it. The Linstrums and others give up and return to the city in defeat. Lou and Oscar are willing to follow their example, but Alexandra is determined to stick with the land and make the farm prosper. Although she is the epitome of common sense and practicality, Alexandra is unable to give reasons for her mystical faith in this land: "You'll have to take my word for it," she tells her brother. "I *know*, that's all" (58). Her thesis that land can be made fruitful if man will but keep struggling with it does not accord with modern ideas of conservation, but it is in keeping with a long-standing belief among Americans which even the droughts of the 1930's did not altogether destroy.

[4] Willa Cather, *My Ántonia* (Boston: Houghton Mifflin Co., 1937), p. 19.
[5] Willa Cather, *O Pioneers!* (Boston: Houghton Mifflin Co., 1937), p. 30.

Alexandra's feeling toward the land, her closeness to it as evidenced by the conviction that it will reward those who stick to it, is the chief feature about *O Pioneers!* that permits one to use the term "romantic" in reference to the novel. John T. Flanagan has remarked that Willa Cather's novels represent the highest achievement in the romantic type of farm novel, a type which prevailed until well after World War I.[6] There is certainly justice in his characterization, for her novels, especially *O Pioneers!*, display several traits usually associated with romanticism in fiction. A dominant theme throughout the book, sometimes obscuring the human plot, is the beauty and inscrutability of the land. Alexandra feels a close rapport with the land, which is personified in a mystical fashion at times reminiscent of Frank Norris' attitude toward the wheat in *The Octopus*. Although most of the novel is written in subdued tones, with largely unspectacular action, Miss Cather has a flair for the dramatic, and there is a certain amount of theatricality, especially in respect to the romance of Emil and Marie Shabata. Emil's exotic appearance at a church bazaar, dressed in Mexican regalia, is pure romanticism, as is the tragic climax which ends this illicit affair. Miss Cather also has a strong sense of the vividly pictorial and makes highly effective use of the striking tableau. A good example of this and one of the most splendid passages in *O Pioneers!* occurs in the scene in which the young men of the French village ride out to meet the bishop who is coming to officiate at a confirmation and also at the funeral of Emil's good friend Amédée Chevalier (whose name and personality are both highly romantic); the scene concludes with this paragraph:

> As the troop swept past the graveyard half a mile east of the town . . . old Pierre Séguin was already out with his pick and spade, digging Amédée's grave. . . . The boys with one accord looked away from Pierre to the red church on the hill, with the gold cross flaming on its steeple.[7]

But Miss Cather cannot be charged with overuse of such pictorial effects, like some later authors who have been accused of writing

[6] John T. Flanagan, "The Middle Western Farm Novel," *Minnesota History*, XXIII (June 1942), 117.

[7] Cather, *O Pioneers!*, p. 214.

with one eye on the motion picture potentialities of their work. Passages such as the one just quoted are not employed to take the place of more significant content but rather to give additional beauty to the solid substance of the novel.

Romantic or not, Willa Cather's handling of the pioneer theme is subtler and hence more effective than the treatment accorded it by her predecessors. There is in her novels a fusion of the physical environment with the characters and their actions. Although the background is by no means neglected, the portions of these novels dealing with it do not have the merely reportorial quality that is evident in, for example, *Moccasin Ranch*—the piling up of descriptive details for their own sake. Yet, on the other hand, the actions of the characters do not usurp the entire attention of the reader. As David Daiches observes, "The human drama is subordinated to the drama of the plains and the seasons, and the characters seem less interesting than the background against which they move."[8]

This subordination of the characters to the setting, if it exists, may of course be a defect of Miss Cather's writing in these novels. There are other defects, chiefly structural faults, such as the extended time lapse between Parts I and II of *O Pioneers!* and the disappearance of the central character for long periods in *My Antonia*. It might also be argued that the characters in *O Pioneers!* express more of their inner thoughts than is quite credible, more than many novelists would permit their characters to express. *My Antonia* suffers from the use of a first-person narrator, who takes up a good deal of the reader's attention, to the neglect of the principal character. Jim Burden is the customary detached narrator, rather colorless but highly receptive to external impressions. He is not interesting enough to be the main character, and yet his position makes it inevitable that considerable attention be centered on him, particularly in the episodes between him and Lena Lingard.

These faults and others that have been pointed out by critics are not enough to detract seriously from the effectiveness of either book. In such matters as character portrayal, restraint in

[8] David Daiches, *Willa Cather: A Critical Introduction* (Ithaca: Cornell University Press, 1951), p. 27.

the handling of emotion, absence of author intrusion, and the use of a polished, flexible style, Miss Cather's novels are clearly superior to the farm fiction discussed previously. Critical opinion seems to be divided on the comparative merits of her early novels of pioneering and her later fiction, but there is a tendency to regard such works as *Death Comes for the Archbishop* and *Shadows on the Rock* more highly than *O Pioneers!* and *My Antonia.* This question does not properly come within the scope of a study of the farm novel, and no judgment on it will be offered here. It is arguable, however—and a point more relevant to the present purpose—that Miss Cather's most significant contribution in the earlier novels may have been her sympathetic insight into the European immigrant rather than her treatment of the pioneer experience. Therefore, it will be necessary to turn now to her fictional treatment of immigrant life in the rural Middle West.

O Pioneers! and *My Antonia* provide the first sympathetic handling of this subject in middle western farm fiction. The issues are largely evaded in the former novel, because no "native American" figures appear in it and there is little friction between different nationality groups. The Bergsons adjust successfully to the new environment, at least as well as the rest of the Nebraska pioneers, and there is little indication that they have special problems. In *My Antonia*, however, the subject is given more searching treatment. Anton Shimerda represents a timid, sensitive type of personality, possessing neither the ability nor the desire to adapt himself to the new country. His heart is in the old country, and he finally kills himself out of loneliness. His wife and children are more adaptable, and they succeed in making themselves part of the new environment, without, however, giving up their language or their religion.

Ironically, it is the immigrant rather than the American who achieves the greater degree of material success, as Miss Cather points out in an interesting digression on a social phenomenon that she had noted during her residence in Red Cloud. No matter how hard-pressed the American farmers were, it was socially impossible for their daughters to go into service (as Mrs. Kirkland had observed on the Michigan frontier of the 1830's); and unless they could find jobs teaching school, they were unable to contribute to the family income. On the other hand, no such restraints were felt by the immigrant farmers. Their daughters took jobs as servants in town homes, earned wages, and helped their fathers prosper.[9] Miss Cather considered it striking that the Americans looked down upon all immigrants; the fact that the ancestors of these servant girls may have been educated men carried no weight in this country (200–201). As she observed in a later essay, "If the daughter of a shiftless West Virginia mountaineer married the nephew of a professor at the University of Upsala, the native family felt disgraced by such an alliance."[10] In Black Hawk, Nebraska, says Miss Cather, the town boys were expected to marry within their own class—and they usually did, even though many of them recognized the greater vitality and intrinsic worth of the servant girls with whom they dallied more or less surreptitiously.[11] Here Miss Cather has put her finger on one of the most important aspects of the immigrant's adjustment problem: the fact that he was not accepted as an equal by members of the older American stock. He had to struggle against an imputation of inferiority and gain full recognition as a citizen before he could feel the kind of loyalty he was expected to display. David Daiches sums up Miss Cather's contribution to the literature of this subject in the following passage:

> *O Pioneers!* is the first of a group of novels in which the impact of a young country on the sad sensitivity of uprooted Europeans is presented with a sympathy and an insight rare in American writers, even the most sophisticated of whom tend to regard the European immigrant as only too happy to leave the bad old world behind and settle down in the land of the free.[12]

Miss Cather also deals to some extent with pioneering and the adjustment of the immigrant in her short stories, although most of her Nebraska stories concern village life rather than life in the country. The best example of her treatment of the immigrant theme in her short stories is "Neighbour Rosicky," which is use-

[9] Cather, *My Ántonia*, pp. 199–200.
[10] Quoted in Edward K. Brown, *Willa Cather: A Critical Biography* (New York: Alfred A. Knopf, 1953), pp. 25–26.
[11] Cather, *My Ántonia*, pp. 201–202.
[12] Daiches, *Willa Cather*, p. 17.

ful here for another purpose in that it illustrates, perhaps better than the passages already cited from the novels, the peculiar beauty of her style. Anton Rosicky is a Bohemian farmer in his sixties who has known hard times as an apprentice tailor in London and New York before coming to Nebraska to achieve comparative success as a farmer. Now he is told by his doctor that his heart is bad and that he must retire from active farm work if he is to live even a few more years. By being as careful of himself as it is possible for a man of his temperament to be, he manages to remain alive long enough to save from disaster his son's marriage to a city-bred girl. But his zest for action is too strong, he overstrains his weakened heart, and he dies quickly, to be buried in the graveyard next to his land.

Anton Rosicky is no coarse, boorish peasant; he has a fine sense of tact and delicacy revealed in his every action. After his visit to the doctor we are told that "Rosicky placed the Doctor's fee delicately behind the desk-telephone, looking the other way, as if this were an absent-minded gesture."[13] When he speaks to his wife in Czech, he tells the doctor what he has said. Miss Cather informs us that he liked soft-voiced women and never raised his own voice, for he was "a city man, a gentle man . . ." (24). It was this urban background that enabled him to comprehend the discontent that lay at the roots of his daughter-in-law's marital troubles. There is a mutual understanding between these two that develops into a fine comradeship before Rosicky's death. The doctor's feeling toward Rosicky somewhat resembles Jim Burden's admiration for Ántonia; Doctor Ed appreciates the old man perhaps more than anyone else outside Rosicky's family, despite the fact that superficially they have little in common.

Miss Cather's descriptive power, at its best in such passages as the opening paragraph of O Pioneers! with its sharply drawn picture of Hanover, Nebraska, appears to good advantage also in "Neighbour Rosicky." Possibly the best example is the description of the scene that lies before Rosicky as he stops at the graveyard on his way home from his visit to the doctor:

> Over yonder on the hill he could see his own house, crouching low, with the clump of orchard behind and the windmill before, and all

[13] Willa Cather, *Obscure Destinies* (New York: Alfred A. Knopf, 1932), p. 7.

down the gentle hill-slope the rows of pale gold cornstalks stood out against the white field [17–18].

Miss Cather is not the only writer of farm fiction who would have used the word "crouching" in this passage, but she is almost the only one who would have stopped there and continued the description in less figurative language instead of overloading it with other striking figures. Her talent lies not only in her possession of all the words that might be employed effectively but also in her restraint in using only those which are really needed. Most of her descriptions are simple and direct, and when she uses figurative expressions, they are not strained or forced but strike the reader as singularly apt. The result is that the reader sees not only what he would see if he were observing the scene himself but also what he would probably not consciously perceive though it was there.

There is no reason to labor the obvious point that Willa Cather's style is excellent, especially since her perceptive treatment of the pioneering venture and the immigrant theme would guarantee her a high place among the writers of farm fiction even if her style were undistinguished. But there is some value in noting that the quality of her fiction is greatly enhanced by possession of this technical polish. On the basis of style alone, no subsequent farm novelist has equaled her. Before passing on to a discussion of other writers, however, it should be pointed out that Miss Cather's chief significance in a chronological survey of the literature of pioneering is that it was in her novels that the story of the pioneer's struggle to subdue the land and of the immigrant to adjust to the new environment was first raised to the level of high art.

The novels thus far treated in this chapter all deal with the pioneering venture in the Great Plains area. Joseph Kirkland had in the 1880's described the settlement of the Illinois prairie, but for the next important account of the pioneer experience in the Mississippi Valley it is necessary to turn to the novels of Herbert Quick. Quick had been born on the Iowa frontier, only a few years after the original settlement, and he became convinced that the history of his state offered legitimate material for fiction. In his sixties when he wrote his important novels, he approached his literary task under several handicaps, of which the most serious was perhaps his lack of formal education. Although Quick, a lawyer by occupation, had done some fugitive writing, mostly of children's books, before 1920, his first significant novel and un- doubtedly his greatest was *Vandemark's Folly*, published in 1922.

Vandemark's Folly is the story of Jacob Teunis Vandemark, like Quick the descendant of Dutch settlers in the Hudson Val- ley. Jacob, whose father has died and whose mother has remar- ried, works on the Erie Canal for a time, then goes west to Madi- son, Wisconsin, where he has been told his mother and stepfather are, only to learn that his mother has died. The stepfather, who is quite in the tradition of cruel stepfathers, has already taken up with another woman and wants to rid himself of his seventeen- year-old stepson. So to avoid possible litigation over the inherit- ance, he pacifies Jacob with a deed to a tract of land in Monterey County, Iowa, and furnishes the boy with the necessary equip- ment to make the journey there. Much of the novel (and the most valuable part) is concerned with Jacob's pilgrimage to Iowa, during which he acquires a herd of cows and the nickname of "Cow" Vandemark; his breaking of the soil he has bought, most of which is covered by Hell Slough, renamed Vandemark's Folly Marsh; and the development of the community of which Jacob is one of the pioneers. Most of the characters who figure impor- tantly in the novel are encountered along the route from Madison to Monterey County, and the rest of the book is concerned with their interrelationships.

Little need be said of the plot, for it has the defects of its models. Both Jacob's stepfather, who functions as the villain in the early part of the novel, and J. Buckner Gowdy, who serves in that capacity through the rest of it, are obviously drawn from Quick's reading rather than from his experience. And the hero- ine, engaging though she is, derives from the stock genteel hero- ines of nineteenth-century fiction. Her geographical origins and her name are evidences of this: she is from Kentucky, and her name is Virginia Royall.[14] The chief merits of the book lie in its author's ability to recapture in words the appearance of the

---

[14] For Quick's boyhood reading, see Herbert Quick, *One Man's Life* (Indi- anapolis: Bobbs-Merrill Co., 1925), especially pp. 171–173. According to his

prairie before it was brought under cultivation, and his creation of a few striking characters, of whom Jacob Vandemark himself is the most successfully realized.

Jacob's first view of the prairie as he reaches the top of the bluffs west of Dubuque is a memorable experience, recreated by Quick in a rhapsodical passage in which he speaks of the shadows of the clouds "walking over the lovely hills like dark ships over an emerald sea."[15] Quick's account describes the Old Ridge Road, the clear streams that laced the prairies before the plow reduced them to mudholes, the native wild flowers and birds, including the now almost extinct prairie chicken, and the diverse personalities thrown together by the westward migration. All these details make of Quick's book a social document in which the narrative seems of comparatively little consequence.

Of the multitude of characters who appear on Quick's canvas, only a few stand out as original creations. Paramount among these is Jacob Vandemark, the tow-headed, buttermilk-eyed youngster, slow of thought and speech, incorruptibly honest yet with his frailties, solid, deliberate, reliable, shrewd in his dealings, eminently practical yet imaginative and capable of deep emotion. So completely does he dominate this first book that the minor characters have little opportunity to be developed to their fullest dimensions. The outlines are drawn, however, for some who appear in his later novels, *The Hawkeye* (1923) and *The Invisible Woman* (1924). These novels are inferior to the first of the series, but they do permit the development of characters hardly more than suggested in *Vandemark's Folly*, such as Roswell Upright, the epitome of corruption in government, and Surajah Dowlah Fewkes, the feckless (and chinless) inventor whose latest scheme is always bound to succeed if only he can complete some minor detail.

The hero of *The Hawkeye*, Fremont McConkey, is clearly modeled on Herbert Quick himself, as is evidenced by the identity of many details in this novel with those recounted in Quick's

own estimate, he read about a ton of New York *Ledgers* and New York *Weeklies*, chiefly illustrated stories.

[15] Herbert Quick, *Vandemark's Folly* (Indianapolis: Bobbs-Merrill Co., 1922), p. 112.

autobiography, *One Man's Life* (1925); yet he somehow fails to carry the impact of some of the author's other creations.[16] In the course of the novel, Fremont, a farm boy, takes up school teaching, becomes a sort of protégé of Captain Ashe, a prominent figure in local politics, elopes with Ashe's daughter Winifred, and after a reconciliation with her irate father, enters the political arena on his own. Although honest himself, he is associated with the corrupt "court house ring" in Monterey Center, and when they are thrown out of office, he goes with them and is obliged to begin a new career as a newspaperman in the neighboring town of Lithopolis. The Bushyager family, introduced in *Vandemark's Folly*, play an important role in *The Hawkeye*, and although not especially memorable as individuals, they collectively represent one of Quick's major achievements. Living on the fringes of the settlement, uninhibited by any regard for the laws of organized society, the members of this clan earn a somewhat more than deserved reputation for horse thievery and other offenses common in a newly settled country. Fremont is on good terms with them, however, as the result of a childhood friendship with one of them, and he gains his first political success by delivering the Bushyager vote to Captain Ashe and his colleagues.

The Invisible Woman includes many of the same characters as the first two novels but centers chiefly about Christina Thorkelson, the daughter of Jacob Vandemark's friend and neighbor, Magnus Thorkelson, and Rowena Fewkes, the one normal member of the otherwise Jukes-like Fewkes family. Like Fremont McConkey, Christina leaves the farm early and finds her place in the town, first as secretary to the law firm of Creede, Silverthorn, and Boyd, later as court reporter when Oliver Silverthorn becomes a judge. The novel's inferiority to its predecessors is due principally to the progressive exhaustion of Quick's material, the increasing distance from the actual pioneering experience with

[16] Among the parallels that might be noted are these: in both Quick's and Fremont's cases the father is a hard-shell Baptist, the mother a Methodist, but the mother turns Baptist in order to persuade the father to return to the church; in both cases the mother, although an uneducated woman, is sought out in her old age by educated people because of her wisdom; and both boys cry easily, are precocious, and read widely.

which he is most successful, the difficulty (for a man) of centering a novel about the life of a woman, and, in the opinion of many readers at least, the author's weakness for riding his hobby—that is, devoting much space to the details of a legal case. Upon the death of J. Buckner Gowdy, his illegitimate son by Rowena Fewkes Thorkelson, Owen Lovejoy Gowdy, is persuaded by Creede, Silverthorn, and Boyd to sue for his share of the estate, and much of the novel is occupied with the subsequent litigation, in which the action centers about the efforts to prove that the elder Gowdy "generally and notoriously" recognized Owen as his son. All this makes for a novel delightful as vacation reading for lawyers but rather tedious to the lay reader. But here as in the earlier novels Quick maintains a high level of character portrayal, which makes the book at least readable, if less significant a contribution than *Vandemark's Folly*.

As an example of Quick's methods of characterization, it may be worthwhile to examine the personality of Roswell Upright, who appears in all three novels. Although "Raws" could readily become a mere caricature or the type venal politician, Quick manages to keep him three-dimensional and very credible. An influential citizen of Monterey County, Upright is a contractor by trade who combines this occupation effectively with the office of chairman of the county Board of Supervisors, to which he is repeatedly re-elected. He makes his living by levying high taxes on vacant land held by nonresident speculators and using the money for public (and private) improvements which he builds, meanwhile not bothering to tax actual settlers on their improvements. Two eastern men come to Monterey to investigate the reasons for their high taxes, and the local lawyer, N. V. Creede, introduces them to Upright. After professing their faith in the desirability of public improvements but suggesting that the roads, bridges, and schools of Monterey County are not quite commensurate with the taxes they have been paying, one inquires earnestly of old "Raws":

> "Mr. Creede has said that you can tell us where our taxes have gone. We shall be glad to be set right if we are laboring under a mistake and doing your county government any injustice. We shall be glad to have you tell us in a general way, where our taxes *have*

gone. What have you to show for these very heavy levies upon our properties? . . ."

Mr. Upright, having finished his dinner, shoved back his chair, wiped his beard and arose.

"Perfectly natural question," said he, with another sly and unobserved wink at Mr. Creede. "Deserves a frank answer. I can't say what the other boys have to show for 'em; but as f'r me, I've got a good house, an' a damn good barn. Good day. See you ag'in, I hope!"[17]

At another time, when Upright is awarded a bridge-building contract, Paul Holbrook, a young reformer, threatens to have an injunction issued against the project. Upright inquires of Paul how much legal information he has as a basis for his injunction and then concludes, "Well, did you know that I've got my pay a'ready from the county for buildin' the bridge? I have you know. Now go ahead and injunct all you please. I never meant to build the damned bridge anyway" (303).

Such anecdotes are easily recognizable as the materials of modern rural folklore. Someone remarks of this story that it will soon be told in every threshing crew in the county. One of Quick's major accomplishments is his successful amalgamation of such folklore with the creation of credible characters, in an effectively realized setting. His novels are full of stories like this, vital with the warmth of reality; yet they never seem to be piled up in catalogue fashion, like the tales of stinginess which make up much of the chapter titled "How the Meanest Man Got So Mean, and How Mean He Got" in Kirkland's *Zury.* Quick's people do not often degenerate into caricatures, and when they do it is not because of the tales about them, but because they are inadequately developed or because they are obliged to speak a synthetic and thus unconvincing dialect.

Fremont McConkey's Uncle Steve Lawless is an example of a purposely bizarre character whose highly figurative and sometimes barely understandable speech puts him on the verge of incredibility. The following exchange, which takes place when Uncle Steve visits a watchmaker to have his watch repaired, affords a fair illustration of his everyday speech:

[17] Herbert Quick, *The Hawkeye* (Indianapolis: Bobbs-Merrill Co., 1923), pp. 280–281.

"Lew," said he, handing the timepiece to the artisan, "gi' me some kind of a turnip that'll sort of prop up my judgment when I look at the sun, an' take another runnin' jump at this regulator of mine."

"Didn't it run after I fixed it?" asked Lew.

"Up hill an' down, with the stage," said Uncle Steve, "when the rig did; an' that's all. Now you've had two guesses at this watch, but I'll give yeh another whack at it. If she don't ecker this time, it's the amen trip" [115].

This comes perilously close to sounding like a parody of a third-rate British novel about the American West. Quick's handling of dialogue is ordinarily more skillful, as evidenced by the earlier quotations from Roswell Upright and by the perfectly natural rendering of the words of the wagon driver who stops his horses barely in time to avoid trampling on the boy Fremont, who is snaring gophers in the grass: " 'Gether up that young one,' said he, 'so I kin drive up' " (19). Quick was not a master at reproducing foreign accents, and consequently the red-haired Norwegian, Magnus Thorkelson, becomes pretty much of a caricature. Quick allows Magnus only one form of the verb "to be"—"bane"—and with the exception of the word "ralroad," which carries conviction, the speech of this rather important character is a typical stage-Scandinavian dialect.

Quick's effective use of the vernacular is less evident, however, in the dialogue of his characters, at least in *Vandemark's Folly*, than in the language of his narration. The "frame" of *Vandemark's Folly* is that of a book of memoirs compiled by Jacob Vandemark himself in his old age. Quick is thus able to use the casual, rambling method of a garrulous old man, but he is also obliged to use the kind of language such a self-educated man would naturally employ. Inevitably this would mean the inclusion of a great number of idioms, a number of which might call for explanation or even defense. Some of these are handled in explanatory notes, ostensibly by Vandemark's granddaughter (such as "emptins" and "possblummies"); others merely occur naturally in the course of the narrative and are explained by their context. For examples, when Jacob is barely acquainted with Virginia Royall, he begins to call her "Virginia," because "Miss Royall" would be the name of the wife of a man named

Royall.[18] He says that it "gravelled him like sixty" to pay an exorbitant price for something; a lawyer tried to practice but "didn't make much of an out of it"; someone "didn't know B from a bull's foot"; Vandemark describes himself as being "wamble-cropped" (confused, stymied, powerless to act); and near the end he says, "What remains to be told here is a short horse and soon curried."[19]

Such use of vernacular idiom is the stock in trade of all writers of fiction trying to catch the flavor of a particular time and place, and there is nothing especially striking about Quick's handling of the technique. Although he employs these peculiarities of language deliberately, perhaps somewhat self-consciously, he does not as a rule overload his narrative passages with them, nor do they appreciably hinder the average reader's comprehension of the story. Quick uses them naturally, probably because they were familiar to him and presumably part of his natural speech patterns. Although *The Hawkeye* is presented as the autobiography of Fremont McConkey, these idioms are not so noticeable, perhaps because McConkey is portrayed as more "literary" than Jacob Vandemark. Nevertheless, they do appear occasionally and add to the flavor of the story.

Herbert Quick's novels are of particular interest because in them one can find expressed several of the attitudes and beliefs described in Chapter I as being characteristic of farm people. For example, the contempt felt by farmers toward any labor other than physical is clearly illustrated in a scene in which Fremont comes home after a day of teaching in the district school and encounters his brother Henry, who has been working in the hayfield. Fremont remarks on the heat, and Henry replies, "You'd 'a' thought it was hot . . . if you'd 'a' been with me pitchin' that slew hay this afternoon."[20] Quick makes an observation doubtless based on his own experience:

> It was assumed on Henry's part that Fremont was doing less than his share of the hard work, and Fremont himself felt a little guilty on the point, for life in the McConkey family was reckoned on a

[18] Quick, *Vandemark's Folly*, p. 164.
[19] *Ibid.*, pp. 95, 136, 213, 414, and *passim*.
[20] Quick, *The Hawkeye*, p. 75.

system which used muscular exertion of a useful nature as the standard of value. Fremont himself looked upon his teaching as a sybaritic indulgence, to which he was seduced by his love for reading and study [75–76].

The sharp social distinction between farmers and townsmen and the resultant hostility between the two groups were also apparent to Quick and receive due attention in his novels. Many of the people Jacob Vandemark meets on the Old Ridge Road are headed for Monterey County, and he speculates on the chances of encountering them again when he arrives there:

> They would be neighbors of mine, maybe; but probably not. They looked like town people; and I knew already the distance that separated farmers from the dwellers in the towns—a difference that as I read history, runs away back through all the past. They were far removed from what I should be—something I realized more and more all through my life—the difference between those who live on the farms and those who live on the farmers.[21]

The last sentence of this passage suggests also the belief on the part of the farmers that they were being exploited by the merchants and bankers. This theme is not ignored in Quick's novels, although it is not pressed to such extremes that they become in any sense tracts. *The Hawkeye* includes a chapter in which the governor, a member of the Republican machine dominated by the railroads, is to speak before an audience of Grangers who have allied themselves with the Anti-Monopoly party. Banners are tacked up reading "As Citizens We Favor the Anti-Monopoly Convention," "As Grangers We Know No Party," and "We Mean Business." When the governor refuses to speak until the banners are removed and orders their removal, Zenas Smith replies, "When this banner is tore down, . . . there'll be guts layin' around this grove."[22] Quick does not explicitly endorse this insurrection, but most of the characters who have been sympathetically portrayed are participants in it. His autobiography indicates that he was an agrarian liberal with strong feelings about the exploitation of the farmer by businessmen and politicians. If his sympathies are with the embattled farmer, however,

[21] Quick, *Vandemark's Folly*, p. 120.
[22] Quick, *The Hawkeye*, p. 103.

and if he wishes the reader to share these sympathies, his narrative method in *The Hawkeye* is not calculated to produce this result. Throughout the novel attention is centered on the "ins"—the railway-dominated machine, of which Fremont is a more or less unwitting beneficiary—and the only picture we get of the farm protest groups is through the eyes of their opponents.

Herbert Quick is not a farm novelist par excellence, for considerable portions of his novels are devoted to town affairs—the activities of the courthouse ring in *The Hawkeye* and Fremont McConkey's life in that circle, the development of Christina Thorkelson in *The Invisible Woman*. His great contribution is the story of settlement on the Iowa prairie. His treatment of pioneering is by no means the most profound in American fiction —Willa Cather and Rölvaag both provide deeper insights into this experience—nor is he the polished artist that these two and some others are. But he dealt with the topic in a locale where it had not been treated previously and proved by his work that Iowa history contained the materials for serious fiction.

The most penetrating treatment of pioneering occurs in what at least one critic, John T. Flanagan, regards as the high point of the farm novel thus far, Ole Edvart Rölvaag's *Giants in the Earth* (1927). Since Garland's bleak tales in *Main-Travelled Roads* there had been little stress on the negative side of the pioneer experience, of the ultimate failure of those who had sung "O'er the hills in legions, boys," of the possibility that the end of the whole effort might be futility. Those who treated the subject superficially evaded the problem altogether and presented a rosy picture of blooming fields and contented people after the initial hardships had been weathered. Miss Cather, whose treatment could certainly not be called superficial, wrote some of her early stories in the naturalistic vein of Garland but later took an affirmative approach, and the picture we get in *O Pioneers!* is, so far as the group is concerned, scarcely distinguishable from that of those novelists who saw only the surface of things. In Quick's novels the pioneers overcome the resistance of nature and build up a society and a state on the prairies at no great cost to the individual. But Rölvaag was determined to give what he considered the true picture, and since his own experience had been that of a Norwegian immigrant, he chose to embrace both the pioneering venture and the immigrant's adjustment to a new environment in his books.

In Garland's stories the struggle is chiefly with an economic structure oriented away from the interests of the farmer; in his tales nature is usually portrayed as beneficent or at least not hostile to man. For example, when Bradley Talcott, the hero of *A Spoil of Office* (1892), returns to the country after a time away from it, "the thought came to him there, for the first time, that nature was not malignant nor hard; that life on a farm might be the most beautiful and joyous life in the world."[23] Rölvaag reverses the emphasis. His pioneers do not find themselves at odds with the economic system—are indeed scarcely aware of it— and the relations of man to man are chiefly benevolent; Per Hansa's relations with his neighbors, with the Trönders farther east, with the Indians, eventually even with the Irish, are all mutually helpful associations. Nature is the force that the pioneers must contend with—in the person of the inscrutable, subtly malignant prairie, which seems to promise rich yields and then destroys the grain with a plague of locusts, which drives women mad with loneliness, and which finally destroys the man who violates its laws by venturing forth in the blizzard.

The importance of *Giants in the Earth* in a study of the farm novel requires that some attention be given to its origins and purposes, to the extent that these can be known or surmised from the facts of Rölvaag's biography. The novel had its inception in the spring of 1923, when Rölvaag learned that the Norwegian novelist Johan Bojer was planning a trip to America in order to collect information for a novel on the Norwegian immigration to the United States. Rölvaag had apparently been considering such a work, and this news provided him with a strong incentive to go ahead with the work, for if Bojer were to anticipate him, his opportunity to do the job for which he felt especially well qualified would pass.[24] Rölvaag asked for and received a leave of

[23] Hamlin Garland, *A Spoil of Office* (Boston: Arena Publishing Co., 1892), p. 263.
[24] Theodore Jorgenson and Nora O. Solum, *Ole Edvart Rölvaag: A Biography* (New York: Harper and Brothers, 1939), p. 324.

absence from his teaching duties at St. Olaf College and in September of that year began writing the novel in a lake-shore cottage in northern Minnesota. As his biographers, Nora Solum and Theodore Jorgenson, point out, he had five choices as to locale: the Muskego community in Wisconsin, the first major Norwegian settlement in the United States; the colony in northeastern Iowa, centering about Decorah; the later movement to Fillmore and Goodhue counties in Minnesota, which ultimately became the most important Norwegian community; the still later settlement in eastern South Dakota; or the final "leapfrog jump" into North Dakota (325). He chose the fourth of these, chiefly because his own first years in America had been spent in that region (although he arrived in 1896, and the period he deals with begins in 1873) and he was therefore familiar with the geography and history of the area. Besides his own youthful experience, he drew upon the recollections of his wife's father, who had followed Per Hansa's route west from Fillmore County and had later become county auditor of Minnehaha County, South Dakota, and upon the recollections of other early settlers who were still living.

The book was written in Norwegian and originally published in Oslo in two volumes in 1924 and 1925. Its immediate success in Norway, coupled with its use of an American subject, made an English version almost indispensable. The process by which such a version was arrived at calls for more than passing mention because of the implications it has for matters of style and even meaning. In his foreword, Rölvaag acknowledges the assistance of nine people in the translation, in addition to himself and Lincoln Colcord, who are chiefly responsible for the form in which the novel finally appeared. Colcord did not work from a Norse original but rather from a rough English version already prepared by several others, notably Ansten Anstenson, one of Rölvaag's former students. He rewrote the novel in his own fashion and submitted each alteration of the original to Rölvaag for the latter's approval. Some of these alterations are quite extensive; sentences and even whole paragraphs have been added, and the speech of individual characters has been considerably modified. According to Rölvaag's biographers, Per Hansa has been made to sound more effusive than in the original, with a great increase in the amount of profanity he uses, and Syvert Tönseten (whose name is Tönset in the Norwegian original) is more of a braggart than Rölvaag had portrayed him (374). Since all these changes were made with Rölvaag's knowledge and approval, it cannot be said that Colcord wrote a new book or that the picture we have of Per Hansa and others is Colcord's rather than Rölvaag's. It is probable that in many cases the recommended alterations struck Rölvaag as improvements which would better express his meaning and his characterization to an English-speaking audience. But it does mean that great caution must be exercised in any effort to interpret Rölvaag's characters on the basis of their speech.[25]

The superiority of *Giants in the Earth* to most of its predecessors lies not merely in a different approach to the pioneering venture, the validity of which might be a matter of dispute, but in the general artistic superiority of the novel. Rölvaag has succeeded in individualizing his characters, so that in spite of the alien culture which surrounds and conditions them, they stand out as real people: Per Hansa, the buoyant, capable, pragmatic pioneer; Beret, the sensitive, timid, Old World type of woman who longs for the familiar and the certain; Hans Olsa, ponderous in his physical build and his mental processes, a man to whom right and wrong are absolutes; Tönseten, unstable, imaginative, emotional, full of fears and enthusiasms. Rölvaag has accomplished this task of individualizing his characters despite the fact that their personal peculiarities of speech are obscured in translation.

Nora V. Lewison, in an unpublished doctoral dissertation, has pointed out a major difference between Willa Cather's and Rölvaag's literary methods. Miss Cather, she says, is primarily interested in individual personalities, and subordinates the external story of pioneering to the internal structure of character development; whereas Rölvaag reverses the emphasis and gives his principal attention to the external story, including the internal story within that. She also points out that Miss Cather takes up, chron-

[25] In this connection Rölvaag's own comment on translations in general is worth noting: "Translated works are but rough approximations, but shadows of the reality they try to convey." *Ibid.*, p. 115.

ologically, where Rölvaag leaves off, and attributes Miss Cather's optimism, in part at least, to the fact that she deals with a later, more hopeful period.[26] Vernon L. Parrington, in his introduction to *Giants in the Earth*, takes a somewhat different approach to the subject. Although Miss Cather displays a warm sympathy with the emotional life of pioneer women and a poignant understanding of their bleak lot, he says, her analysis, like Garland's, "draws back from the threshold of final tragedy, pausing before it has penetrated to the hidden core of futility."[27] Whatever the validity of these two views, which seem to represent different, if not conflicting, approaches, it should be pointed out that Rölvaag's way of making his point in the *external* realm (the whole pioneer experience) is by means of the successful portrayal of the *internal* problem. People of Beret's kind pass off the stage early in Miss Cather's novels and occupy no more of our attention, which is then focused on the successful pioneer. Rölvaag keeps Beret in the center of the narrative and in this way emphasizes the tragic side of the process. The death of Per Hansa, the sort of person who would be expected to succeed, underscores this tragedy and gives it a broader significance.

The two main characters in *Giants in the Earth* are, of course, Beret and Per Hansa. They represent not merely two types of personality but two fundamental attitudes toward life, and they lend themselves to two different kinds of literary treatment. Rölvaag's biographers see Per Hansa as essentially a romantic character, while Beret is treated both realistically and naturalistically.[28] One of the four literary influences they find evident in the novel is Norwegian fairy lore, centering about the figure of the *Askeladd*, who, like Per Hansa, is characterized by such traits as resourcefulness, inventiveness, a *joie de vivre*, ambition, and the gambling instinct (344). Per Hansa's repeated good fortune in everything but the mental state of his wife and his final defeat

[26] Nora V. Lewison, "The Achievement of Willa Cather" (doctoral dissertation, State University of Iowa, 1944), pp. 71–76.

[27] Vernon L. Parrington, *The Beginnings of Critical Realism in America* (New York: Harcourt, Brace & Co., 1930), p. 393. Reprinted from "Editor's Introduction" to Ole Edvart Rölvaag, *Giants in the Earth* (New York: Harper and Brothers, 1927), p. xvi.

[28] Jorgenson and Solum, *Ole Edvart Rölvaag*, p. 347.

also identify him with the *Askeladd,* who is the child of fortune.
Hence it is inevitable that so long as the novel centers about him
it must be essentially romantic. Beret, on the other hand, is passive rather than active, the product of her environment rather
than the molder of it. A dark theology that emphasizes fear has
accentuated what may be presumed to have been a natural timid-
ity; the physical emptiness and spiritual loneliness of the Dakota
prairie provide the culminating influence needed to shake her
sanity.

Beret's fear is revealed early in the novel. In the opening
chapter, while she and Per Hansa are seeking the rest of the
party, whom they have lost, she expresses her feeling: " 'I wonder
if we shall ever see them again,' she said, as if speaking to herself,
and looked down at the ground. 'This seems to be taking us to
the end of the world . . . beyond the end of the world!' "[29] It
continues after they have found the others: "How will human
beings be able to endure this place? she thought. Why there isn't
even a thing that one can *hide behind!*" (29). Something of this
vague fear is felt by the rest of the settlers, too:

> No one put the thought into words, but they all felt it strongly; now
> they had gone back to the very beginning of things. . . .
> This mood brought vague premonitions to them, difficult to
> interpret. . . . No telling what might happen out here . . . for almost
> anything *could* happen! . . .
> They were so far from the world . . . cut off from the haunts of
> their fellow beings . . . so terribly far! . . . [32–33].

Per Hansa is the one to break the hold of this mood, though he
is clearly affected by it himself. As time goes on, the feeling
wears off among the other members of the party, but in Beret it
lingers and grows stronger. When Per Hansa is away, she puts
heavy cloths over the windows and pushes their great trunk (a
symbol of the old stable world they have left) against the door,
not so much as a matter of practical protection as to shut out
the vastness and emptiness of the prairie. The loneliness finally
breaks Beret, and she dwells for a time "on the border of utter
darkness." Her mind is restored by Per Hansa's love for her, but
she slips into the religious fanaticism which is the ultimate cause

[29] Rölvaag, *Giants in the Earth,* p. 8.

of her husband's futile journey into the blizzard during which he loses his life. Her obsession with the sinfulness of all men infects the dying Hans Olsa, and he asks Per Hansa to go for the minister. Per Hansa's body is found the next spring, facing west.

Although little can be said of the use of the vernacular in a book written in a foreign tongue and then translated into English, the explanatory notes in *Giants in the Earth* indicate that the author knew and employed with conscious skill the Nordland dialect which all his characters speak. Folklore and folk beliefs figure importantly in the novel. Tönseten's wife Kjersti tells the story of a childless couple (like herself and Syvert) who wished to have a child. The wife consulted a witch-woman, who gave her both *"devil's drink* and *beaver-geld,"* without effect. Finally, one summer a fleet of strange fishermen came to the fjord, and the woman bore a child to one of them. The husband was as fond of the child as if it had been his own, but on the day it was to be christened, a storm came up as they were crossing the fjord, and both mother and child were lost. Syvert tries to dispel the sobering effect this story has had on the group by saying, "We're through now with all that troll business over in Norway!" (206–207). But trolls figure in the thinking of these people; even Per Hansa thinks of the trolls when he finds stakes with Irish names on them at the corners of his neighbors' land. When Beret discovers that he has removed the stakes, she is appalled, for in Norway removing a man's landmarks was both a serious crime and a sin for which a special punishment was reserved in the hereafter. The religious beliefs of these people are important and distinctive. The devil is very real to them, and he is responsible for much of their misfortune. The exaggerated respect shown the minister, who is quite an ordinary man in appearance and manner, is also characteristic of the Old World people.

Instead of the anti-intellectualism evident among some pioneer groups, these people show a tremendous desire for education. Henry Solum is appointed to keep a school in his house, and later the school is made a community institution, held by turns in all the houses of the settlers and attended by adults as well as children. Although Henry's pedagogy consists of nothing more than telling stories in both Norwegian and English and having the children memorize them, this effort is indicative of the hunger for knowledge in the Spring Creek settlement.

The title of the final section of *Giants in the Earth* is "The Great Plain Drinks the Blood of Christian Men and Is Satisfied." The last two words are important. After Per Hansa and Hans Olsa have died, the settlement of the prairie continues and is finally completed. The locust plague has ended several years earlier, and from this point on, the struggle is never again so desperate. In Rölvaag's two succeeding novels, *Peder Victorious* and *Their Fathers' God*, the conflict is no longer between man and a hostile nature but between man and man; these novels concern the cultural and religious conflicts that arise in the new land. So in the final analysis, the pioneering venture is successful so far as the whole society is concerned, however futile it may have been for the individual. The kingdom is founded, after all, even though the cost has been tremendous.

Rölvaag's purpose, then, was not to show the futility of the whole pioneering process but to indicate the cost at which this achievement was made. His biographers state that Rölvaag "to his dying day . . . insisted that he was primarily interested in the cost, culturally and psychologically, of pioneering."[30] The price which had to be paid had not previously been stressed; Willa Cather emphasized the successful people, like Alexandra Bergson and Ántonia Shimerda, rather than those who failed, like John Bergson and old Anton Shimerda. Rölvaag was therefore making an essentially new contribution on the ideological level while clothing his interpretation of a historical event in artistically satisfying garb. The optimism of Per Hansa is symbolic, but it is not merely symbolic; it is also highly individual, and the character of Per Hansa is realized to a degree that Alexandra Bergson was not. As David Daiches points out, Alexandra is more effective as a symbol of the Earth Mother or Ceres than convincing as a person.[31] Similarly, Beret's fear is depicted with a degree of realism that makes it understandable and Beret herself thoroughly

[30] Jorgenson and Solum, *Ole Edvart Rölvaag*, p. 323.
[31] Daiches, *Willa Cather*, p. 28.

believable. Besides this, Rölvaag provides the detailed and accurate treatment of the physical setting that we have come to expect in any competently written farm novel of the period.

Rölvaag was concerned about another kind of cost different from the one discussed in the preceding paragraphs: the loss of cultural continuity suffered by the immigrant who cut himself off physically from the Old World. In dealing with this subject he made a contribution almost as significant as his treatment of the pioneering theme, if not more so. The most penetrating fictional treatment of the immigrant's adjustment problems would logically come from one of his own group. Rölvaag gave the subject some attention in *Giants in the Earth,* but the absence of any real contact with people outside the Norwegian community (except for the Irish) limited the possibilities in this book. The men face up to the necessity of substituting legally acceptable surnames for the old Scandinavian patronymics, and there are a few other passing references to the problem of being a Norwegian in America, but the matter is not taken up in detail. In Rölvaag's next novel, *Peder Victorious* (1929), he makes this problem the central theme. The struggle is carried on between Peder, Per Hansa's son, who is eager to adopt American ways, and his mother, Beret, who is determined to retain the customs, traditions, and language that she brought from Norway. Her position is that it is impossible to deracinate oneself to the extent of becoming a mere unhyphenated American and blasphemous to attempt to do so.

The conflict takes several forms, most prominently in the areas of the school, the church, and the family. Peder for a time attends a mixed Irish-Norwegian school taught by the fiercely patriotic Clarabelle Mahon, who would feel at home at a D.A.R. convention. Here Peder's growing preference for the English language and his friendliness with the Irish persuade Beret to have him transferred to an all-Norwegian school. The conflict in the church centers about the liberal Pastor Gabrielson, who, seeing that English will ultimately supplant Norwegian, conducts informal services in the adopted tongue. Because Beret feels that discarding the old language will lead to the loss of national identity, Gabrielson's gift to Peder of an English Bible precipitates a long-continued antagonism between them. The family conflict, ultimately the most serious because it involves not only language but religion as well, concerns Peder's interest in Susie Doheny, the daughter of one of the Irish Catholic families who settled in the Spring Creek district in Per Hansa's time. Beret strenuously opposes the alliance and is persuaded to allow it to ripen into marriage only when she believes she has seen Per Hansa in a vision and he has advised her not to interfere.

Rölvaag's precise position on these issues is not easy to determine from the novel itself, for he presents both sides with scrupulous objectivity, just as he does the Catholic-Protestant conflict in the next novel, *Their Fathers' God* (1931). Fortunately, his other utterances on the subject, cited in the Solum-Jorgenson biography, do much to clarify the point. The fact is that Rölvaag was profoundly concerned about the loss of cultural and "racial" (i.e., national) identity by the Scandinavian immigrants to the American Middle West. His concern centered especially about the matter of language, for he felt that the most difficult adjustment the immigrant had to make was adopting a new language and making it his own to the extent that his mental and emotional life would be identified with it. He said once in a public address, "The giving up of one language and acquiring a new necessitates a spiritual readjustment far beyond the power of the average man. The old he cannot let go because that would mean starvation to his soul. The new he cannot master because the process is beyond human power."[32] In the light of this attitude, it is clear that Rölvaag's sympathies are not with Peder in his determination to shake off the old allegiances and become an American indistinguishable from Americans of other national origins.

Since Rölvaag believed that each immigrant group could make its greatest contribution to American society by preserving its national identity, he naturally found himself in opposition to the melting-pot concept that has fascinated Americans since Crèvecoeur's letter titled "What is an American?" His biographers state that "throughout his mature days, Rölvaag was a racial and a cultural purist. He believed that high values come into the human realm by way of personalization rather than

[32] Quoted in Jorgenson and Solum, *Ole Edvart Rölvaag*, p. 396.

through diffusion, through purity of strain rather than through any melting pot" (413).

The tragic consequences of a marriage contracted in defiance of cultural and religious differences is the thematic issue in Rölvaag's third novel in this series, *Their Fathers' God*. From the beginning of their marriage, Peder and Susie have conflicts over religion. Susie retains and practices her Catholic faith; Peder, although nominally a member of the local Lutheran congregation and contemptuous of Catholicism, actually takes no part in the religious life of the community; Beret, the third element in this triad, is of course an orthodox Lutheran, opposed alike to her daughter-in-law's faith and to Peder's religious indifference. Thus there are really three positions in the equation, rather than a simple Catholic-Protestant dichotomy. In fact, the specifically religious opposition is more or less incidental; as Rölvaag's biographers remark, the book is "not a contribution to the literature of ecclesiastical controversy" (419). The idea of the novel apparently was conceived before that of *Giants in the Earth* and in its original form involved characters of the same religious affiliation. What Rölvaag is concerned about are the consequences of efforts at cultural amalgamation and rejection of old cultural patterns. Susie represents one cultural stream, Catholic in religion; Beret represents another, Lutheran; Peder represents the synthetic American who deliberately severs himself from his cultural moorings and then finds himself adrift. As a rationalist, he is in conflict with his wife's religious beliefs and practices. The same problem would have arisen had he been an orthodox Lutheran or had she been a Lutheran and he a rationalist unfamiliar with the externals of the Lutheran faith. The essential problem would have existed had they been of the same faith but of different cultural backgrounds (at one time Rölvaag believed that immigrants should not marry members of their own national group born in America); Rölvaag provided a religious difference to dramatize his case.

Rölvaag's fears of cultural chaos if the old languages were given up and intermarriage permitted may seem unjustified in the light of subsequent history, but there is no doubt that he understood and clearly depicted the tensions experienced by the immigrants and the first-generation Americans while the process was going on. It is his comprehension and his effective treatment in fiction that give Rölvaag his pre-eminence among interpreters of the immigrant psychology. By including these problems in the story of pioneering and presenting them with unequaled insight and understanding, he adds a new dimension to the fictional treatment of the pioneer experience. Although neither of the later novels reaches the artistic level of *Giants in the Earth*, they do increase Rölvaag's stature as a novelist by giving attention to a subject not dealt with extensively in the first of the series. There is little doubt that *Giants in the Earth* is the most satisfying treatment of the pioneering theme that has thus far appeared in the literature of the Middle West, perhaps the finest achievement in the realm of the farm novel.

After Rölvaag a number of writers attempted to deal with the pioneering venture, with varying degrees of success. Their products generally suffer by comparison with *Giants in the Earth*, especially if the theme is fairly close to that of Rölvaag's book. This is illustrated by Walter J. Muilenburg's *Prairie* (1925), technically subsequent to the appearance in Norway of *Giants in the Earth*, although it is highly unlikely that Muilenburg was familiar with the earlier work. *Prairie* concerns the settlement of the Nebraska region and centers about the experiences of a young couple who go there from the Mississippi Valley, presumably Iowa. Elias Vaughn becomes increasingly dissatisfied with his father's rigid discipline; and when the elder Vaughn refuses to let his son go out with Lizzie Dalton, the daughter of a shiftless neighbor family, Elias elopes with the girl and runs off to the new country west of the Missouri. Here the young people are nearly driven to the wall by drought during a series of difficult years but finally achieve economic success and status in a settled community. Life on the prairie, however, is too much for Lizzie, and she dies of sheer exhaustion, after her mind has begun to waver. Their son leaves the farm (against his father's will) and takes work in the nearby town; after his mother's death and his own disillusionment with town life, he returns to the farm, only to be disowned and refused admittance by his father. The wheel has come full circle.

Muilenburg had apparently been considering his theme a decade before the publication of *Prairie*, for the August, 1915, issue of *The Midland* contains a story by him entitled "The Prairie" in which the basic outline of the novel appears. The main characters in the story are John Barrett and Lizzie Delton and the course of their fortunes roughly parallels that of Elias and Lizzie in the novel.[33] Another story published by Muilenburg in 1915, "Heart of Youth," deals with a boy discontented with farm life and doomed to operating the family farm while his parents go west in the interests of the mother's health.[34] Rölvaag gave definitive treatment to the theme of a man and woman unequal in psychological stamina and in their enthusiasm for the pioneer experience together "facing the great desolation," and compared with his achievement the work of Muilenburg seems ineffective. There are touches of grim realism in *Prairie*, but the action (covering about twenty years) is described in too few pages, and hence Lizzie's disintegration fails to carry the conviction that Beret's does. The novel is really only an expanded short story, not sufficiently expanded for the scope of the theme. In its treatment of a woman unable to endure the trials of prairie life, however, it does display a recognition of the cost at which the conquest of the continent was achieved. Since the English version of *Giants in the Earth* did not appear until 1927, *Prairie* may be considered an anticipation, crude but not negligible, of Rölvaag's epic.

Among the many writers who used the pioneering theme in the later 1920's and in the 1930's were at least three women novelists—Bess Streeter Aldrich, Josephine Donovan, and Rose Wilder Lane. Of these only Mrs. Lane is important enough to require much attention here. Mrs. Aldrich's books, *A Lantern in Her Hand* (1928) and *Song of Years* (1939), contribute nothing essentially new to the story of pioneering in Iowa and Nebraska,

[33] *The Midland*, I (August 1915), 260–270. Muilenburg published six stories in *The Midland* between 1915 and 1922, at least half of which include the motif of a conflict between parent and child. Among other farm novelists whose early work, either fiction or poetry, appeared in *The Midland* were Ruth Suckow, Paul Corey, Henry Bellamann, Grace Stone Coates, Paul Engle, David Cornel DeJong, Josephine Johnson, and K. Eleanor Saltzman.

[34] *The Midland*, I (November 1915), 362–377.

already competently treated by more perceptive writers, and are marred by sentimental plots and much bad writing. Miss Donovan's *Black Soil* (1930) is a more satisfying piece of work, but it too suffers from its author's tendency to sentimentalize and romanticize her material. One critic remarks that "it is difficult to take seriously a novel in which a girl named Sheila Connors is discovered to be part Indian and in the last chapter rides off into the sunset with her Indian lover. . . ."[35] Although this comment includes some distortion of fact, it is a fair enough estimate of the book as a whole. The chief distinction of *Black Soil* is that it, almost alone among farm novels, deals with a group that consists chiefly of Catholics, the Irish and German settlers of northwestern Iowa.

Rose Wilder Lane found in the settlement of the Dakota prairie a theme for fictional treatment. Although her handling of the subject is clearly not comparable to Rölvaag's, it has points of distinct superiority over the work of Mrs. Aldrich and Miss Donovan. Her two novels, *Let the Hurricane Roar* (1933) and *Free Land* (1938), are parallel treatments of the same subject, the first very brief, scarcely more than an outline, the second a full-scale novel with an announced purpose and a wealth of detail to give it significance. *Let the Hurricane Roar* (a line from a hymn—there are no hurricanes in Dakota) is the story of a couple who homestead in present-day South Dakota. Afflicted with the usual quota of misfortune, they see their first crop eaten by grasshoppers just when they have gone deeply into debt. The husband goes to Iowa to find work during the winter and leaves his wife in the care of the Svensons, recent immigrants who know little English and less about farming on the prairie. When the Svensons give up, the young wife and her baby decide to stay at the townsite during the winter but find that the village affords no place to stay except on a charity basis. So they return to the sod hut and contend with blizzards until the husband unexpectedly appears in the midst of one of the nearly continuous storms. They look forward hopefully to the approaching season.

Free Land is a more detailed development of essentially the

[35] Charles T. Dougherty, "Novels of the Middle Border: A Critical Bibliography for Historians," *Historical Bulletin*, XXV (May 1947), 87.

same story, with modifications and additions. The situation here is not quite so desperate, because the young couple in this novel are more ingenious and more fortunate than those in the first book. A number of incidents are added, such as the Indian scare that results from the theft by an amateur anthropologist of the mummified body of a Sioux child. Although somewhat theatrical, this story has about it a certain air of plausibility. In a brief foreword Mrs. Lane suggests that this novel is intended as an attack on the public land system of the United States, which she tells us was the last nation to give away large tracts of public land to settlers. For a long time the policy was to allow the land to fall into the hands of speculators and railroads instead of those who wished to cultivate it. Since this theme is not, however, developed in the novel, its mention at the beginning impresses the reader as somewhat irrelevant.

More important is Mrs. Lane's treatment of the attitude settlers have toward the government and railroads. Cheating the government and the railroads is regarded almost as a moral duty. The law requires that a prospective settler file his claim in person, but Dr. Thorne (the amateur anthropologist) files a claim in his son's name. The author comments:

> Dr. Thorne was so excessively honest that he was helpless in a horse-trade, but dealing with the Government is another thing. . . . Beating a legality was a satisfaction, like paying something on an old grudge. A man knew instinctively that Government was his natural enemy.[36]

The same attitude prevails in respect to the railroads. The hero of the novel works one summer for Gebbert, a contractor who is helping to build the Northwestern railroad line. Gebbert buys his supplies from the company and is expected to pay for them at the end of the season. But instead of economizing, as he is expected to do, he feeds his men well and surreptitiously sells the rest of his supplies to storekeepers and settlers. Of course he goes into debt. But he is not worried; by the end of the season he will owe the railroad more than ten times the value of his outfit, so there will be no way of getting the money out of him,

[36] Rose Wilder Lane, *Free Land* (New York: Longmans, Green and Co., 1938), p. 29.

for he has his illegal gains secretly salted away in the East. None of the men who work for him see anything dishonest about this business. One says of him, "The old man's straight as a string. Hell, a man that won't steal from a railroad ain't honest" (107). The settlers who have invested in townsite lands reflect the same hostility as they tear up a boxcar and use the boards after the railroad has decided to make another town its division point, depriving them of their hope of speculative profits (108). This odd ethical position is perhaps the chief original contribution of the novel, although it has other merits as well as several defects.

A flavor of the authentic is provided by snatches from the popular songs known to the prairie dwellers. There are many versions of this one (268):

> O Dakota land, sweet Dakota land!
> As on thy burning soil I stand
> And look away across the plains
> I wonder why it never rains.
>
> O Dakota land! Sweet Dakota land!
> Thy skies are great, thy prairies grand—
> But we don't live here, we only stay
> 'Cause we're too poor to get away!

Another realistic feature of her books stems from her interest in the economics of homesteading. So detailed are her lists of the supplies and equipment needed by homesteaders that one critic has observed that "many of her pages read like a kind of auditor's report."[37]

Although Mrs. Lane offers a suggestion of the ordeal suffered by women in the new land, the subject is handled with much less deftness than in Rölvaag. Some of her incidents seem contrived, as when at the very end of *Free Land*, the husband is saved from bankruptcy by a gift of two thousand dollars from his father, to be deducted from his prospective inheritance. Mrs. Lane's style leaves something to be desired, but is adequate. The reader tires of her habit of linking independent clauses with commas and her insistence upon bringing the young couple's baby into the discussion on little or no pretext, usually as "the little shaver"; but in general, she does not overwrite, and so the simplicity of

[37] Dougherty, "Novels of the Middle Border," 86.

the subject is appropriately treated. *Let the Hurricane Roar* and *Free Land* do not rank with the finest work in their genre, but they are a contribution to the literature of the Dakota frontier.

The only farm novelist since Rölvaag to handle the immigrant theme with much penetration is Sophus Keith Winther, the author of the "Grimsen trilogy," *Take All to Nebraska* (1936), *Mortgage Your Heart* (1937), and *This Passion Never Dies* (1938). The first of these tells of the efforts of Peter and Meta Grimsen, Danish immigrants, to establish themselves on a rented farm in Nebraska. Besides having to contend with the usual difficulties of pioneer farmers—drought, grasshoppers, blizzards, low prices, and avaricious moneylenders—the Grimsens are further handicapped by being aliens in a largely English-speaking community. More than Rölvaag's people, they are made to feel their alien status with its putative inferiority. Hans, one of their five sons and the author's central intelligence, is ridiculed in school because his mother cannot speak English.

Taken by itself, the first novel seems to suggest an optimistic view of the pioneer experience. Although the Grimsens are thrust off the farm where they have lived for seven years, they find a better one and at the end of the novel are about to begin anew. More significant, the parents take out citizenship papers. Their emigration to America began tentatively, as something of an experiment, and all through the years of their struggle they have talked of returning to Denmark some day. However, they discover that they have become part of the New World—that they are facing west.

The second and third novels carry the story from 1905, when the first one ends, to the early 1920's and concentrate on the lives of the Grimsen sons, particularly Hans, who goes off to the university and for a time escapes the financial difficulties of his parents. Since Hans and his brothers are no longer acutely conscious of their immigrant background, the immigrant theme is somewhat muted in these books. The final defeat which Peter Grimsen suffers, when the post-war depression so depreciates land values that he is unable to pay for the farm he has bought at inflated war prices, is not peculiarly the fate of an immigrant, for as Paul Corey shows in his Mantz trilogy (discussed in Chapter IV), the depression hit farmers with equal severity regardless of their national origins. But the immigrant theme is not forgotten; at the end of the third novel a Bohemian family are about to move on to the Grimsen farm and repeat the cycle traced in the trilogy.

As might be expected of a novelist whose background somewhat resembles that of Hans Grimsen, Winther handles his materials realistically and treats his characters with sympathy and understanding. There is no idealization of either the farm or its inhabitants. In sharp contrast to Rölvaag's people, the Grimsens and their neighbors are largely untouched by religion. There is occasional preaching in a church nearby, but the Grimsens never attend. The boys are all hard-boiled swearers (in both English and Danish) and tobacco-chewers and can hold their own in purely physical combat with others of their age. Hans and David at least have some sensitivity, which in part alienates them from their father. The relationships of the characters with one another are treated with unsparing realism, especially the unhappy marriages of both Hans and David. Instead of the group solidarity displayed by Rölvaag's pioneers, the Danes in this novel prey on one another almost as ruthlessly as the "native Americans" prey on them; the most hateful character in the trilogy is the moneylender, Jacob Paulsen, illiterate but materially successful until the collapse of land values in 1920.

A professed determinist, Winther tries to tell his story in a strictly cause-effect sequence, with a minimum of coincidence. In his piling up of incremental detail he anticipates Corey, without, however, creating as artistically satisfying a piece of work as the Mantz trilogy. One defect of Winther's writing is a rather bumbling, unpolished style, noticeable particularly in *Take All to Nebraska*. No doubt this is partly deliberate, designed to render the mind of his central character as accurately as possible, but it does make for somewhat undistinguished writing. Another weakness of these novels is that, in spite of his insistence on realism, Winther sometimes allows melodrama to intrude upon his story. After the death of his first wife, Hans takes up with Janice Melville, who turns out to be the daughter of the very man who is behind local interests that are buying up farms at mortgage sales —the enemy, in short. Both Melvilles disappear, and Hans pursues Janice to New York, where he finally marries her. This portion of the trilogy is perilously near the bounds of realism, if it does not actually cross them.

On the whole, however, the Grimsen trilogy is a significant achievement in the realm of farm fiction. Although the ending is ambiguous, the Grimsens' struggle has ended in failure, at least for the immigrant generation, and the outlook for the next generation is only partly hopeful. Whatever Winther's intention, it can be argued from the evidence presented that the movement to America has cost more than it was worth.

Except for Winther, no other author who has treated the immigrant theme since Rölvaag requires more than passing mention. Mrs. Aldrich introduces a character somewhat like Ántonia Shimerda in *A Lantern in Her Hand*, but her treatment of this woman, Christine Reinmueller, is unsympathetic and emphasizes her coarseness at the expense of her good qualities. The Svensons in Mrs. Lane's *Let the Hurricane Roar* are generous-souled but rather ineffectual people, and her depiction of them is strictly an external view, as they are seen by the native American hero and heroine. The nearest approach to Rölvaag's achievement in recent farm fiction is to be found in the work of Feike Feikema, now writing under the name of Frederick Manfred. In *This Is the Year* (1947) the author provides some valuable insights into the mind of the immigrant through the thoughts and utterances of Alde Romke, a Frisian-born farmer in northwestern Iowa who clings to his memories of the old country and fails to adapt himself to the large-scale farming methods of the American Middle West. He resembles in many respects Willa Cather's Anton Shimerda, despite having spent the greater part of his life in America. He uses the old Frisian language frequently and disapproves of his son's marriage to a girl who is one-fourth Norwegian; he wants the family line to remain 100 per cent Frisian.

Treatment of the immigrant in the farm novel has been extensive, but, with the exception of the work of Cather and Rölvaag, it has lacked the psychological penetration and the sense of artistic form that would raise it to the level of high art. Most of the writing has been done by people with several generations of American ancestry behind them, and the authors have lacked the profound insight into the immigrant mind that makes Rölvaag's work a superior achievement. As the period of heavy immigration recedes further into the past, the number of writers who know the subject at first hand must necessarily diminish. So the possibility of any great work of this type in the future depends on the appearance of authors of unusual sensitivity and perceptiveness, like Willa Cather, who are able to understand and give expression to a phenomenon they cannot know from experience.

All the novels thus far discussed which treat of the settlement of the West have one feature in common: the land is ultimately conquered, and an agricultural society is firmly established. Whatever the fate of individuals may have been in the course of this conquest, the success of the enterprise, in terms of group achievement, is as complete as in the eastern portion of the country. It remains to discuss a novel that departs from this consistent pattern and describes a group of people trying unsuccessfully to bring under cultivation a region in which the rainfall is too scanty for agriculture.

Henry Nash Smith traces, in *Virgin Land*, the process by which the myth of the Great American Desert was transformed into the myth of the Garden of the World, so that the American people came to believe that the Great Plains region was as suitable for intensive agriculture as the Mississippi valley.[38] The long-held belief that the area between the ninetieth meridian and the Rocky Mountains was an uninhabitable desert was gradually dispelled following the Civil War, as the result of the Republican administration's need to justify its promises concerning the Homestead Act and to promote settlement in this region. The idea was advanced by competent authorities that rainfall would increase as more land was brought under cultivation. "Rain Follows the Plow" was the popular slogan, and in the years of abnormally heavy rainfall immediately following the Civil War, it seemed as if this theory were sound. In the minds of the settlers the old suspicion of the prairie had proved unfounded; many persons had refused to settle the Illinois prairies on the grounds that where God had neglected to plant trees it was no use to try raising them, but trees planted on the prairies had flourished

[38] See Smith, *Virgin Land*, Chapter XVI, pp. 174–183.

there, as had farm crops. As far west as the eastern parts of Nebraska and the Dakota Territory this had been true, even though droughts had given the settlers real trouble.

This experience lies behind the plot of Horace Kramer's *Marginal Land* (1939), which centers about Stephen Decatur Randall's attempt to raise wheat on the central South Dakota prairie. After all, his father had made trees and crops grow in the southeastern corner of the state when the odds seemed against it; why shouldn't he do likewise farther north and west? He remembers what his mother has told him and what he has heard often since then: " 'Remember, son,' she would say, 'the good Lord is not making any more land. He has given us a generous heritage of his bounty, and time alone will make us rich.' "[39] Randall is unwilling to heed the advice of his father's old friend, Simon Peter Voorhees (rather too obviously the "rock" of the novel), who insists that the land is not suited to agriculture. Steve has read the literature of the railroad promoters and insists,

> "Well, you must admit that at least there's good soil here. . . . And with a little more rain—"
> "Yeah. That's also one of the little drawbacks of hell!" exploded the old man. "I'll bet that when all these land agents go to hell—and that's where they're going if there is any justice—they'll be assuring the fresh arrivals that everything is going to be all right just as soon as they get the brimstone plowed up and some trees planted. Climate changing! Bah!" [76].

Voorhees, who brings forty years of living in this country to bear upon the subject, has seen several waves of settlement break upon the land, each new group of hopefuls led astray by advertising and unusually wet weather, only to be forced to give up and leave when the dry years returned. He advises Steve not to follow their example: "These lands here are what the sharps down at the Agricultural College call marginal lands—lands which have virtues maybe, but which ain't good enough for farming. The soil is good, but there's not enough rain. They're on the margin, as they say" (84). Steve concentrates on cattle, but the example of

---

[39] Horace Kramer, *Marginal Land* (Philadelphia: J. B. Lippincott Co., 1939), p. 15.

his neighbor, Felix Bohak, who is trying to get rich on wheat, induces him to break a good deal of prairie and sow it to grain. When the dry years return, he of course loses all he has put into the wheat enterprise and has to fall back on his cattle. Other settlers, who have tried to raise beans, raspberries, and everything but bananas, are defeated and driven out of the country or else die victims of the severe winters. The words of Voorhees have proved true: this country is suitable only for grazing and should never be plowed up.

Marginal Land is more than a tract on agriculture, however. The inexhaustible topic of human relations comes in for some attention as well. Steve Randall is a Chicago white-collar worker with a tubercular tendency. Before moving out to his claim, which he has inherited from his father, Steve marries his landlady's daughter and leaves her in Chicago until he has built up the place so that it will be fit for her reception. She arrives unexpectedly at Christmas and soon develops a strong dislike for the country. Unlike Beret Holm or the heroines of Mrs. Lane's novels, Josephine Randall is a pampered, self-indulgent city girl who is repelled by the farm animals and wants no part of the schemes her husband wishes to share with her. After about a year, she goes back to Chicago and eventually divorces Steve, who afterward marries a neighbor girl, Trina Bohak. Thus the old theme of the frontier woman and her problems is given a new twist by the introduction of a woman who lacks the most basic materials of a frontier wife.

Despite mediocre writing (Kramer makes no consistent distinction between "lay" and "lie") and some stock characters, *Marginal Land* is considerably above the run of farm novels dealing with the pioneering venture. The events are plausible, not contrived, and most of the characters are sufficiently complex to be credible. Voorhees is perhaps too wise, too perfect for complete plausibility, but he is an interesting personality, with a fine sense of humor. The humor of the book is one of its best qualities and provides a refreshing contrast to the work of the women writers discussed earlier. Although Herbert Quick employs humor, it tends to be rather labored, with only an occasional flash of real spontaneity; but Kramer seems to to have a natural sense of the comic, and in this book there is more than a dash of rollicking, earthy humor.

Since *Marginal Land* pioneering has received little serious treatment in farm fiction. By the 1930's the attention of farm novelists was shifting to depiction of more or less contemporary scenes or to the writing of psychological novels in which the farm background was largely incidental. The persistent fascination of the frontier experience is evidenced, however, by the appearance in 1956 of a novel about pioneering in Dakota Territory entitled *The Land They Possessed*, by Mary Worthy Thurston and Muriel Breneman, writing under the pseudonym of Mary Worthy Breneman. Here are all the stock elements of this type of fiction: a cultivated family possessed by the westering instinct that moved Garland's father in the years after the Civil War, a boom town at the end of the railroad, a plethora of blizzards, drought, and prairie fires, a gang of bandits led by a somewhat incredible villain, and, to make it complete, a horde of Russo-German immigrants whose assimilation is demanded and yet hindered by the "native Americans," who regard them with contempt. If all these materials had not been handled before, and more skillfully, *The Land They Possessed* would require extended treatment here. Unfortunately, however, despite a certain technical finish that such writers as Muilenburg and Lane might envy, this novel strikes the critic as little more than a rehash of themes that had demonstrated wide appeal in the early decades of the twentieth century.

It may be significant that most of the novels about the pioneer experience were written in the generation or generation and a half following the pronouncement of the Turner thesis (1893). Once the frontier was irrevocably gone, interest in the story of its settlement rose high and remained so until other events and issues, such as World War I and the farm depression of the 1920's, intervened and sent the novelists off in new directions. The revival of the pioneering theme in *The Land They Possessed* probably shows only that this subject can never entirely lose its charm for the general reader and does not augur any major return to it by authors of the stature of Cather and Rölvaag.

IV.

Escape and Return
The Farm Novelist as Arbiter of Values

ONE WRITER has remarked that there have been two popular attitudes toward the farmer: God bless him, and Devil take him.[1]
Much the same might be said of the attitudes toward the farm
taken by the writers of rural fiction. Aside from the nostalgic
approach popular in the nineteenth century, there are two prevalent views: the notion that the farm is narrow and stultifying
and that the person of breadth and ability will do well to leave
it as soon as possible, and the attitude that life close to the soil
is more wholesome and more satisfying to human beings than
life in the city. The former view is the earlier and can be traced
back to nineteenth-century farm fiction. The fiction endorsing
this view does not bulk large, however, and is restricted almost
entirely to the period before 1930. The second, or affirmative,
approach became popular in the 1920's and virtually supplanted
the earlier, negative approach in the depression decade of the
1930's, when farm life seemed especially attractive to many city
dwellers.

The negative view of the farm corresponds philosophically
and to some extent chronologically to the revolt-from-the-village
movement in American literature typified by Edgar Lee Masters'
Spoon River Anthology (1915) and Sherwood Anderson's *Winesburg, Ohio* (1919). For a variety of reasons, of which the most
important may be the general literary inferiority of most farm
fiction endorsing it, the manifestation of this attitude in rural
fiction was overshadowed by the more famous movement and
never developed independently. The disillusionment of the 1920's
did not affect farm novelists so intensely as it did those writers

[1] Nelson Antrim Crawford, "The American Farmer in Fact and Fiction,"
Literary Digest International Book Review, IV (December 1925), 25.

who were more directly in touch with its sources. Only a few of the writers of farm fiction (of whom Glenway Wescott is the most conspicuous example) participated in the disillusionment or reflected it in their novels.

The seeming continuity between the nostalgic, sentimental view of the farm prominent in nineteenth-century fiction and the affirmative view taken by many writers of the 1920's and 1930's is more apparent than real and may be a mere matter of coincidence. The two differ in the fundamental respect that the nineteenth-century view was essentially romantic, whereas the twentieth-century approach is emphatically realistic. To the nineteenth-century author the farm was good because it was devoid of faults; to the twentieth-century novelist holding the affirmative view it is good in spite of its faults, which are never ignored and seldom underplayed in novels of any consequence. Thus the recent "God bless it" approach is based upon a much solider foundation than that of the sentimental novelists of the last century.

This is not to suggest that the romantic approach was dominant throughout all of the nineteenth century. The late nineteenth century was, so far as its most significant fiction is concerned, predominantly an age of realism. In keeping with the vogue, the farm, as we have seen, received harsh treatment at the hands of Howe, Kirkland, and Frederic. One of the best illustrations of the "Devil take it" attitude toward the farm is found in *Seth's Brother's Wife*; one of the more perceptive characters in this novel says:

> The nineteenth century is a century of cities; they have given their own twist to the progress of the age—and the farmer is almost as far out of it as if he lived in Alaska. Perhaps there may have been a time when a man could live in what the poet calls daily communion with Nature and not starve his mind and dwarf his soul, but this isn't the century . . . get out of it as soon as you can.[2]

Frederic was speaking, of course, of the East, where industrial development had already (1886) largely displaced agriculture in the regional economy; but this dark view of the farm was an

[2] Harold Frederic, *Seth's Brother's Wife* (New York: Charles Scribner's Sons, 1886), pp. 32–33.

anticipation of a condition which was to become increasingly apparent in the Middle West in the twentieth century.

Something of the tendency of the farm to starve the mind and dwarf the soul was recognized by Garland about the time Frederic's novel and Kirkland's *Zury* appeared. It may be said without much hesitation that Garland's best stories show a decided preference for the unpleasant side of farm life and suggest a notion of economic determinism that was not consistently maintained in his later writings. The ambivalence in Garland's attitude toward the farm somewhat blurs the indictment, but the general effect of his stories is one of hostility toward the farm. In "Up the Coulé," one of his strongest stories, there is a sharp contrast between the son who has attained financial success in the city and his brother who has met with dismal failure on the farm. Furthermore, the story contains no suggestion that those who have remained on the farm have gained spiritually or that the one who has gone to the city has lost in this respect.

Rose of Dutcher's Coolly (1895) provides a better example of Garland's negative view of farm life, however, because it is largely free of the reform overtones that figure importantly in *Main-Travelled Roads*. The misfortunes of the farmers in the short stories might be prevented by changes in the economic set-up in the country, Garland seems to say; but the narrowness of the environment that forces Rose Dutcher to break her father's heart and leave the farm is an essential and ineradicable characteristic of the rural world. Rose is the intelligent and talented daughter of John Dutcher, a widowed farmer in southwestern Wisconsin. Through a series of somewhat improbable events, Rose is enabled to attend the state university, where she is introduced to a world that makes her father's little farm near Bluff Siding seem pretty insignificant. She has a natural grace and beauty that endear her to everyone she meets, and influential people want her to go to Chicago and pursue her studies (which are never clearly defined). But her father has planned for her return to the farm and has remodeled the house to make it attractive to her. There she is to live, he intends, until she is ready to marry, and then she and her farmer-husband can take over the place. But after a few months of life on the home farm, Rose determines to leave, goes

to Chicago, becomes the darling of a rather exclusive and enlight-
ened group, and finally agrees to marry a newspaperman fifteen
years her senior.

Rose of Dutcher's Coolly is in some respects a weak novel,
less important artistically than historically. Rose's meteoric rise
to prominence in the social world of Chicago seems too rapid for
complete credibility, and her peculiar talents are never made altogether clear to the reader. But the novel provides an almost ideal
illustration of the success-story myth in which the leading character, of farm background, rises above that background, leaves it
behind, and finds a place of importance in urban life. This myth
is almost as pervasive as the log cabin–to–White House legend,
and of far more frequent occurrence. Most of the fictional treatments of it are not examined here because they are not farm
novels; the hero may start, like Howells' Silas Lapham, from the
farm, but the portion of his life with which the novelist is primarily concerned takes place in the city. In many cases, the farm
background is dismissed rather quickly as a relatively minor matter requiring little elaboration.

Herbert Quick tells stories of this kind in *The Hawkeye* and
The Invisible Woman, both of which begin with the farm childhood of the central character and then move to the town where
that character carves out a career for himself. In neither case is
there a return to the farm at the end of the novel. Neither of
these books is as effective as Quick's earlier novel, *Vandemark's
Folly,* which is concerned almost entirely with farm life, and the
earlier portions of *The Hawkeye* are more effective than the later
sections.

The stereotyped success-story theme, however true it may have
been to the actual experience of many readers of the novels that
used it, was not invariably satisfying to such readers, nor did it
in all cases correspond to the attitude toward the farm held by
novelists. Hence the farm novel never developed a distinctive
"revolt-from-the-farm" pattern corresponding to the "revolt-from-
the-village" vogue. Instead there came into being the "God bless
it" approach to the farm which has prevailed in the majority of
farm novels since the early 1920's. Since that time few novelists
have deigned to write of the farm at all unless they believed that

they saw in it values which seemed absent from town and city life or overwhelmed there by the competition of other, less praiseworthy values.

The first really significant expression of this positive approach to the farm appears in two novels by John T. Frederick: implicitly in *Druida* (1923) and explicitly in *Green Bush* (1925).[3] *Druida*, although inferior to its successor as a work of fiction, is valuable for our purposes because it roughly parallels *Rose of Dutcher's Coolly* but with a conclusion the very opposite of that in Garland's novel. Druida is the intelligent, sensitive daughter of Mrs. Oscar Horsfall and Ed Brown, a hired man of the Horsfalls. She does not learn until maturity that she is not the daughter of Oscar, a coarse, tyrannical man addicted to heavy drinking, and he never finds it out. "Discovered" by Leonard Willoughby, an English teacher at the nearby Riverton Normal School, in much the same fashion that Rose Dutcher is "discovered" by Dr. Thatcher, she leaves the farm and goes to the Normal School, where she soon absorbs all the place has to offer her. Her innocuous but misinterpreted relationship with Willoughby leads to his dismissal and her expulsion from the school, but he is convinced that he can obtain a position elsewhere and asks her to marry him. Instead of accepting him and becoming part of the urban world of which she has read, she marries a neighbor boy, Bud Madsen, and goes with him to Montana, where he is homesteading. She gives as her reason for this choice her desire to be a participant in life rather than a mere observer.

Frederick has made Druida's choice a more courageous one than Rose's would have been had she determined to go back to

---

[3] The popular Canadian novelist Arthur Stringer offers his readers a sort of romantic primitivism in his books *Prairie Wife* (1915) and *Prairie Mother* (1920), which appear superficially to represent the affirmative view of farm life. But in the light of the fact that Stringer "poured out thrillers, westerners, poems, and one-act plays in great profusion" (Stanley J. Kunitz and Howard Haycraft, *Twentieth Century Authors* [New York: H. W. Wilson Co., 1942], p. 1362), one may seriously doubt whether these novels are to be regarded as valid expressions of a point of view toward the farm. In addition, their melodramatic plots and forcibly imported domestic triangles make these novels of Canadian ranch life unworthy of much consideration as serious fiction.

her father's farm, for Druida has known the brutality of farm life under the dominion of Oscar Horsfall, whereas Rose's early life seems to have been largely free of drudgery, lived in the company of a kindly and understanding father. There is nothing to indicate that Druida will escape hard work on the plains of Montana, and Bud Madsen is certainly not an intellectual companion for her. The characterization in *Druida* is thin, the machinery sometimes creaks, situations often seem contrived, and the conclusion is somehow unconvincing, but the moral is clear: a life lived in touch with reality, preferably close to the soil, whatever its hardships and deprivations, is superior to the vicarious life of the observer, secure in his detachment.

The case for the farm is made out more clearly and more convincingly in Frederick's next novel, *Green Bush*. Green Bush is a small Michigan town on the shores of Lake Huron where Frank Thompson helps his father edit the local newspaper and cultivate a small farm near the village. Father and son are both interested in the farm, but the mother regards farming as a pursuit unworthy of her menfolk and does what she can to steer her son away from it. He has already completed four years at the state university but is persuaded to go back for some graduate work, although his professional objectives are vague. The death of his father obliges him to give up this plan for a time and return to Green Bush to publish the newspaper. The mother meanwhile sells the farm without his consent and, when he seems to be settling nicely into the life of Green Bush, also sells the newspaper. When she dismisses from the house the girl Frank loves, he storms out and returns to Ann Arbor, never to see or communicate with his mother again. After he marries and makes various attempts to work on a Detroit newspaper and continue his graduate work, Frank returns to Green Bush and buys a farm near his wife's home. At the end of the novel a tempting offer comes from Ann Arbor, where he is desired as an English instructor; but he rejects it to remain a farmer.

Frederick makes Frank's decision a difficult one. The farm he operates is no rich prairie homestead in the West, but a sandy patch of cutover timber land (he buys a quarter section for $1,200); and the academic world to which he is urged by his friend Steen to return holds many attractions for him. To make the problem still more difficult, Frederick arranges for Frank to be seriously injured while pulling stumps, so that he is incapacitated for many months and never fully restored to health. But the newspaper has come back into his hands, and he thinks he can follow his father's example, though with greater emphasis on the farming part of his career.

The case Frederick makes out for the superiority of farm to city life is the strongest early presentation of this position and perhaps the strongest case that has been or can be made for it. What is the life of the average city dweller? Frank tries to talk to his fellow workers in the Detroit newspaper shop:

> But he discovered that to most of them the work of the shop was all alike—just so much to be done and got out of the way, so that they could be free for the bowling-alley or the movies or the dance-hall. They did not care what they were doing, but they would discuss vociferously the need for better wages and new equipment in the plant.[4]

Frederick's imagery is interesting. Frank looks out upon the streets of the city: "From the corner near him the avenues curved away like long golden talons. He saw the hurrying thousands, and it seemed to him that he and Rose like all of these were caught and impaled in a huge and torturing trap" (210). But this is not the alternative to farming that Frank faces; Ann Arbor is not Detroit, and newspaper make-up work is not the same as teaching English. What then is it about the farm that attracts him so powerfully? It is something almost mystical. Once he senses it as he looks at his plow: "Earth and the plough: an exultant sense of kinship with elemental things—of self-sufficing strength and conquest . . ." (237). He states his position explicitly in his letter to Steen, turning down the offer of an instructorship. "I think," he says, "I see that prolonged contact with the earth has brought me finally the power to confront my life, my fate, and myself at once with clearness of vision and with peace of mind" (301). Those who live in cities manage to cloak the essential reality of life "with the glitter of achievement, and of pleasure" (301); but

[4] John T. Frederick, *Green Bush* (New York: Alfred A. Knopf, 1925), p. 207.

if this cloak is removed they are helpless, while the farmer knows life and death at first hand, and for him they hold no terrors. Life in the city would mean surrounding himself with the temporary edifice of man's creation—"brief devisings whereby to mask oblivion"—and he would suddenly realize the futility of what he was doing instead of being contentedly aware of his insignificance all the time. He insists that he writes with no evangelical intention: "I would not urge the course I choose on you or any other" (303). One is reminded of Thoreau's "I would not have any one adopt *my* mode of living on any account. . . ."

In view of the clear-cut statement of the superiority of farm to city life to be found in this novel, it is not surprising that a reviewer wrote, shortly after its appearance,

> So far as interpretation of the deepest aspect of farm life is concerned, John T. Frederick's "Green Bush" reaches the high point in recent fiction. Here, as in no other American novel, implicit unity with the soil is given adequate and coherent expression.[5]

That is to say, the notion, valid or not, that the farm is a better place to live than the city is a characteristically rural belief, and its expression in this novel makes *Green Bush* an authentic piece of rural fiction, despite the fact that most of its important characters are educated people with urban ties of some sort. There is no studied attempt to reproduce the vernacular of a given region; and except for the central theme, there seems to be no particular effort to represent typically rural attitudes. In fact, the surprisingly deft treatment of the phenomenon Philip Wylie was later to call "momism" might entitle the novel to some consideration as a psychological study of a more typically urban situation.

Whatever the technical faults of his novels (and they are less evident in *Green Bush* than in *Druida*), Frederick was eminently qualified by experience to write farm fiction. In an article on "The Farm in Iowa Fiction," written in 1951, he defended his fitness to write on such a topic, saying,

> I was born and grew up on an Iowa farm—a rather small and poor farm, duly equipped with a mortgage. And although I no longer live in Iowa, there has been no year in the more than fifty since I was

[5] Crawford, "The American Farmer," 101.

old enough to ride the horse hoisting hay in which I have not done a considerable amount of common farm work with my own hands.[6]

Druida and *Green Bush*, although they do not deal with Iowa farm life, were both written against a background of personal experience. The "Riverton Normal School" of the first book is rather transparently the Moorhead State Teachers College in Minnesota, where Frederick taught from 1917 to 1919. In the two following years, like the main character in *Green Bush*, Frederick operated a farm near Glennie, Michigan, in the cut-over country described in that book.[7] Authenticity of background does not, however, guarantee a superior literary product, and it is safe to say that Frederick is less successful as a novelist than as a critic and editor. His services to young authors as editor of *The Midland* are mentioned elsewhere in this book, while his critical pronouncements on earlier and contemporary writers have been consistently useful in evaluating particular novelists.

If *Green Bush* qualifies as the strongest fictional defense of farm life, G. D. Eaton's *Backfurrow*, published the same year (1925), must surely deserve to be called the bitterest attack on it. Closely paralleling Frederick's novel in locale and incident, it arrives at quite the opposite kind of resolution; the meanness and futility of farm life are set forth in all their brutal nakedness. Critics who reviewed the novel upon its appearance agreed in their interpretation of its message. One reviewer observed that "if there are any vestiges of glamor still clinging to farm life, Mr. Eaton has made it his business to dispel them."[8] Another, calling it a "hymn of hate" and a "paean of loathing," commented, "One may seek in vain among travels of rural life for one wrought with more savage, cumulative, acid intensity than G. D. Eaton displays in his morbidly gloomy picture of life on a Michigan farm."[9] Still another critic said of *Backfurrow*: "Here is no light and no sweetness, no cloud-vaulting beauty and no starry flights; here is only bleakness and desolation, the level monotony of labor, the tear-

[6] John T. Frederick, "The Farm in Iowa Fiction," *Palimpsest*, XXXII (March 1951), 123.

[7] *The Midland*, XX (March–April, May–June 1933), 56.

[8] "Books in Brief," *Nation*, CXX (May 6, 1925), 524.

[9] *New York Times Book Review*, February 15, 1925, p. 16.

less tragedy of stunted lives and puny loves and monstrous futilities."[10] Such comments, although severe, are not mere rhetorical flourishes, for the picture of farm life presented in *Backfurrow* is extremely dreary, even for a novel clearly in the naturalistic tradition.[11]

Ralph Dutton begins life under a cloud, for he is illegitimate, his father unknown, his mother dead. He is brought up by his maternal grandparents on a stony, hilly farm where even the hardest work is no guarantee of a living. When his grandparents die, Ralph, only fifteen, works for a farmer briefly, then goes to Detroit and tries one job after another. He grows intellectually while in the city, but jobs are scarce, and finally he is forced to return to the country, where he works for several farmers in succession. He comes to spend an increasing amount of time in the local pool hall and bar, which, bad as it is, provides a better influence than the homes in which he lives. Just when he thinks he will try city life again, he becomes interested in Ellen Tupper, marries her, and is soon trapped on the farm for life. Like Frederick's Frank Thompson, he suffers a crippling illness and, after convalescence, returns to the farm, not, however, cheerfully and hopefully like Frank, but in a spirit of futile resignation.

The people in *Backfurrow* are selfish, vindictive, hypocritical, grasping, and thoroughly miserable. At one of the places where Ralph works, the husband and wife hate each other passionately, and eventually the husband kills the wife and then hangs himself. Illegitimate births are frequent, although the people are conventionally pious; they refuse to let Ralph hunt on Sunday,

[10] Stanton A. Coblenz, "A Realist Portrays American Farm Life," *Literary Digest International Book Review*, III (April 1925), 331.

[11] Eaton's short and mercurial career included a farm background near Plymouth, Michigan, and *Backfurrow* is reputedly autobiographical. As a student at the University of Michigan, Eaton antagonized faculty and students by writing violent letters to the student publication, the *Michigan Daily*, attacking complacency. Elected to Phi Beta Kappa, he refused the honor. In the seven years of life that remained to him after graduation, he had a varied journalistic career, including the co-editorship (with Burton Rascoe) of *Plain Talk*, which he founded. He died in 1930 at the age of thirty-five. *Michigan Alumnus*, XXXII (1926), 561, and XXXVI (1930), 655; *Bookman*, LXX (January 1930), 539.

and they say grace at meals. They drink to forget their misery, but the state goes dry in an election, and prohibition leads to bootlegging. In the matter of religion, Ralph discovers that one farmer, of whom he had had hopes, was just as orthodox as the rest: "Pete had occasional outbreaks when things went wrong, but in the main he made an effort to be pious and he was filled with the fears spread by the minister and the inwarped creed of generations."[12] In the case of the husband and wife who hate each other, divorce is out of the question, because a "divorce, or separation, was a more choice bit of scandal even than illegitimate childbirth" (117). The farmers lack foresight and a broad perspective; Ralph says, "I read in a magazine of a plan where the farmers'd get nearly twice as much for their stuff and the city folks wouldn't have to pay any more for it. But they're so stupid and they can't get together" (129). Ralph's dim view of farming emerges in his reaction to an article titled "Why Farmers' Sons Should Remain on the Farm," which he finds "a mixture of romanticism and of commercial logic . . ." (179). In the same article he finds "not a word about the smaller chances for an education, not a word about cultural pursuits, not a word about the small farmer whose chances would be even lessened by the placing of agriculture on more of a production basis" (180). He concludes that the only reason why farm boys should stay on the farm is that they might be even worse off in the city because of their early deprivations. His experience has indicated to him that farm boys are at a decided disadvantage in the competitive struggle of urban life because their own background has been different from that of the city boys. Though fully as brutal in its own way, their early training has not fitted them for the peculiar demands of city life.

As a novel, *Backfurrow* has many faults. There are large unassimilated chunks, like the passages describing Ralph's reading and the development of his philosophy while he is in Detroit. People like Aikman, a professor of philology, come and go, helping Ralph toward his nihilistic position, but they fail to merge with the plot or setting. Most of the characters, including Ralph, are rather wooden. But in spite of these and other faults, the

[12] G. D. Eaton, *Backfurrow* (New York: G. P. Putnam's Sons, 1925), p. 111.

novel has a corrosive power in destroying the positive view of the farm that Frederick expressed in *Green Bush*. Farming could scarcely be portrayed in gloomier colors than it is in this novel. There is a constant futile struggle with a hostile environment— poor soil, weather too wet or too dry, debts, accidents, dissatisfaction. Ralph's final position is far from the kind of optimistic acceptance that Frank Thompson achieves; it is a weary resignation to the inevitable, by a person too dulled and beaten by misfortune to struggle any longer.

Backfurrow is not, however, typical of farm novels written since 1920; the approach taken by Frederick in *Green Bush* is much more frequently encountered. We may then legitimately ask this question: if the farm is fundamentally superior to the city as an environment, as many novelists insist, why do young people leave it? What kind of young people are those who leave the farm? And what kind are those who stay? A commonly held belief among fiction writers is that the pioneers were made of sterner stuff than their children, that the second generation lacks the moral, intellectual, and physical stamina to maintain the high standards and ideals of their parents. Having fallen victim to the idols of the market place, they are interested only in acquiring fortunes and an urban social status. So they seek the easy road to success, leave the farm, and enter upon urban careers, which typically lead to material failure and almost always to spiritual impoverishment. A characteristic treatment of this pattern appears in Edna Ferber's *So Big* (1924). Since this book is not properly a farm novel, although John T. Flanagan so designates it,[13] and since the topic is treated more effectively elsewhere, there seems no need to discuss this modern handling of the old theme of gaining the world and losing one's soul, except to remark that it apparently endorses the view that the virtues of one generation are not necessarily inherited by the next.

For a really vigorous treatment of this theme it is necessary to turn to Frederick Philip Grove's *Our Daily Bread* (1928). John and Martha Elliot, pioneers on the Saskatchewan prairie, raise a family of ten, of whom not one remains on the original home-

[13] John T. Flanagan, "A Bibliography of Middle Western Farm Novels," *Minnesota History*, XXIII (June 1942), 156–158.

stead. Several attempt farming, but lacking the qualities of character and intelligence their parents possess, they hover perpetually on the brink of bankruptcy, kept solvent through the efforts of the bank, which hopes somehow to get its money back. Others have gone to the city, where even those who succeed financially are harried by a constant round of social activities and responsibilities. In their domestic affairs all are hopelessly maladjusted and miserable. No wonder a reviewer said of this novel:

> "Our Daily Bread" is probably one of the most depressing tales penned by an American writer. There is no relieving touch of humor or fancy, small departure in any case from dull routine, sorrow and death. Mr. Grove, without question, has drawn a grim design and adhered closely to it.[14]

What is the cause of all this concentrated unhappiness? The author would say it is the abandonment of old John Elliot's high ideals by the second generation. John Elliot "had come to view all occupations except that of the farmer with suspicion."[15] His beliefs concerning the relative importance of the farm and the town are summed up in this paragraph:

> Empires rose and fell: kings and high priests strove with each other: wars were fought: ripples on the sea of life. Underneath, deep down, that life itself went on as it had gone on in Abraham's time: the land was tilled to grow our daily bread. And this life, the life of the vast majority of men on earth, was the essential life of all mankind. The city with its multifarious activities was nothing but a bubble on that sea.[16]

---

[14] *New York Times Book Review*, October 7, 1928, p. 20.

[15] Frederick Philip Grove, *Our Daily Bread* (New York: Macmillan Co., 1928), p. 78.

[16] *Ibid.*, p. 190. This passage should be compared with the following quotation from Grove's autobiography: "I gained an insight into the lives of men in the country, a straighter, juster view of things. . . . What were cities and towns? Mere specks on the map. Here was the ground-mass of the nation— the soil from which cities sprang, like strange, weird, sometimes poisonous flowers in the woods. For the first time I saw the true relation: the city, the town working for the country: the farmer, though not yet realized as such, the real master of the world who would one day come into his own. I understood that, before I could say that I had a fair view of America as it is, I should have to mingle with the men who tilled the soil." Frederick Philip Grove, *A Search for America* (New York: Louis Carrier & Co., 1928), pp. 310–

Elliot knows how to farm, and he has crops when his careless, ineffectual neighbors do not. Furthermore, he refuses to go into debt under any circumstances, for he knows the malignant nature of its growth once it has established itself. To him these convictions are eternal verities, immune to the trivial changes of the times. His son-in-law, a university professor, tries to convince him (although he himself is in sympathy with old John's views) that things are changing: " 'The spirit of the times is commercial,' said Woodrow. 'Commercial!' John Elliot exploded. 'That means, don't *make* a thing. Shave a little piece off it while you are handling it! The spirit of the times! The spirit of nonsense!' "[17] The Elliot children and their mates abandon the father's stern creed. They farm carelessly, in the hope of a sudden fortune, and they go deeply into debt with no certainty of being able to pay it off. The fundamental mistake lies in their motive: they want to get rich. John Elliot says, "You whippersnappers of today are not satisfied to make a home and a living on the farm; you want to make money!" His son John agrees: "We want to make money like everybody else" (210). Woodrow Ormond, the professor son-in-law, agrees with old Elliot, so far as farming is concerned; but he is active in Dominion politics and has to live lavishly in order to maintain his political position.

Grove overstates his case in *Our Daily Bread*. His main point is clear as John Elliot states it; the multiplied and compounded misery of the Elliot children only gives it unnecessary emphasis. Consequently the novel fails to attain the stature such a theme deserves. But as a repository of characteristic rural beliefs and attitudes, reflected in the words and thoughts of John Elliot, it is an important contribution to rural fiction. The fact that its people are essentially dirt farmers rather than ranchers brings it closer to the typical farm novel than the popular fiction of Grove's fellow Canadian, Arthur Stringer, despite the fact that the locale is roughly the same. By 1928 the failure of the ideals of those men who sang "O'er the hills in legions, boys!" could be

---

311. Elsewhere (p. 382) he observes that "I have since come to the conclusion that the ideal as I saw and still see it has been abandoned by the U.S.A. That is one reason why I became and remained a Canadian."

[17] Grove, *Our Daily Bread*, p. 177.

seen in terms quite different from those that dominated Garland's stories in 1891. No longer was it chiefly a question of economics, which a new social system might remedy; now it could be seen in terms of human character, of a second generation unable to maintain the high standards of their fathers.

Another, somewhat cruder illustration of the position taken by Grove may be found in an inferior novel, *Glass* (1933), by Howard Stephenson. Covering about twenty years in the life of George Rood, a farmer in northwestern Ohio, this book states more explicitly than necessary that life on the farm is better than life in the city. The contrast between the two is set up when the discovery of natural gas in the vicinity leads to the construction of a huge glass factory across the road from Rood's farm. A village grows up adjacent to the factory, and farm boys are lured away by the enticement of steady work there. Although Rood's son Georgie joins the exodus from the land and becomes a glass-worker, George himself stubbornly refuses to lease his land to the gas companies and keeps right on cultivating the soil, largely oblivious to the successive booms and depressions that characterize the gas industry. Rood may be intended as the author's spokesman, but his almost total ignorance of cities and city life weakens his testimony against them. He blames most of the world's troubles on urban congestion: "Why, the devilment that goes on is mostly caused by people bein' too close cooped up together."[18] At the end of the novel the glass factory is closed, apparently for good, and George Rood is still peacefully tilling his acres.

Since about 1930 a dominant theme among farm novelists has been one of reconciliation to the soil. In developing this theme writers have tended to follow one of two approaches: they have made explicit the contrast between rural and urban life by taking their characters to the town, allowing them to be disillusioned, and then bringing them back to the farm; or they have assumed the question of relative superiority of town and farm to be settled and have contented themselves with depicting the wholesome life on the farm, without offering any overt contrast to city life. Whichever approach is taken, the narrowing, stultifying influence of farm life is played down or omitted altogether, so far as

[18] Howard Stephenson, *Glass* (New York: Claude Kendall, 1933), p. 149.

the characters the author is chiefly interested in are concerned.

Paul Corey's novels afford good examples of the first approach described above. In his trilogy about the Mantz family, *Three Miles Square* (1939), *The Road Returns* (1940), and *County Seat* (1941), Corey follows the lives of the family and their neighbors through the twenty years from 1910 to 1930. His purpose is indicated in a letter, addressed to the author and signed "Otto Mantz":

> To improve the social and economic conditions of our country, its [sic] seems to me that all of the people must know intimately all sections of it, and the books you want to write sound to me like a first-rate way of getting that across, at least for us in the corn-hog belt.[19]

Together Corey's novels constitute a sort of economic and social history of the region they describe during the twenty years they cover. The main theme, however, is the conflict among members of the Mantz family over the issue of farm versus city life. Mrs. Mantz, left a widow at the beginning of the first book, is determined that her children will have good educations so that they will be able to make "somebody" of themselves. Andrew, the eldest, is to stay on the farm until he is twenty-one and then turn the management over to the next in line and so on until all four children have been given the opportunity to prepare themselves for careers. Mrs. Mantz thinks of these careers in essentially urban, professional terms. Her husband had wanted to become an architect but was prevented from obtaining the necessary training because of his marriage, so the oldest boy, who has a taste for architecture, will study in that field.

The first crack in the structure of this plan appears when Andrew is taken out of college in 1917 and drafted into the army. When he returns from service, his interest in further schooling has waned, and he drifts from one job to another. The second son, Wolmar, is uninterested in farming and wants to become a mechanic. The daughter, Verney, marries a man with no experience or interest in farming. The youngest son, Otto, is as yet too young to manage the farm, and in any case his mother has deter-

---

[19] Paul Corey, *County Seat* (Indianapolis: Bobbs-Merrill Co., 1941), p. 418.

mined that her dream of education for her children shall come true in one instance at least. So the farm is sold, the family moves to town, and Otto eventually goes away to the state university. His educational aims are vague, tending in the direction of sociology and political science rather than toward architecture. Upon graduation he takes a job in Chicago with a telephone company, which he loses when the depression of 1929 strikes. At the end of the third novel, he finally persuades his mother to let him take over the home farm, which has fallen back into her hands when the buyer was unable to meet his payments on it.

The conflict in values in Corey's trilogy places Otto on one side and the rest of the family on the other. Wolmar looks upon the farm almost with loathing: "A guy got like a lump of dirt working on the farm—a lump of dirt. You picked corn day after day until you couldn't stand the sight of a cornfield. And what did it get you? Nothing! Not a thing."[20] Andrew runs the place dutifully for seven years, but he has no real love for farming. Otto looks at a cornfield and remarks that it is beautiful. "Andrew looked at him but saw only a field of corn. The farm was two things to him: the home place because his father had conceived it as that, where he had been born and raised, and the means to make a living, a springboard to something in life."[21] Mrs. Mantz is obsessed with the notion of her sons, particularly Otto, as successes in the urban business world. She is distressed when she learns that Otto has lost his job: "Phrases which she had played with in her thoughts: my son the manager, my son the vice-president, my son the president—all came back to taunt her now" (362).

But Otto sees his Chicago job in quite a different light. When his mother asks him if he isn't working up, he replies, "To what? Unit supervisor, office supervisor, division supervisor? I spend all my days trying to chisel a few extra cents out of somebody who can't afford it so that the stockholders of the company'll be paid for doing nothing" (325). By contrast, running the home farm has a lot of possibilities, he insists: "There's a chance for honor and

[20] Paul Corey, *Three Miles Square* (Indianapolis: Bobbs-Merrill Co., 1939), p. 266.

[21] Corey, *County Seat*, p. 51.

success and respectability in making it into a good farm. . . . I don't see why the production of food isn't as respectable as sitting in an office with my name on the door, producing nothing" (377).

By this time, Otto's college training has enabled him to analyze and define the family conflicts that he has been contending with in his efforts to take over the home farm. These conflicts he says, "had been the result of thought patterns which shouldn't exist. It was the family desire to be somebody which meant in reality to be better than somebody else; it was the wish to excel for the sake of excelling and not just to give always one's best" (401). Otto's point—and Corey's—is that farming is a legitimate occupation for those who enjoy it, as honorable as any white-collar job in the city, despite Mrs. Mantz's disappointed hope that Otto will be something "better" than a dirt farmer. That it takes Corey three books to say this indicates that he did not wish to make his case too obvious. Throughout the trilogy Corey handles his theme with restraint, just as he treats the emotional struggles of his characters with reserve and delicacy. For this reason, as well as for others, Corey's novels are definitely superior to the general run of farm fiction.

Rose Feld said in a review of *County Seat* that "the novel achieves distinction through virtue of its accent on mediocrity; through Corey's deep-rooted respect for the dignity and endeavors of ordinary men."[22] The accent on mediocrity is clearly evident in all three books. With the possible exception of Ed Crosby, there is no major character who is distinctly superior in intellect; even Otto has to be helped through his eighth-grade examinations by questionable means. Nor are these people without moral fault; all the Mantzes act from selfish motives a good share of the time, Wolmar nearly always. But Corey manages to give these quite ordinary people a dignity that enlists the reader's sympathy for them in their struggles.

Corey's realistic treatment of farm life, including his accurate reproduction of the speech of his characters, also contributes to the general superiority of his work to most other farm novels of the time. His accuracy is not surprising, inasmuch as Corey grew

[22] *New York Times Book Review*, September 7, 1941, p. 22.

up on a farm in southwestern Iowa. Although he has lived outside the Middle West in recent years, the impressions he gained
during his formative years have stayed with him and enabled
him to recreate farm life with unusual fidelity. He displays a
familiarity with every farm task, from repairing machinery to
delivering a calf. The language of his characters is not only an
accurate representation of farm speech generally but is carefully
suited to each person, in accord with his intellectual and educational level. Rural beliefs and attitudes are effectively treated in
these novels. The conflicts between old and new methods of
farming, between the old individualism and the new interdepend-
ence, and between those who work for immediate gain and those
who take a broader view are all given adequate treatment. Crosby
organizes a meat ring to assure the farmers of fresh meat in the
summer months, but he meets with resistance from many who
have no concrete objections to offer but who are simply suspicious
of the idea because it is new. Anti-intellecutalism is strong in
Moss County, Iowa. Wolmar's constant deriding of Otto's superior education may be merely a manifestation of his own sense
of having been underrated and neglected by his family, but it
reflects an attitude prevalent in the community. When Andrew
is going with Bernodette Farrel, he is unable to convince his
prospective father-in-law of the value of his plan to study architecture; Farrel thinks education is a waste of time and money
and wants Andrew to settle down on a farm and take Bernodette
off his hands.

Considered in respect to the prevalent literary movements of
the twentieth century, Corey's novels, like Eaton's *Backfurrow*,
conform most closely to the criteria of naturalism, or at least of
post-naturalistic realism. Besides the frankness that has come to
be so generally adopted by writers as to be no longer the identi-
fying mark of a particular school, all these novels display a pervasive sense of determinism, an effort at amorality, and a high
degree of objectivity. Ralph Dutton in *Backfurrow* is "trapped by
life" as surely as Dreiser's Clyde Griffiths or any of the characters
in Sherwood Anderson's *Winesburg, Ohio*. Similarly, the Mantz
brothers seem to have little or no influence over what happens
to them. Andrew blunders into marriage with a woman who is

certainly no asset to his future; his mother's hopes for her children are uniformly unfulfilled, despite her best efforts; and Otto gets a girl into trouble and narrowly escapes having to marry her. In this incident, Otto's behavior, scarcely admirable, is portrayed in thoroughly naturalistic fashion, with neither approval nor condemnation from the author. If Corey does not show the amorality that early naturalism professed (e.g., in his mildly propagandistic defense of farm life), this should not trouble the reader of other naturalistic novels with more obviously reformist aims. Corey's objectivity, like that of Dreiser, results in an accumulation rather than a selection of details. Perhaps the novelist he most closely resembles in this respect is James T. Farrell, who also required three books to complete his story of Studs Lonigan. Like Farrell, Corey stresses average rather than exceptional people and piles up details to produce almost a case history of a group representing a particular locale and economic stratum.

In terms of the criteria set forth in the first chapter of this book, Corey's fiction represents the farm novel in its most highly developed form to date. Nearly all the distinguishing features of farm life are to be found, given effective and artistic treatment. The chief criticism that might be leveled at these novels is that the slender thread of plot in each one is all but buried under the wealth of detail, and as a result they lack emotional intensity and have less impact on the reader than some tightly knit but otherwise inferior novels. Nevertheless, evaluated in terms of Corey's apparent purpose, they are among the most important contributions made during the past generation to farm fiction.

Some novelists have preferred to remain outside the controversy of whether farm life is or is not preferable to town life. Accepting as fact the assumption that farm life has its satisfactions, they have gone on to show what some of those satisfactions are, without offering overt comparisons to city life. Among the novels of which this may be said are the light fiction exercises of Phil Stong, surely one of the most prolific of farm novelists. From *State Fair* in 1932 to *Blizzard* in 1955, Stong turned out a long succession of cheerful rural idylls whose only real justification for inclusion here is the fact that they illustrate this approach to the farm-versus-city issue. There is in Stong's novels no serious effort to come to grips with social or economic problems; they are patently intended for entertainment only. *State Fair*, probably the best of them, concerns the adventures of an Iowa farm family who take their prize hog to the state fair. The late-adolescent children, Wayne and Margy, undergo a measure of emotional maturation through short-lived liaisons with young people from the city, but the analysis of the process and its results is superficial.   *1 0 b 5̄ 8 1*

The final impression Stong's novels leave is one of gay inconsequence. Their explanations (when explanations are offered) are simply too facile, too shallow to be convincing except to the reader who does not require explanations of any sort. When contrasted with such novels as those of Paul Corey, Stong's books seem to evade all the issues, particularly those peculiar to farm life. Even the author's reproduction of dialogue has nothing distinctive about it. The speech of his farm families conforms more closely to that of Americans in general, rural and urban, than to that of Iowa farmers; and although the topics they discuss are largely rural, his characters seem to be able to talk equally well about anything else on which they have any knowledge.

When, as in the case of Phil Stong, a novelist begins with the assumption that farm life is wholesome and satisfying and requires no defense, it is natural for him to place his emphasis upon the personal and emotional conflicts of his characters, conflicts which do not grow specifically out of the farm environment. Many novels of this type are discussed in Chapter VI. If one were to consider the love story in Paul Engle's *Always the Land* (1941) the most important feature of the novel, a cogent argument could be offered for placing this story of Iowa farm life in Chapter VI rather than here. Since several issues involving judgments on the desirability of farm life are taken up in the novel, however, it is most appropriately discussed here.

Although the farm of Jay Meyer and his grandson, Joe, a few miles from Cedar Rapids, raises corn and hogs as its principal source of income, the attention in *Always the Land* is chiefly on its side line of horses, raised mainly for exhibition and sale. Consequently it is a story of the race track and the stable rather than

the land itself. The plot, which revolves about a fairly conventional romance between Joe Meyer and Jerrie Holmes, another
horse enthusiast, requires little attention here. On the ideological
level, the major theme is the conflict between individualism and
collective action. Jay stands for the old way of life, each man
working as hard as he can and (supposedly) getting a proportion-
ate reward. Joe says things are more complicated now, and since
individuals will not work together voluntarily, the government
has to bring pressure on them to cooperate. He is undogmatic,
but he believes in going along with corn loans, price support
programs, and other government policies aimed at helping the
farmer. To old Jay, his grandson's attitude amounts to a desire
on the part of modern farmers to work eight hours and be paid
for not working another eight, instead of working sixteen hours
as the pioneers did.

Jay's attitude is tied in with a strong element of anti-intellectualism. He has sent Joe to Iowa State College, but he has misgiv-
ings: "I don't believe much in this edjamacashun business. Seems
to me all these college graduates want to do is sit around picking
slivers outa their pants all day."[23] And when Joe tries to convert
him to modern research-developed techniques, he generalizes:
"That's just what college is—half-baked ideas put out by a lot
of half-cracked dopes who never did an honest day's work in
their life. Just sit around on their big butt all day talkin' " (37).
There is no arguing down this point of view, especially since old
Jay has a staunch ally in Henry Hope, an old horseman who
appears at the Meyer place as the novel begins. But when Henry
dies, at the end of the novel, there is a suggestion that Joe will
be able to pressure his grandfather into accepting some of the
despised innovations.

The dialogue in *Always the Land* is accurate and appropriate,
the characterization is convincing, and the conflicting positions
of Jay and Joe Meyer are sharply defined and plausible. Here, as
in Paul Corey's work, there is a good picture of the shifting attitudes taken by farm people toward such questions as individualism versus collective action. In Grove's *Our Daily Bread* it was
the pioneer who represented sound thinking and conduct, the

[23] Paul Engle, *Always the Land* (New York: Random House, 1941), p. 27.

next generation who failed because they fell prey to false modern notions. By 1941 the present generation could be seen as the one with foresight, while the old views of their fathers and grandfathers seemed reactionary, inadequate for present-day conditions and needs.

Thus in the novels of the 1930's and 1940's one finds not only a skillful portrayal of farm people and their characteristic beliefs and attitudes but a recognition that some of these beliefs are changing and a sensitive handling of the process of change. Most of the novelists who attempted to deal seriously with the process found themselves taking sides, either for or against the change. In doing so they were acting as moralists, for such questions as the comparative merits of farm and city life and the conflict between individualism and collective action are, in the final analysis, moral issues, matters on which the author brings to bear certain ethical presuppositions. Some of these authors went beyond the realm of moral values and entered the arena of economic and political controversy, where they advocated or denounced specific policies. Novels written with such objectives in mind will be discussed in the next chapter; the novels treated in this chapter are not the vehicles of propaganda or reform, but rather a commentary, in literary form, on questions fundamentally moral rather than economic or political.

V.

Man Against Man
The Farm Novelist as Social Critic

THE NOVELS discussed in the previous chapter dealt with questions which are basically matters of individual morality. Whether the farm is a more desirable place to live than the city is a question for the individual to decide for himself, not a matter for legislation by political bodies. If the children and grandchildren of the pioneers have failed to live up to the ideals of their parents, this too is a matter of individual failure, outside the scope of social agencies. Even the conflict between self-reliant individualism and collective social action, as it has been discussed thus far, is essentially a question of the individual's ability and willingness to reconcile himself to a changing social order.

By contrast, the novels to be treated in this chapter deal with the desirability or undesirability of certain aspects of the social order, and most of them recommend specific changes in that order, such changes to be achieved through group action. Thus they differ in both aim and method from the novels discussed in Chapter IV. Individual morality is not ignored in these novels, but there is in them a common belief that the problems which face the rural world are not the results of individual acts, nor are they to be solved by individual means.

Despite the almost chronic discontent that has characterized American agriculture since the Civil War, the literature of social criticism does not bulk large in middle western farm fiction. The farm novel offers nothing really comparable to the body of social protest literature extending from the utopian fiction of Bellamy and Howells, through the socialistic novels of Upton Sinclair and Jack London, to the proletarian fiction of the 1930's. Novelists have generally found the struggle with nature a more attractive subject than the struggle with the economic system. Besides the considerable number of books that touch incidentally and not very significantly on minor aspects of economic problems, however, there is a handful of novels which take those problems as their main theme and seek at least to describe objectionable situations and, in some cases, to arouse a public demand for remedial action. In dealing with such novels the chronological pattern followed in earlier chapters will be observed, although the novels are too few to permit any clear-cut case for a development from decade to decade.

Like the fictional treatment of the pioneering venture and the escape-from-the-farm theme, rural fiction of social protest began with Hamlin Garland. "Under the Lion's Paw," surely the best-known story in *Main-Travelled Roads*, is essentially a single-tax tract. Garland, a disciple of Henry George, here gave fictional expression to his conviction of the evil effects of unearned increment. The farmer who has made extensive improvements in the farm he intends to buy is rewarded by having the price raised beyond his expectations in consequence of his improvements. Garland at this stage of his career, with his belief that truth is superior to beauty, was perhaps more of a propagandist than an artist in motive, but as his interest in reform waned, his art also declined in merit.

Garland's first attempts at novel-length fiction were also propagandistic in motive. The two that deal most directly with farm life were *A Spoil of Office* and *Jason Edwards*, both of which appeared in 1892. The former concerns the political career of Bradley Talcott, an Iowa farm boy whose oratorical skill leads him into politics, although at first he has no definite convictions and is largely indifferent to the content of a speech by Ida Wilbur, a Populist agitator, whom he hears early in his career. Political experience leads him to political convictions, however, and he shifts from the status of an independent Republican to that of a Democrat, and finally, under Miss Wilbur's influence, allies himself with the Populists. The rather distant and tepid love affair between Bradley and Ida gives the novel a mild romantic appeal, but attention is centered chiefly upon the struggle of the farmers to overcome the dominance of railroads and big business in government. The actual treatment of farm life is limited to the opening chapters, which resemble the stories in *Main-Travelled Roads* and *Prairie Folks* in the use of authentic detail.

Jason Edwards is considerably wider in scope than *A Spoil of Office*, because it concerns not merely a particular political movement but rather the whole economic balance of the American nation. Jason Edwards (who is the main character only in a titular sense) is a laborer in a Boston foundry who seeks to escape the chronic poverty and insecurity of his lot by coming west and taking up land near Boomtown, South Dakota. There a succession of bad seasons reduces him to bankruptcy and he is forced off his land. Fortunately he and his family are saved from penury by Walter Reeves, a Boston newspaperman, on whom the novel's attention is chiefly centered. Reeves has become interested in Edwards' daughter and has followed the family west, where he is able to step in at the opportune moment with an offer of marriage to the daughter and financial security to the rest of the family. The moral of the novel is clear: the West used to be the outlet for urban labor, but now there is no free land left, and a man who buys land is likely to be ruined by mortgages in bad seasons. Nature, which seemed friendly to man in *A Spoil of Office*, is here portrayed as altogether indifferent. Out on the prairie "Reeves felt again the force of Nature's forgetfulness of man. She neither loves nor hates. Her storms have no regard for life. Her smiling calms do not recognize death. . . . She knows not, and cares nothing."[1] Man, in the person of the mortgage holder, is pitiless, unsympathetic to the misfortunes of the farmer, which he attributes to bad management and a lack of determination. *Jason Edwards* is good in its realistic portrayal of the harsh prairie life and the bleak western town and also of working class conditions in Boston. In the latter, Garland's unsparing brutality can be compared with that in Stephen Crane's *Maggie*.

Farm fiction was not always intended as the stimulus to reform; sometimes it was the imaginative re-creation of a reform movement already past. An example of a novel serving the latter function is Lorna Doone Beers' *Prairie Fires* (1925), a fictional

[1] Hamlin Garland, *Jason Edwards: An Average Man* (Boston: Arena Publishing Co., 1892), p. 182.

treatment of the rise of the Nonpartisan League in North Dakota. The "prairie fires" concerned are the fires of economic and political discontent which resulted from exploitation of the farmer by Minneapolis and St. Paul milling and railroad interests and their stooges, the small-town businessmen in North Dakota. The novel captures effectively the disgruntled mood of the farmers and their hostility toward the bankers and merchants of the towns who hold them in contempt, and in this way it makes a significant contribution to middle western farm fiction. Upon its publication, it was extravagantly praised, both for virtues which it possesses and for some that it does not possess. A reviewer for the New York *Times* described it as "a cool, serene, adult comedy . . . a refreshing and powerful and stimulating novel."[2] It has merits, to be sure, but they are not so great as those attributed to it by the reviewer just quoted.

Unfortunately, *Prairie Fires* is handicapped by its author's belief that a novel is a love story. Tacked onto a historically accurate treatment of the Nonpartisan movement but never adequately fused with it is a somewhat implausible romance between Christine Erickson, the sentimental, romantic farmer's daughter who spends most of her time fantasizing, and Christian Lövstad, the coarse, egotistical banker, a sort of exaggerated and vulgarized Torvald Helmer.[3] Just to complicate the situation, the author throws in a disturbing element in the form of "Doctor" Benjamin Paul, a dissatisfied chemistry instructor at the Agricultural College, as romantic as Christine, a man who shifts periodically from maudlin sentimentalist to highly practical organizer and back again. The effect of trying to combine such a plot, in which there is infatuation but no love, with the theme of the farmers' rebellion resembles in many respects those portions of *The Gilded Age* in which Twain and Warner wrote alternate chapters without consulting each other. The result is that as a work of art *Prairie Fires* is inferior to the author's later novels, *A Humble*

---

[2] "Social History of the Dakota Prairies in a New Novel," *New York Times Book Review*, May 17, 1925, p. 8.

[3] The resemblance between Lövstad and Ibsen's Torvald is intentional, for the latter is mentioned in connection with Lövstad's forgiving his wife (p. 338).

Lear (1929) and *The Mad Stone* (1932). It has considerable importance in a study of the farm novel, nevertheless, because of its presentation of certain characteristic farm attitudes and their influence in determining political action.

In dealing with social-protest fiction, it is more important to know something of the historical background and the relationship between that background and the fiction itself than is the case with the novels previously discussed. Hence there is considerable value in pointing out the parallels between the incidents in *Prairie Fires* and the actual historical events that accompanied the formation of the Nonpartisan League.[4] The three characters mentioned previously are introduced solely for the sake of the love plot and appear to have no prototypes in historical fact. Two other major characters, however, are drawn directly from life. The chief organizer of the League, Tom Everly, who was once known as "the Flax King of the Northwest" but who was ruined by a sudden drop in the price of flax caused by speculators, is clearly a fictionalized portrayal of A. C. Townley (pruned of his colorful profanity), the actual founder of the League, whose career followed the same pattern. One of his chief supporters, Hans Erickson (Christine's father), is modeled on Fred B. Wood, a respected farmer who at first opposed the League but later became one of its most ardent advocates. Several other minor characters also seem to be modeled on men who took an active part in the formation of the Nonpartisan League.

The situation facing the farmers at the outset of the novel also has a basis in fact. The abuses they suffered at the hands of the country elevators and the railroads have been documented, as have the exploitative practices of the small-town bankers.[5] Several incidents recounted in the novel closely parallel historical fact. Betrayed by the legislators who promised to help them, the farmers hold the annual convention of the state union of the American Society of Equity in Bismarck, the state capital, while the 1915 legislature is in session. They prowl through the halls of

---

[4] The historical background for this section is drawn from Robert L. Morlan, *Political Prairie Fires: The Nonpartisan League 1915–1922* (Minneapolis: University of Minnesota Press, 1955), Chapters 1 and 2, pp. 3–46.

[5] In *Ibid.*, pp. 3–21.

the capitol, annoying the legislators with their inquiries. Finally, irritated beyond endurance by what the legislators consider unjustified snooping, one of the House members (Lövstad) shouts that lawmaking is not the business of the farmers and that they should "go home and slop the hogs."[6] All this is a matter of historical record, although the final taunt has been variously interpreted and denied so that its authenticity is doubtful. The reaction of the farmers, the methods employed by Everly to organize them, and their sweep of the primary elections the next summer are all part of the story of the Nonpartisan League.

What we are primarily interested in is the accuracy of the author's portrayal of characteristic farm attitudes and beliefs. The purpose of detailing these factual parallels is to suggest that a novel in which the incidents and characters so closely follow historical fact would in all probability be equally accurate in its treatment of the attitudes which underlie the historical incidents. It is particularly important to do so in the case of *Prairie Fires*, because in it greater emphasis is given to the hostility between farm and small town than in any other work treated here. This hostility is not merely a matter of mutual suspicion due to ignorance; it is a matter of contempt on the part of the townsmen and hatred on the part of the farmers. When the farmers attempt to hold an organizational meeting in the town of Besserud, they find no place open to them. Although the schoolhouse has been advertised as a community center, the superintendent has been pressured into refusing permission to the farmers to use the gymnasium. Even earlier, however, it has never served the farmer. It is described as a fine building, "with the nice little waiting-room for farmers' wives; never used by them, of course, because it was always full of teachers who felt superior and eyed the country wives out of countenance."[7] The townspeople snicker at the heavily bundled farmers searching for a meeting place; to them "it was as though cattle were having a convention to discuss the slaughter-house problem" (141). Children shout insults at them as they wander about the streets. They finally meet in an un-

---

[6] *Ibid.*, p. 21; also Lorna Doone Beers, *Prairie Fires* (New York: E. P. Dutton & Co., 1925), pp. 243–244.

[7] Beers, *Prairie Fires*, p. 143.

heated barn on the edge of town and decide to boycott the village
—a device which eventually brings an apology from the mayor
but no real improvement in the treatment of the farmer. Benjamin Paul, in his rational phase, states the case lucidly: "The only
excuse a little town has to exist is because it serves the agricultural community. . . . If the town stops doing that efficiently, and
begins to prey on the farmers—then, presto! It ought to be
cleaned out" (82). Hostility to the town may, of course, go much
deeper than the immediate issue of exploitation. Farmers tend to
think of the town—any size, from small village to metropolis—as
the dwelling place of evil. After the farmers in *Prairie Fires* have
been told to "go home and slop the hogs," they head for home,
and Hans Erickson remarks to a friend, "Men like me should
never get off the soil, Pat. We are out of place here amongst all
the devilment" (245). The "devilment" is not merely the political
chicanery going on in this particular legislative session; it is what,
to the farmer, normally goes on in cities and towns, something
for which he is unprepared since it is not encountered in the
country.

Although farm people tend to be conservative in politics,
such a stereotype does not always hold true, particularly in the
Great Plains states. A study of voting records has shown that
North Dakota leads all the other states in "insurgency," measured
in terms of frequency of shifts from one party to another.[8] The
psychology of the Great Plains wheat farmer is fundamentally
that of a gambler. Instead of emphasizing the cardinal virtues of
prudence, thrift, and industry and clinging to tried and true
methods of farming, he is likely to risk everything he has in the
hope of a good year in which he can recoup all his losses of previous years. The wheat farmer does not succeed by being cautious
but by trying something new whenever the old techniques fail.
Consequently he might be more receptive to new ideas than the
farmer in areas where the climate is more favorable to agriculture.
For this reason the conservatives in *Prairie Fires* are not the
farmers but the village bankers and businessmen. One morning
Christine (who has no political views worth mentioning) hears
snatches of Lövstad's political creed: ". . . state-owned elevators

[8] Carl C. Taylor *et al.*, *Rural Life in the United States*, p. 497.

would never do. It's Socialism. . . . gotta keep the government out of business. . . . for getting in a damned Democrat. . . . Huh? . . . What? . . . Wilson a professor? . . . need a good sound business man in the White House."[9] It might be noted parenthetically that Lövstad's remarks also reveal the anti-intellectualism of rural areas—not, however, as the distinctive possession of the farmer, but as characteristic of the small town; Hans Erickson sends his son to the Agricultural College and has a high regard for education, while Lövstad affects a scorn for schools and colleges.

The truly radical basis of the Nonpartisan League is indicated by the fact that most of its original organizers were card-carrying members of the Socialist party, which was more highly organized in North Dakota at this time than in any other predominantly agricultural state.[10] This aspect of the situation is not emphasized in the novel, perhaps because it was written in the early 1920's, but there are suggestions of something less than complete satisfaction with the existing economic system on the part of the author. Referring to the speculators' manipulation of the flax market which ruined Tom Everly, she says sarcastically in one of her many author intrusions, "What if hundreds of farmers were ruined? It is only those who are weak who fail in our competitive system."[11] Everly himself makes no direct attacks on the economic setup but reserves his strictures for the political system, particularly the phenomenon of party politics, with its patronage and its opportunities for graft. His ideal is simple: "A government run by impartial scientists responsible in aims but not in methods to the representatives of the people—that would be the ideal democracy" (251).

Although Hans Erickson may be somewhat idealized, the author of *Prairie Fires* does not attempt to portray the American farmer as godlike in wisdom or to place the entire responsibility for his misfortunes on circumstances external to himself. In Axel Johnson she shows the improvident, ineffectual farmer whom no alterations in the economic system can save; in others she shows the lack of vision, the lack of comprehension that prevent many

[9] Beers, *Prairie Fires*, p. 135.
[10] Morlan, *Political Prairie Fires*, pp. 23–24.
[11] Beers, *Prairie Fires*, p. 25.

farmers from knowing where their best interests lie. But the conditions she describes as existing in North Dakota before the organization of the Nonpartisan League are such that only the exceptional individual, like Erickson, can make more than a bare living, and the careless or unfortunate farmer goes down to inevitable disaster. The argument is that through intelligent and bold political action a new economic environment can be created, more favorable to the farmer who exercises reasonable diligence. This is the contribution of *Prairie Fires*: not the formulation of a new economic or political doctrine by the author, but the reflection in fiction of such a doctrine already formulated and put into practice.

In the year that *Prairie Fires* was published, another novel of farm life, Lynn Montross' *East of Eden*, appeared, describing the activities of the Nonpartisan League in Illinois. One of the organizers of "Grain Growers, Inc.," Jack Rothermel, had been a farmer in North Dakota and had gone to Bismarck with the group told to go home and slop the hogs by "one of the senators who was bought and paid for by the Minneapolis gang that owned us."[12] Instead of following the suggestion, he gave up farming and became an organizer for the League. In Illinois he finds a great deal of discontent among the farmers and persuades them to form a cooperative grain-marketing association. So severe is the farmers' plight and so persuasive the arguments of Rothermel that even stolid, conservative Fred Derring decides, reluctantly, that farming is part of a world economy and lends his support to the movement. Derring is the central character in the story, which is told largely from the point of view of his teen-age daughter, Louise. As in *Prairie Fires*, there is a love story, between Lou and a local no-good, Milt Bowen, but it is so incompletely fused with the major theme that it can be conveniently ignored.

To the businessmen of Dry Creek, Illinois, it at first seemed "impossible that the discontent which had started among a few Scandinavian farmers in North Dakota could have swept across their own state—their own county" (23). When they recover from the initial shock, however, they prove more effective adversaries

[12] Lynn Montross, *East of Eden* (New York: Harper and Brothers, 1925), p. 72.

than Lövstad and his cronies. Despite the inspired lobbying of Rothermel, the farmers are defeated in their attempt to push through the legislature a bill that would grant farm organizations a seat on the Board of Trade. The reasons for their defeat and the subsequent collapse of the association are never made quite clear, but internal dissention and jealousy seem to be the principal causes. The League's opponents spread the report that executives in the organization are receiving high salaries, and in time even the members themselves come to believe the rumor. The incorruptible Derring, who has spent money rather incautiously on household improvements, is thought to be a beneficiary of these salaries; his inability to speak effectively before a group prevents him from denying the charge, and the decline in his personal reputation parallels the disintegration of the association to which he has committed himself.

A better novel artistically than *Prairie Fires*, though suffering from a lack of effective characterization, *East of Eden* makes a less significant contribution to the literature of agrarian protest. The clash tends to be more one between individuals than between town and country. Throughout the novel Derrick's arch-enemy is Tom Nicholson, a local elevator owner and the richest man in Dry Creek, but the antagonism between them is never raised to the symbolic level of a rural-urban opposition. Unlike *Prairie Fires*, Montross' novel ends in defeat for the farmers. In this respect it is more prophetic than Miss Beers' work.

If *Prairie Fires* can be regarded as an optimistic account of a successful farm revolt in a predominantly agricultural state, Louis Bromfield's *The Farm* (1933) may be seen as a bitter epitaph on the tomb of agrarianism in an overwhelmingly industrialized state. Nostalgic to the point of sentimentality, it advocates no economic program, offers no hope for the restoration of the old order, but merely endeavors to recapture the flavor of that order and to contrast it with the modern materialistic industrial order which Bromfield passionately detested. His ideal is what he understands as Jeffersonianism. In his introduction to the novel he states his case succinctly:

"The Farm" is the story of a way of living which has largely gone out of fashion, save in a few half-forgotten corners and in a few families, which have stuck to it with admirable stubbornness in spite of everything. It was and is a good way of life, . . . It has in it two fundamentals which were once and may be again intensely American characteristics. These are integrity and idealism.[13]

The Farm is less a novel than a volume of reminiscences and genealogical information—"a somewhat fictionalized biographical account of the family," as Bromfield's biographer, Morrison Brown, calls it.[14] The central intelligence (to the extent that there is a central intelligence) is Johnny Willingdon, and the book is mostly a historical account of the people and forces that have gone to produce him, most of it centered about a piece of land in northern Ohio which has been in and out of the family for several generations since Colonel MacDougall took up the land shortly after the War of 1812. The Colonel is the true Jeffersonian who, though aristocratic to the core, believes that a good worker should know equality with his master and so invites his help to eat at his table.

> It was a part of his dream of this new country that it should be like this—simple and direct, in which good citizens, no matter what their station under any other scheme of things, should respect one another and live in a state of absolute democracy.[15]

One of his employees, Jamie Ferguson, later marries the Colonel's daughter and succeeds him in possession of the farm. From here on, a multitude of characters enter and leave Bromfield's panoramic canvas, most of them striking in one way or another. There is Great-aunt Sapphira, for example, who continues to treat her son as though he were a child under her direction, until her death when he is 86 years old and she is 104. The novel traces the decline of the old pattern of lavish living and vast estates, showing how the old families fall into decay as farming becomes less lucrative and are replaced by tenant farmers and immigrant peasants. The town grows and becomes a city, with huge ugly mansions and acres of slums, and the farmer becomes less and less important in the political equation.

[13] Louis Bromfield, *The Farm* (New York: Harper and Brothers, 1933), pp. v–vi.

[14] Morrison Brown, *Louis Bromfield and His Books* (Fair Lawn, N. J.: Essential Books, 1957), p. 2 n.

[15] Bromfield, *The Farm*, p. 48.

Bromfield of course is deeply grieved by the transformation he chronicles. He looks back fondly on the state of society on the eve of the Civil War, when "the town had not yet imposed itself upon the County; it was merely a market place where things were bought and sold" (67). All this changed after the war, when the robber barons took over and prostituted the country to materialism. He hopes that the old house of John Sherman will be preserved as a monument to the "tasteless and pretentious ugliness" of the period:

> Over it hung the shadow of men like Gould and Fiske, Drew and "public-be-damned" Vanderbilt, who had contempt for the common people whose judgment Jamie and the Colonel honored and believed that the country should be ruled by men who knew how to make money [120].

Who is to blame for the catastrophe that has overtaken the agrarian ideal of Jefferson? Bromfield places the blame squarely on the New England mercantile spirit, as embodied in the Yankee peddler. Colonel MacDougall has only contempt for New Englanders; to him, "they were tradespeople and shopkeepers, interested only in making money and swindling one another and the rest of the country" (8). At times the assault on New England, especially when expressed as Jamie's thoughts, approaches hysterical vituperation:

> [Jamie believed] that it was New England which had corrupted the democracy, the New England which long ago talked of a king and worried over titles and precedence, the New England which swindled the Revolutionary veterans and whose clergy preached privilege from their pulpits and soiled their cloth with obscene abuse of Jefferson [336].

It is not the New England of Cotton Mather or Jonathan Edwards that is to blame, for Jamie concedes that Puritanism at its best was a force for good; it was the mercantile spirit which began with that "genius without character," that *arriviste* and opportunist, Alexander Hamilton, who died none too soon for his own reputation (336–337). Bromfield takes some pains to dissociate his characters from the New Englanders he despises. Contrary to popular belief, the people he admires did not have "Yankee common sense":

Common sense, thrift, practical qualities, despite legends to the contrary, do not go with frontiersmen, and they were all children by blood, tradition, and experience of the frontier. If the men who conquered the wilderness of America had been thrifty and cautious shopkeepers, they would never have adventured into the wilderness [233].

The ideal which Bromfield sets up in opposition to that of the New England shopkeeper is clearly in the tradition of American agrarian thought. He says of old Jamie:

He had been born on the land. All his life he had lived by it, detesting towns and cluttered communities. Even as an old man he continued to fight the losing battle of the farmer. In the depths of his soul he believed the land to be the finest and most honorable of all that which might occupy the energies of man [295].

Expressed in less personal and more philosophical terms, Jamie

had believed that honest democracy was practical and good, that virtuous, dignified government was not impossible, and that in a new country, with a fresh start, man could escape greed and dishonesty and enjoy a life which was at once both rich and simple [335].

Despite the remark by a *New Republic* reviewer that what Bromfield is writing about is "fake,"[16] this expression of the agrarian ideal and the superiority of farm to city life is in accord with characteristically rural attitudes and beliefs.

Is there any hope for a return of the old way of life? No, says Bromfield, although some of its values may still be usable. Johnny's parents make an attempt to restore the farm, but their effort soon ends in failure, since the kind of life they seek to revive is no longer economically possible. The only farmers who can make even a bare living are the immigrant peasants who rise before dawn and use their women and children in the fields; these people have a passionate love for the land, and they do restore its fertility, but they are not the materials on which a Jeffersonian democracy can be built. The only ray of hope suggested in the novel is old Jamie's lingering belief that some day "there will come a reckoning and the country will discover that

[16] T. S. Matthews, "Fiction vs. Blurbs," *New Republic*, LXXVI (September 20, 1933), 162.

farmers are more necessary than travelling salesmen, that no nation can exist or have any solidarity which ignores the land."[17] This has about it a ring of childish petulance, as coming from one who is beaten and knows he is beaten but derives some satisfaction from muttering that his victorious opponent will be sorry. The reckoning Jamie envisions will take the form of an economic and social upheaval, he suggests, which will make the farm more attractive than the city. Since the novel was written during the depression period, when there was a temporary "back to the land" movement, such a claim possessed a measure of validity that it did not have in the previous decade.

It should perhaps be pointed out that the basic philosophy expressed here is Bromfield's and does not necessarily represent the views of any large numbers of farmers. His attitude toward the city may be attributable in part to the fact, noted by his biographer, that "the Bromfields did not belong to the new group that was taking over the leadership of Mansfield [the 'Town' of the novel]. They were more a part of the group that was being superseded."[18] He was described in 1942 as one of the most strongly agrarian of contemporary authors, a practicing farmer, a theorist on agricultural matters, and a self-announced candidate for the position of Secretary of Agriculture.[19] Born in Mansfield, Ohio, he moved with his family when he was sixteen to a farm which had been in the family for several generations. During the years that his maternal grandfather, Robert Coulter (the original of Jamie Ferguson), had operated the farm, it had been the family gathering place; sometimes as many as fifteen hundred relatives had been invited to a family reunion there. Expecting to take over the farm, young Louis spent a term at the Cornell University Agricultural College. But after a year and a half of actual farming, he decided that it was not the career for him and entered Columbia University to study journalism. Later in life, after writing several successful novels, he purchased a thousand-acre farm which he named "Malabar Farm," and he

[17] Bromfield, *The Farm*, p. 342.
[18] Morrison Brown, *Louis Bromfield and His Books*, p. 1.
[19] Stanley J. Kunitz and Howard Haycraft, *Twentieth Century Authors* (New York: H. W. Wilson Co., 1942), pp. 198–199.

lived there until his death in 1956.[20] As evidenced in *The Farm*, Bromfield's point of view is that of landed gentry, not that of the small farmer struggling for economic survival.[21] R. L. Duffus in a review of *A Few Brass Tacks* speaks of Bromfield as "An angry gentleman farmer striding up and down his sitting room . . . dictating and not revising."[22]

In its power to recreate an earlier period of history when agrarian dominance was a reality, *The Farm* makes a valuable contribution to the body of farm fiction. Its characters are generally believable, although the emphasis is on the more spectacular of them. There is no point in attempting to make it fit the conventional definition of the novel, since its plotless construction renders it more a series of portraits, but this in no way diminishes its artistic effectiveness. But its chief interest for the present purpose lies in its expression of a particular attitude toward the American scene, an attitude distinctively agrarian in its hostility to cities and to the relative decline of the farm.

The proletarian novel is virtually unrepresented in middle western farm fiction. Probably the nearest approach to it is Fannie Cook's *Boot-Heel Doctor* (1941), and it deals with a more typically southern situation and is laid in a part of Missouri which is called a "sixth finger on the hand of the South."[23] It is useful in this study, however, as an illustration of the application of the techniques of proletarian fiction to an agricultural situation.

The animus of the novel is revealed in the quotation from

[20] Morrison Brown, *Louis Bromfield and His Books*, pp. 9–11, 23–24, 109.

[21] Bromfield's ideals show a curious similarity to those of John Ward, the central character in *The Land They Possessed*. Although Ward has a greater propensity toward money-making than the characters sympathetically portrayed by Bromfield, he too is adventurous, a speculator, contemptuous of the immigrants (because they oblige their women and children to grub in the dirt and they pinch pennies), fond of horseflesh and of hunting, and much concerned that his family live like members of "their class." It may be significant that these are the very characteristics that Thorstein Veblen identifies with the predatory stage of man's development.

[22] Quoted in Stanley J. Kunitz, *Twentieth Century Authors: First Supplement* (New York: H. W. Wilson Co., 1955), p. 125.

[23] Fannie Cook, *Boot-Heel Doctor* (New York: Dodd, Mead & Co., 1941), p. 111.

Goldsmith's *The Deserted Village* that appears on the title page:

> . . . a bold peasantry, their country's pride
> When once destroyed, can never be supplied.

The main theme is the small independent farmer's struggle for survival against the expanding cotton-plantation system imported from the South. The relations between Negro and white receive consideration as a secondary theme. The incidents in the novel center chiefly about a flood in the boot-heel section of Missouri which results in the inundation of low-lying areas and the temporary displacement of the economically depressed population. Dr. Joel Gregory, the somewhat idealized hero of the novel, gives medical assistance to the Red Cross in caring for the farmers and share-croppers, who are temporarily housed in tents on the edge of the town of North Cotton. As the flood waters recede, he attempts to get community cooperation in planning for the time when the inundated areas become habitable again. He is interested chiefly in seeing that the bankers and businessmen make the loans that will be necessary to put the farmers back on their feet. But he finds that the influential men of the community see the flood as an opportunity to extend the plantation system over the whole area and eliminate the independent farmer altogether. This is precisely what they do, as Dr. Gregory's efforts go for nothing, and soon discontent becomes desperation as the share-croppers are driven deeper and deeper into poverty and dependence on the landowners.

Although race feeling is strong in the region (Negroes are allowed in North Cotton only to trade), the debt-ridden, poverty-stricken croppers accept the leadership of a Negro, Reuben Fielding, and organize a union. When the landowners try to force the ignorant croppers to sign over their government crop-control checks to them, the union acts to prevent this open fraud by apprising the croppers of their rights. The result is that the landowners decide to expel the union members (who constitute most of the croppers) from their shacks and hire day laborers to do the work. The expulsion is to take place in January, when the croppers can least afford to be driven outdoors, but they decide to anticipate the move and camp along the main highway, U.S. 61, to advertise their plight to the world. The organized exodus takes place, and Dr. Gregory involves himself in it in the course of his professional duties. His sympathy for the oppressed croppers and his defiance of social custom in allowing Reuben to leave his home by the front door bring down upon him the indignation of the community, and he is the victim of smear attacks. At the end of the novel he rather melodramatically saves Reuben from lynching and is content in the knowledge that the situation has been brought to the attention of the nation, which will act to relieve it.[24]

Of particular interest in a study of farm attitudes is the breaking down of extreme individualism and parochialism in the face of a situation that neither the individual nor the immediate group can cope with. In *Boot-Heel Doctor* the people are suspicious at first of the "foreign" Red Cross personnel, including the somewhat patronizing St. Louis doctors. They are especially disturbed when one of the nurses addresses a Negro as "Mister"; she is warned not to repeat the offense or she will be run out of the community. Dr. Gregory has never in his life called a black man "Mister," but "it sickened him to hear Odin [the owner of a cotton gin] bragging in the Cafe about all that sass of his to the round little Red Cross nurse. . . . Could give her a bad opinion of the boot-heel."[25] Even Dr. Gregory resents outside interference. At one time he considers writing to Washington about the planters' bare-faced steal of the crop-control checks, but he hates "so bad to take our quarrels out yonder to strangers" (194). This provincialism gives way to a realization that help from the federal government is the only salvation. Reuben tells his followers that they are all Americans and have their rights; although he knows little of the outside world, he is convinced that if he and the other croppers make the whole country aware of their plight,

[24] The incidents which form the background of this novel are matters of historical record. The flood took place in 1938 and the demonstration in January, 1939. The moving spirit in the latter was Owen H. Whitfield (Reuben Fielding in the novel), a farmer and part-time Baptist minister. The number who took part is variously estimated as from 1,000 to 1,300. State officials gave it as their opinion that the demonstration was fostered by subversive elements. New York *Times*, January 11, 12, 13, and 17, 1939.

[25] Cook, *Boot-Heel Doctor*, pp. 202–203.

help will be forthcoming. But to do so necessitates group action and a greater degree of group solidarity than these individualistic people have ever before shown. Somehow Reuben is able to weld together even such unpromising material torn by racial differences into a unified force held together by their common misery and a semireligious fervor which he fans with all the techniques of the camp-meeting evangelist.

Besides the element of individualism and the suspicion of outsiders found here, a characteristically rural hostility to the city appears now and then in *Boot-Heel Doctor*. Odin Hattock, the gin owner in league with the planters, suffers symptoms that any physician would recognize as psychosomatic in origin. Dr. Gregory tells him,

> You're all right, Odin. Haven't got a thing in the world to be ashamed of. It's just that you're a mite too enterprising for the rest of us around here. You belong up in the city where that sort of thing is respected. Come you'd move up and not live so close to the misery you profit from, I reckon you'd be a well man in no time [52].

Needless to say, "enterprising" here is the equivalent of "grasping." Dr. Gregory's speech also illustrates the author's handling of boot-heel dialect, particularly in the use of "come" as a synonym for "if." Her use of local speech patterns is consistent and gives an impression of studied accuracy, just as her reflection of rural attitudes carries conviction.

Paul Corey's novel *Acres of Antaeus* (1946) provides the best example of rural social-protest fiction in a typical middle western setting. Through the character of Ed Crosby, Corey had preached in his earlier novels the doctrine of the desirability of collective action as against the individualism that had put the farmer at the mercy of well-organized industrial and financial combines. Crosby insisted that farmers saw only their immediate advantage or disadvantage and were unable to look ahead, in part as a consequence of the occupational peculiarities of farming:

> Things that happen to the farmers have no immediate effect; their effect is cumulative. It isn't felt until months after the trouble happens. . . . That's why you can't get farmers to work together: they

can't see that what they do today will benefit them a year from now. . . .[26]

There was nothing very original about his diagnosis of the problem or his recommendations for its solution: "What was needed was organization and direction. Business, industry—the middleman—were integrated and could dictate terms to the farmer; the farmer, the producer of food, should be the one to set the prices" (295).

He does what he can to demonstrate the effectiveness of organization and direction by organizing a meat ring, which succeeds, and a cooperative elevator scheme, which fails when the bank buys a controlling interest in it.

Organization and direction are present in *Acres of Antaeus*, but they are provided not by the farmer or in his interest but by a corporation called Midwest Farms which is trying to create an agricultural empire by buying up farms on which mortgages have been foreclosed by an insurance company in league with Midwest. Jim Buckly, out of work because of the depression and unable to finish his course at Ames because he needs to support a wife, accepts a supervisory job with Midwest Farms. Although he likes the work, his loyalty to the organization is half-hearted at best, since he does not sympathize with its contemptuous attitude toward the small farmer; furthermore, his wife's family is in danger of foreclosure by the insurance company that is backing Midwest, and Jim is looked upon as a sort of traitor to his own people. His divided loyalty is the source of most of Jim's troubles, including his separation from his wife, but his problems are multiplied by office jealousies and a power struggle within the corporation. A farmers' protest meeting results in violence and the imprisonment of Jim's father-in-law just at the time he is about to lose the farm. Labor troubles in the nearby town get involved in the plot and culminate in the merciless beating of a youth who has given at least tacit support to a strike.

The conclusion to Corey's novel is unsatisfying in terms of the basic problem treated. Externally the problem seems to be re-

[26] Corey, *Three Miles Square*, p. 413.

solved. Midwest Farms has been taken over by a group interested in efficient farming rather than exploitation for immediate gain, and the insurance companies have decided to resell on the open market the land on which they have foreclosed, rather than sell it to Midwest. To Jim Buckly this is a satisfactory arrangement. He thinks that

> The days of building empires were over, even agricultural empires. The land had to belong to the people who farmed it; the land was too much of a living thing to be left to the quarreling and bickering of men interested only in making money. The farmers would have to learn to own the machines of mass production co-operatively; then they could compete with the growing corporation farms.[27]

But Midwest Farms is still in existence, and Jim is apparently still working for the corporation. And corporation farms are still growing, although Jim says the day of the agricultural empire is over. This unresolved contradiction weakens the novel and makes the reader wonder what chance there is for the land to belong to the people who farm it. The title of the novel refers to the Greek myth of Antaeus, who was unconquerable so long as he could renew his strength by touching the earth but was overcome by Hercules, who discovered his secret and lifted him off the ground. The farmer is not perceptibly nearer the attainment of the necessary contact with the soil at the end of this novel than at the beginning, and so the renewal of his strength still remains to be accomplished.

Most of the generalizations made in the previous chapter about Corey's skill as a novelist apply also to *Acres of Antaeus*, although its comparative brevity (it is shorter than any one of the three earlier novels) deprives it of the cumulative power of the trilogy. The major characters are also weaker than those in the earlier books; even Jim's difficult position between the exploiters and the exploited cannot fully account for the unreasonable behavior of both husband and wife in their always strained relationship, although one cause for the continued tension is the wife's refusal to have a child. A miscarriage early in their married life has had a traumatic effect on her, and it is only after she has

[27] Paul Corey, *Acres of Antaeus* (New York: Henry Holt & Co., 1946), pp. 387–388.

assisted her husband in delivering a calf, at the end of the novel, that the effect of this experience is erased and she is reconciled to the idea of having a child.

In *Acres of Antaeus* some attention was given to soil conservation, a subject that becomes a major theme in Feikema's huge novel about farm life among the Frisians of northwestern Iowa, *This Is the Year* (1947). Already mentioned briefly in Chapter III, *This Is the Year* resists classification on the basis of the categories employed here; since it includes the mildly reformist aim of conservation, however, it seems most appropriately treated in this chapter.

Pier Frixen is the central figure in *This Is the Year*. The illiterate, ignorant, and yet withal sensitive son of Frisian immigrants, Pier is a complex and convincingly portrayed individual. When he comes of age and marries, he attempts for a time to run the family farm in partnership with his father, but the father's hidebound traditionalism is too much for even the conservative Pier to stomach, and soon he sends his parents off to the town of Starum, where they live in disconsolate retirement. Both Pier's farming and his marriage succeed for a time. Unfortunately, his tendency to be ignorantly, but not viciously, domineering leads him to mistreat both his wife and his land; later a son, Teo, bears the brunt of his mistreatment and is consequently disillusioned with farm life. Pier's wife Nertha dies after two miscarriages but no more children, and Pier marries his gypsy neighbor, Kaia, but drives her out of the house after a few months of domestic disharmony.

Meanwhile Pier has been ignoring the advice of the county agent, Old Dreamer Pederson, and allowing his land to suffer permanent erosion damage. A reactionary in matters of modern farming practices, Pier stoutly refuses to have his cows tested for tuberculosis until forced to submit at gunpoint, and he refuses to join the government support programs for corn and hogs. He does well enough in good years, but when the droughts of the 1920's and 1930's come along, his profits are reduced, he is forced to mortgage the land, and at the end of the novel, in 1936, he loses his farm and is turned out to wander alone, his first wife dead, his son alienated, his second wife expelled. All through the novel he has been consistently lucky in minor matters, and he accepts his final misfortune with cheerful optimism.

In the previous chapter a resemblance between Paul Corey and James T. Farrell was noted. If Feikema can profitably be compared with any modern novelist outside the realm of farm fiction, it would probably be Thomas Wolfe. Like Wolfe, Feikema takes his work seriously and writes enormous novels; as in Wolfe's writings, there is in *This Is the Year* a mixture of realism and mysticism, of coarseness and poetry, of bathos and beauty. Frankness in language and in the physical details of farm life has seldom if ever been carried farther than in this novel; every indelicate and repulsive feature of Pier's life is given sober treatment, with especial reference to Nertha's miscarriages. Terrifying experiences are reproducd with great fidelity, as in the case of Pier's sensations as he feels himself slipping from a barn roof (to land in a manure pile) or from the top of his windmill. Gory details are the author's specialty; the picture of Pier's father being sliced in half, vertically, by a fragment of a whirling saw reminds one of Wolfe's description in *You Can't Go Home Again* of C. Green after he has leaped from a twelfth-story window onto a sidewalk.

Yet coupled with all this blood and brutality there is in the book a vein of poetic beauty, not always handled with the deftness and delicacy it deserves. The novel begins with an account of a robin's arrival in spring and ends with its departure in the fall; snatches of Frisian legend and language are interspersed with the narrative in highly effective fashion; and Pier himself has poetry in his soul, as evidenced by the little songs he composes for himself as he goes about his work and by the delight he takes in an operetta he attends and in the stories from the *Odyssey* Teo recounts to him. Feikema is not always successful in fusing the disparate elements that his novels include, but in *This Is the Year* he probably does not merit the scathing treatment accorded him by Granville Hicks in a review of a later novel, *The Giant*:

> The commonplace and the melodramatic, the banal and the would-be poetic, lie side by side. . . . The trouble is that Mr. Feikema has been unable to communicate his passion and seriousness, principally

because he cannot command the necessary resources of style. By no means a careless writer, in fact almost too self-conscious in his handling of words, he achieves an infelicity of language that is staggering in its consistency.[28]

Comparing Feikema with Faulkner, Hicks remarks that Faulkner's experiments with language now and then result in something pretty bad, but in Feikema the proportions are reversed: "He misses nearly every time" (5). Perhaps the most striking form taken by his experiments with language in *This Is the Year* is his free coinage of words, a device not always necessary to his purpose. Among the coinages found at least once (and usually only once) are swervelings (noun), wapping, nincing, fluped, sussing, craking, ruckling, bibber (all verbs), gulking, and ludding (verbs used adjectively).

The principal theme of *This Is the Year* appears to be Pier's mistreatment of his land and, by extension, the almost universal mistreatment of the land by American farmers. In developing this theme the author employs a prolonged analogy, amounting almost to allegory, between the soil and a woman. The land is personified as a fecund woman caressed by the rain and sun, raped by man, who loses her charm and her fertility when she is mistreated. Old Dreamer Pederson, the author's mouthpiece, tells Pier, "When you've married the land, you've got to learn to protect her."[29] In a long, impassioned soliloquy he says, in heightened language, "Man, the fool, has been reckless with his wife. He has behaved foolishly on her breasts and her thighs. Here in America he is losing her, will lose her, has already lost half of her" (480). Pier's marriage then becomes the symbol of his management of his land; in both situations he "bulls his way" to his immediate objectives, without consideration for his partner and without listening to anyone's advice.

Pier's reaction to the advice repeatedly offered by Pederson illustrates his independence, conservatism, and anti-intellectualism. His own view on the matter of conservation is stated suc-

---

[28] Granville Hicks, "The End of Mighty Thurs," *New York Times Book Review*, December 30, 1951, p. 5.

[29] Feike Feikema [Frederick Manfred], *This Is the Year* (Garden City: Doubleday & Co., 1947), p. 315.

cinctly: "I still say, a farmer should farm according to his own idees. Too many of them high monkey-monk idees don't get y'u nowhere" (23). It is this attitude which leads him to resist having his cattle tested for tuberculosis and to reject the government corn-hog program. When Pederson explains to him that the program is entirely voluntary and asks if that is not fair enough, he replies, "Fair or not, I'm agin anybody tellin' me what to do. I'm independent, I am. I run this farm myself. I don't ask nobody about nothin', do as I please, an' am my own boss" (468). Although Pier has been a leader in organizing the forced sale that saved his friend Red Joe from ruin, the cooperative aspect of the corn-hog program means nothing to him; cooperation on a local scale he can comprehend, but when it extends beyond his immediate neighborhood it is outside his grasp. For the same reasons he later refuses to seal his corn and receive a government loan on it.

Feikema's use of historical background resembles that of *Prairie Fires*, except that of course it is only incidental to the main plot. When Pier and Red Joe attempt to take a load of hogs to market in Sioux City in 1933, they encounter both the milk strike in Sioux Center and the Farm Holiday strike which centered about Le Mars. The treatment of these movements may represent some telescoping, for artistic purposes, of the historical facts. The best-known phase of the milk strike occurred in 1932, and was restricted to the immediate Sioux City area, while the Farm Holiday strike occurred early in 1933. The incidents most readily identifiable with Feikema's story are those connected with picketing that went on in October, 1933, when livestock trucks headed for Sioux City were stopped.[30] Pier and Red Joe are, somewhat implausibly, in complete ignorance of these disorders; this is less surprising in the case of Pier, who cannot read, than in Joe's case. Coupled with the fact that Red Joe, who ordinarily ships to Sioux Falls, a much closer market, has decided on the spur of the moment to ship to Sioux City now, Feikema's

[30] For background on these incidents see Frank D. DiLeva, "Iowa Farm Price Revolt," *Annals of Iowa*, XXXII (January 1954), 171–202; and "Attempt to Hang an Iowa Judge," *Annals of Iowa*, XXXII (July 1954), 337–364. The reference to stopping livestock trucks is on p. 356.

introduction of the historical event strikes the reader as awkward and unnecessary.

This Is the Year contains an interesting echo of the passage from *Seth's Brother's Wife* quoted at the beginning of Chapter IV. The doctor who attends Nertha in her final illness asks Pier's son Teo where his interests lie. Upon being told that Teo is more interested in machinery than in farming, he replies, "Huh. Good. You're smarter than I thought. The age coming at us is going to be a buzzer age and you might just as well be right in the middle of it as not."[31] This may not represent Feikema's own position, but his subsequent novels have had less to say about the farm background of some of their heroes than about the later urban careers of those figures.

Not propaganda in the same sense as *Boot-Heel Doctor* or *Acres of Antaeus*, *This Is the Year* nevertheless has a persuasive theme: the land must be used, not misused, if it is to continue supporting the human race; the pipe dream of substituting the laboratory for the farm, if it is ever realized, will come too late for mankind. In the meantime, man must learn to live with the land.

A somewhat more sophisticated but equally stubborn Pier Frixen appears as the central figure in a recent—and very good—farm novel by Lois Hudson, *The Bones of Plenty* (1962). Like his famous namesake, George A. Custer is rash and impulsive, and although cynical about many things, he tends to be over-optimistic where his own chances of success as a North Dakota farmer in the 1930's are concerned. Handicapped by drought, rust, grasshoppers, low farm prices, and the extortions of a landlord interested only in immediate profits, Custer gambles on a new kind of wheat and loses, borrows from his father-in-law and goes deeper into debt each season, and finally tears up his lease in a fit of pique when his landlord refuses to lend him money. At the end of the novel, which covers a fifteen-month period in 1933 and 1934, the Custer family are having an auction and preparing to go west, perhaps to Alaska.

Although *The Bones of Plenty* is a farm novel with a message, the author does not go out of her way to make clear just what

[31] Feikema, *This Is the Year*, p. 486.

the message is. To the extent that she speaks through George Custer, no rational solution is suggested. Custer is scornful of government action, believing that the government is run in the interests of bankers and industrialists, but he is equally scornful of the Farm Holiday movement and of a Marxist named Oblonsky, who blames the farmers' troubles on the capitalist system itself. At times Custer talks about the farmers' taking things into their own hands in a revolution, but it is obvious that he fails to understand the implications of his suggestion. He is ignorant of economics and suspicious of those who might enlighten him. The only character who might plausibly function as the author's mouthpiece is Will Shepard, Custer's father-in-law, but he is only bewildered at the farmers' plight, unable to offer any answers. There is no question but that the author intends to stress the farm problem. It figures prominently in the novel itself, and in a concluding note Mrs. Hudson points out the continuing problem—that for a large part of the farm population the depression has never ended.

Aside from its somewhat ambiguous point of view, *The Bones of Plenty* has artistic merits that justify the critical praise bestowed upon it on its appearance.[32] It is a polished performance, in sharp contrast to such a novel as *Prairie Fires*, whose social reform purpose has to sustain its clumsy artistry. Its rather underwritten style relies heavily on the vernacular of the characters to convey their thoughts and generally does this effectively. Like many modern novels, it treats in detail a restricted period of time; more correctly, it restricts itself to a series of incidents—

[32] A reviewer for the New York *Times*, for example, thought it possible "that literary historians of the future will decide that 'The Bones of Plenty' was *the* farm novel of the Great Drought of the Nineteen-Twenties and Nineteen Thirties and the Great Depression." He thought that Mrs. Hudson had presented this saga with "intelligence and rare understanding" and "skill and compassion." (Victor P. Hass, "No Chance of Victory," *New York Times Book Review*, August 5, 1962, p. 20.) Another reviewer said, "It is a bitter novel, written in an objective and finished style, with a piling up of agonies which creates a parable for modern times with an argument that natural malevolence combined with human frailty leaves men not only unable to endure but unlikely even to escape." (George McMichael in *New York Herald Tribune Books*, September 2, 1962, p. 6.)

"epiphanies," as Joyce might have called them—and relies on indirect exposition of earlier events and of those which occur between one recorded scene and another. The author of numerous short stories about North Dakota farm life, Mrs. Hudson has here compressed into one sustained piece of writing the indignation that grew out of her own childhood experiences on a prairie farm in the depression years. If the novel offers no solution to the problems of the Great Plains farmer, it is perhaps because the author does not see any.

Several reasons may be suggested to account for the relative infrequency of literature of social criticism in middle western farm fiction. For one thing, it can be argued that the farmer's plight has seldom been as desperate as that of the urban laborer. In this respect his situation is comparable to that of the merchant or banker or newspaperman, all capitalists like himself, who might indeed fail in business but whose lot after failure was not nearly so hopeless as that of the urban laborer out of a job. The middle western farmer who went down to defeat did so at a comparatively high economic level, and there were stages beneath him before he reached the rock bottom of the unemployed coal miner or railway worker. If he lost his farm, it was usually possible for him to remain there as a tenant, or else he could go to the city and look for work there. If he failed to find it, he would be dealt with in literature as a part of the unemployed urban proletariat, not as a farmer.

Another factor which might be involved was the physical dispersion of farmers, which meant that a farm failure was a relatively isolated phenomenon geographically, while the unemployed in cities constituted a body of men too large to be ignored by the rest of the populace. Furthermore, much of the misfortune that afflicted the farmer was the result of natural forces, such as drought, grasshopper plagues, and the like, which played a negligible role in the economic life of the urban laborer. Literature of social protest is necessarily predicated upon the assumption of a vicious or inadequate economic system; proletarian fiction cannot be written about men driven to the wall because of drought, unless, as in *The Grapes of Wrath*, such a natural force can be shown to be a contributory but incidental factor in a situation resulting principally from defects in the economic system.

The result of these and presumably other causes is that middle western farm fiction has been singularly lacking in genuine novels of social protest. The specifically economic problems of the farmer have been touched upon in many novels and have formed the main theme of a few, but a body of social protest literature comparable to that dealing with urban situations has not yet developed.

VI.

Men and Women on the Farm
The Farm Novelist as Psychologist

NOT ALL farm novels written during the past half-century can be seen in terms of an implicitly or explicitly expressed didactic or historical purpose. Many, especially on the sub-literary level, are concerned only with telling a good story. Some, written with an eye on Hollywood, are little more than first drafts of movie scenarios. Other novels are attempting to do what literature has been doing through the ages, exploring the mysteries of human character and personality through the creation of fictional beings. Such farm novels tend to subordinate or ignore the historical and sociological aspects of their material and to concentrate on the psychological problems of their characters. These characters are primarily human beings and only incidentally rural Americans of the nineteenth or twentieth centuries. If such a character is happy or unhappy on the farm, it is not so much because the farm is a desirable or undesirable place to live as because of certain emotional peculiarities of the person himself which fit or unfit him for country life. If a character goes into debt or loses his farm, it is likely to be less the result of an iniquitous economic system than the consequence of some inadequacy on the part of the unfortunate person.

The one feature all the novels treated in this chapter have in common is an emphasis on individual personality and character. All present some psychological problem or problems which are given greater importance than any social or economic issues that may enter into the story. The use of farm background, authentic though that background may be, is usually more or less a matter of accident; the author writes of what he knows, and many of these authors grew up on or near farms or had some first-hand acquaintance with farm life. In a few cases, writers with very little knowledge of rural life attempted to capitalize on the vogue of farm fiction in the 1920's and 1930's and turned out novels to order with the mechanical precision of the poets and artists in the nightmare scene of *Beggar on Horseback*.

A chronological survey of these novels of human character can be of especial value in a study of farm fiction because it affords a view, so far as technique is concerned, of the whole genre in miniature. The complete range is not apparent in this group of novels, however, for it includes neither the very best nor the very poorest; and since most were written between 1920 and 1940, they do not provide a really complete picture of the entire developmental process from Garland to the present time.

One of the earliest twentieth-century attempts to deal with psychological problems in a farm setting is Mrs. Dell H. Munger's *The Wind Before the Dawn* (1912). The central theme of this Kansas novel is the domination of women by their husbands. Elizabeth Farnshaw has seen the suppression of her mother's personality by a brutal, domineering husband, and she is determined to avoid a similar misfortune in her own life. But when the superficially cultured John Hunter appears in her drab world of rural school teaching, she is quickly dazzled by his charms and overlooks the fact that he is subtly overruling her wishes and getting his way in every important matter. Once they are married, his domination becomes much more overt. He employs various subterfuges to avoid taking her to visit friends of whom he does not approve, makes decisions affecting her without consulting her, and even directs the details of her housekeeping on the pretext of helping her with the work. Blessed with too great an ability to see both sides of every question, she submits to her husband's impositions and blames herself for the growing dissatisfaction she feels. At length she rebels, however, when a close friend dies thinking that Elizabeth has forsaken her, unaware that it is only that John refuses to allow Elizabeth to visit her. But she is still virtually helpless, since she has no independent income, and so her rebellion is almost entirely passive. The solution to a well-nigh impossible situation is found when John's business partner, who has secretly fallen in love with Elizabeth, dies and wills his share of the farm to her. Obliged now to recognize her as an equal and consult her on financial matters, John at first refuses to accept the situation and runs off to Chicago. Eventually, however, he returns, and he and his wife take up their marriage on what looks like a more satisfactory basis.

The weaknesses in this story are evident even from this brief outline of the plot. We have only the author's word that John has changed enough by the end of the novel to be willing to accept his wife as an equal, and there is nothing in his previous performance to suggest that he would ever undergo such a change. Divorce is apparently not seriously considered. Elizabeth's mother, bullied and beaten as she is, is horrified when her daughter suggests it as a solution to the older woman's problem; and Elizabeth herself refuses to make any move in that direction even when she has been separated from her husband for some time and admits that she no longer loves him. Perhaps in 1912, among the readers of this kind of fiction, it was not possible to recommend divorce in any but the most extreme cases.

The diagnosis of the problem dealt with in *The Wind Before the Dawn* is more searching than the proposed remedy. The causes for the tyranny exercised by men over their wives are explored with considerable insight. Men in general are not brutal by nature; except for a few like Elizabeth's father, they are not intentionally tyrannical. The process may begin with men ordering their wives around; as Mrs. Farnshaw says, "A man begins right from th' first t' tell her what to do an' she loves 'im and wants t' please 'im, an' before long she don't have her way no more'n a nigger."[1] But the real fault lies in the woman's acquiescence; the man is acting in what he thinks are his wife's best interests, and it is up to her to let him know that she is a better judge of these interests than he is. Elizabeth concludes "that if a woman were enslaved it was because she herself permitted it, that to yield where she should stand fast did not secure a man's love, it only secured his contempt and increased his demands" (375). But the solution Mrs. Munger offers is likely to strike the modern reader as somewhat shallow. The problem is essentially psychological, but the solution is expressed in eco-

[1] Dell H. Munger, *The Wind Before the Dawn* (Garden City, N. Y.: Doubleday, Page & Co., 1912), p. 82.

nomic terms. Elizabeth's own escape comes through a fortuitous gift of money, and so she decides that "a woman, to be free, must have money of her own. She must not be supported by a man" (552). Any reader can see that it is Elizabeth's bitter experience rather than her lover's bequest that really emancipates her from the bondage she has been in since her marriage.

The Wind Before the Dawn is long for a farm novel of its period (564 pages), but its length is not an index to its merit. Much space is consumed with over-documentation of its case or with largely irrelevant side plots. There are altogether too many jarring stylistic infelicities and syntactical blunders:

> Elizabeth saw that if John Hunter must needs run a farm that he would do his best at it. . . . to Elizabeth it was working in fairyland to have John make one side of a bed's clothes lay smooth. . . . She . . . began to see the many whips which a determined husband had at his command, chief of which was the crippling processes of motherhood.[2]

Although Elizabeth herself is a well-drawn character, if rather too long-suffering, none of the other figures is consistently or credibly done. There are several people of little learning but possessed of hearts of gold, and Hugh Noland, the lover whose will gives Elizabeth her freedom, is a romantic figure straight out of a sentimental novel. Because he is sympathetically portrayed and because at the same time proper respect must be paid to the institution of marriage, the only solution is to have him die. His death provides the most notable of several examples of melodrama in the novel.

Mrs. Munger's novel qualifies as farm fiction chiefly because it takes place against a farm background. This background is portrayed with apparent fidelity, but there is little else that is characteristic of farm life or farm people in the book. Some attempt is made to reproduce the speech of the people, but the result seems like a fairly conventional stage-rustic dialect. Locust plagues, floods, and drought receive their usual attention, and there is a hint of the economic difficulties facing the farmer. The novel resembles much nineteenth-century fiction in that the characters on whom attention is chiefly centered are relatively culti-

[2] *Ibid.*, pp. 117, 240, 349–350.

vated and, except for Elizabeth, are outsiders; the attitude taken toward the indigenous figures can only be described as patronizing. For all these reasons, *The Wind Before the Dawn* fails to accomplish what the profundity of the theme and the author's insight into it would lead the reader to expect.

The decade of the 1920's, a rich period in American literature generally, witnessed the coming of age of the farm novel. Early in that decade Emanuel and Marcet Haldeman-Julius published a grim novel of Kansas farm life titled *Dust* (1921). Contrary to the suggestion contained in the title, this bleak tale has little to do with drought and includes not a single dust storm; the dust is in the soul of Martin Wade, a Kansas Zury who comes west with his parents and learns, through hard experience, to sacrifice everything to economic security. After the death of his parents, he builds up a highly productive farm and becomes one of the substantial men of the community. To climax his good fortune, a coal mining company pays him $16,000 for the right to tunnel under his land. Despite this wealth, Martin is puzzled and disappointed: "it came to him that he needed something by which to measure his wealth, someone whose appreciation of it would make it real to him, give him a genuine sense of its possession."[3] Marriage appeared to him, as it did to Zury, chiefly a matter of expediency; "marriage with the men and women of his world was a practical business, arranged and conducted by practical people, who lived practical lives, and died practical deaths" (36). Not quite so "practical" as Zury, who would have proposed to any one of three sisters, he selects a woman of emotional and intellectual depth, Rose Conroy, who is surprised by the offer and asks him if he thinks she could make him happy: "Martin felt embarrassed. He was not looking for happiness but merely for more of the physical comforts, and an escape from loneliness. He was practical. . ." (45–46). Rose, in her late twenties and impressed by Martin's stature in the community, allows herself to believe that he possesses or will develop a real affection for her and agrees to the somewhat precipitate alliance.

The rest of the book is a study of marriage rather than of

[3] Emanuel and Marcet Haldeman-Julius, *Dust* (New York: Brentano's, 1921), p. 31.

farming. Rose soon discovers that Martin considers her his chattel, whose function is to support him in his enterprises and efface her own needs and desires as much as possible. His selfishness and her disillusionment are entirely believable, and the picture of the deterioration of the marriage is accomplished by swift, sure strokes. One child is born dead as the result of Rose's being kicked by a cow during the late stages of her pregnancy; another child learns early to fear and hate his father, who accuses the mother of turning the boy against him. But the boy has seen a sow eating one of her litter, and the remembrance of it "floated near the surface of his consciousness, his first outstanding memory of his father and the farm" (122). The boy is reluctantly allowed to go to high school, where he rebels against the farm and refuses to come home for the summer. Instead, he takes a job as firer in a mine and is killed in an explosion.

Martin Wade is no conventional villain, devoid of qualities worthy of admiration. He is portrayed with as much sympathy as so self-centered a person can be expected to arouse; he is simply unable to think in terms other than those of utter practicality, and hence he cannot conceive of any justification for anyone's thinking in other terms. Furthermore, he has, like Zury, an emotional strain in his make-up that can be touched by the right person, in this case his niece, also named Rose. When she first appears, as a small child, she captivates Martin, and he reveals a side of his nature that his wife has never seen and can scarcely comprehend. The short visit of the little girl leads to a brief reconciliation between Martin and his wife, but the effect is temporary. When Rose next appears, she is a lovely young woman of about eighteen, and Martin, now in his fifties, is swept off his feet. He declares his love for the girl to his wife in language as passionate as that of any conventional lover in fiction. But the girl suspects his infatuation and soon leaves, before Martin can bring himself to sacrifice his material possessions in order to run off with her, as he at one point thinks of doing.

The end of all Martin's striving is dust and ashes. He contracts infection while treating a sick cow and dies soon afterward, leaving his wealth to the woman he never loved and who stayed with him through the years, partly because of a sense of propriety but mainly because of a very real, though repressed, affection for him. Even the splendid buildings he has erected will not long survive Martin Wade, for the mining company is going to build a road directly through the farmstead. At the end of the novel everything Martin has lived for has turned to dust.

The point must be made that *Dust* is not just another anti-farm novel, showing by the example of Martin Wade the dwarfing and desiccating influence of farm life. This may be true of Martin's childhood experiences, but his later affluence might well have opened the door to a spiritual development such as that which Zury underwent. If Martin has the potentialities for such development, Rose Conroy is not the woman to enable him to realize them. Outwardly at least, the farm has produced quite opposite effects on these two. The younger Rose

> marvelled that the same years on the same farm which had given one person added polish and had made him even more good looking than ever, could have changed another so completely and turned her into such a toil-scarred, frumpy, oldish woman [146].

Inwardly, of course, Martin has suffered quite as much as his wife. But given the qualities of character and personality he has, their marriage would have produced the same result in different surroundings. If farm life is to be blamed at all for the misery in the book, it is only the experiences of Martin's early years, when the burdens of breaking the soil and harvesting crops were on his young shoulders.

In *Dust* the usual attitude of superiority taken by town people toward farmers is reversed. Martin jokingly pretends to the humility becoming to a farmer, but actually he looks down on city folk:

> He had the confidence in his superiority that comes from complete economic security and his pride of place was even more deeply rooted. Men of Martin's class who are able to gaze, in at least one direction, as far as eye can see over their own land, are shrewd, sharp, intelligent, and far better informed on current events and phases of thought than the people of commercial centers even imagine [142–143].

This is a far cry from the humble peasant or untutored rustic who still figures now and then in the urban mythology of the farm.

Parallels between *Dust* and Kirkland's *Zury* have been noted. There are also resemblances to Norris' *McTeague*, chiefly in the husband-wife relationship, and it is these resemblances that entitle the novel to whatever claim it may have to being called a naturalistic work. There is less melodrama than in *McTeague*, but on the other hand there is also less of a sense of determinism. The reader does not necessarily feel, as he does of McTeague, that Martin is the helpless product of his early environment, important though that may have been in molding his views. Yet there is a sense that he and Rose are driven, if not by external circumstances, at least by the consequences of their own acts. As in the determinism of *The Scarlet Letter*, there is a feeling that once the initial act has been performed (in this case marriage), the rest is grim necessity. Thus, the naturalistic influence is evident in *Dust* to a degree that it certainly is not in such a novel as *The Wind Before the Dawn*.

It should perhaps be pointed out that Haldeman-Julius' own background did not fit him especially well to write on farm life. Born in a Philadelphia tenement, he went in 1915 to Girard, Kansas, to help edit a socialist periodical, *Appeal to Reason*. His wife was the daughter of a local banker, reputed to be one of the state's wealthiest citizens.[4] Both undoubtedly knew much of village life at first-hand and probably a good deal about farm life but only at second hand. Perhaps for this reason, *Dust* is occupied more with emotional maladjustments in marriage than with the physical or economic problems of farming. There is in the novel no perceptible element of the social criticism that Haldeman-Julius' interest in socialism might suggest to the reader.

The subject of material satiety and spiritual starvation in a rural situation is treated in less dramatic but more typical form by Ruth Suckow in her novel of Iowa farm life, *Country People*

---

[4] William J. Fielding, "Prince of Pamphleteers," *Nation*, CLXXIII (May 10, 1952), 452–453; and Albert Mordell, comp., *The World of Haldeman-Julius* (New York: Twayne Publishers, 1960), p. 6. In a "Profile," (p. 8) his second wife, Sue Haldeman-Julius, says they had a ten-acre farm on the edge of town, but this was subsequent to the publication of *Dust*.

(1924). This straightforward, unembroidered account of the lives of the August Kaetterhenry family is notable especially for its remarkable veracity. The behavior, language, beliefs, and attitudes of Miss Suckow's stolid German farmers have a ring of authenticity that is encountered in only a few of the best farm novels. Of plot, in the conventional sense, there is very little. August Kaetterhenry, the son of German immigrants to northeastern Iowa, marries Emma Stille and with her help and the help of their children builds up a good farm. In accordance with the pattern of the region, August and Emma turn the farm over to a son when they reach late middle age and retire to the nearby town of Richland, where they build a house and become part of the retired-farmer element in the town. August finds himself unable to make the adjustment to his new status, his health fails, and he dies, leaving Emma to make decisions for the first time in her life.

Miss Suckow has expressly repudiated any intention of showing the drabness or emptiness of farm life. Written at a time when American self-consciousness was very touchy, she says, the purpose of this book "was frequently mistaken for an indictment of American rural and small town life, particularly in the Middlewest. . . ."[5] The fact is, she insists, it is "neither indictment nor celebration," and it was "not written primarily for the sake of social criticism" (ix). The truth of her denial would not, however, necessarily obviate the possibility of regarding *Country People* as an unintentional indictment of farm life. The lives of August and Emma Kaetterhenry certainly do not present a glowing picture of happy, healthy people going joyously about their tasks; the people are narrow and at least mildly discontented, and their tasks are just plain drudgery.

Nevertheless, the farm environment does not affect these people uniformly; those who have inner resources and potentialities for growth come off perceptibly better than those who lack such qualities. Grandpa Stille, for example, finds in his religion a satisfaction denied to the more materialistic generations that follow him. It is not that the younger people are irreligious; they are almost as rigorous in their outward observance of religious cus-

[5] Ruth Suckow, *Carry-Over* (New York: Farrar & Rinehart, 1936), p. vii.

toms as their elders. But their religion is inextricably bound up with a highly materialistic morality. To August, "Going to church, and being steady and a good worker, and not drinking, and paying his bills, and saving money, were all part of the same thing."[6] The Germans in *Country People* are all stern Methodists. Although most of them were Lutherans or Catholics in Germany, they were required to change their faiths by the man responsible for bringing them to America, for he was a zealous convert to Methodism. Hence they were quickly assimilated into the American Methodist churches and exposed to the American moral doctrine of thrift, industry, and prudence. The transition to English-speaking churches was not accomplished without resistance, however. The immigrants themselves objected to going to the town church in Richland, where the services were in English; "they thought that it meant, too, that the young people were getting away from them" (33). Grandpa and Grandma Stille are also displeased because Emma and August do not speak German in the home. Here is expressed the double fear of the immigrant who wishes to retain his native language and culture and of the farmer who wishes to keep his children on the farm and away from corrupting urban influence.

The conservatism, anti-intellectualism, and hostility to the town that we have defined as characteristic of farm attitudes are found in this novel, too. August fights the consolidated school plan on the grounds that it will mean increased taxation, and he resists highway-building programs for the same reason, although he admits, when the program has gone into effect, that the good roads make things handier for the farmers (97). One of the daughters, attending the local school, talks of going to town school, but "August couldn't see but that they got about as good as what they'd get in town. All they needed, anyway" (64). When she suggests going to college, August rejects the idea with a typical rural argument: "He had too many children to send them away to school. She'd settle down and marry like the rest of them, and there'd be his money wasted" (87). The country children are made to feel inferior when they go to church services in town: "The children were shy, and wouldn't say much in Sunday

[6] Ruth Suckow, *Country People* (New York: Alfred A. Knopf, 1924), p. 155.

school, Mary and Elva because of the town girls, who wore better dresses than they did" (65). But the Kaetterhenry family gains attention in the local weekly and status in the community when Emma goes to the Mayo Clinic in Rochester; and when she and August move to town, they gradually gain admittance to some village organizations. After August's death, Emma becomes a member of the local sorority of widows.

Miss Suckow's use of the vernacular and of the physical details of her characters' lives is also extremely effective. Her ear for speech patterns is good, as evidenced not only by her use of such German locutions as the placing of an unnecessary and actually meaningless "already" at the end of a sentence, but also by her ability to write expository passages in a language close to that of her characters, as when she speaks of a sister of August: "She afterwards married Rudy Nisson, and had a hard time of it" (20). Her description of the house in which the Kaetterhenrys live shows sharp observation and adds materially to the ring of conviction evident throughout the book: "Their living was done in the kitchen and bedroom. The front room, which had the rag carpet, the stand, the vases, and the album, and a large German Bible, they kept shut off" (56). In many farm homes of the late nineteenth and early twentieth centuries the parlor or "sitting room" (in which the family rarely sat) was kept shut off from the rest of the house and used only on such special occasions as weddings, funerals, and family reunions.

Another characteristic rural attitude is suspicion of the expert —including the doctor, although he gained acceptance sooner than most specialists. Miss Suckow dramatizes this behavior during the illness of Mrs. Casper Kaetterhenry, August's mother. She has been ailing for months, and little has been done about it:

> But finally, when she was almost confined to her bed, could digest virtually nothing, and could hardly drag herself into the kitchen . . . Casper thought it might be time to drive into town and have the doctor come out with him. Of course it was too late then. Otherwise it would have been foolish for the doctor to be called [26].

In the preface to a collection of her works Miss Suckow suggested that a sequel to *Country People*, if written, would enter the arena of social criticism. Carl Kaetterhenry, representing continuity, would successfully operate the home place, but Frank would come near losing his farm and would be saved only by the device of having his neighbors monopolize his sale, buy up everything at low prices, and then sell it back to him (the device used at Red Joe's sale in *This Is the Year*). Joe Fields, who married one of the Kaetterhenry daughters, would lose his farm, which would then fall into the hands of tenants with no knowledge of or love for the soil. He would then become a "radical," and even Carl, conservative as he is, would come to wonder "if folks might not pitch in together more than they did."[7] This sequel was never written, but its projection indicates that Miss Suckow was thinking along lines later to be developed by Paul Corey.

Ruth Suckow employed farm background in some of her short stories and incidentally in some of her novels such as *The Odyssey of a Nice Girl* (1925), where she displayed the same scrupulous accuracy of detail and the same objective, unemphatic treatment of her materials, without, however, contributing anything new to her handling of farm life in *Country People*. The daughter of a small town minister, she was better fitted by experience for the depiction of village life than farm life, and her later novels, like *The Folks* (1934), take place chiefly or wholly in towns and cities. For this reason, however important she may have been in the middle western regional movement, her significance in a study of the farm novel is less than that of many writers of inferior ability. Her chief contributions, as she probably intended, were in matters of style and in the accurate rendering of detail. A conscious regionalist, she showed how the fictional materials of her own part of the country could be given artistic expression and thereby helped dispel the sense of inferiority that still afflicted the Middle West in the 1920's.

Late in the year that *Country People* was published (1924), Miss Suckow reviewed for the *Nation* another first novel by a middle western writer. The novel was *The Apple of the Eye*, and the author was Glenway Wescott, whose familiarity with Wisconsin farm life parallels Miss Suckow's acquaintance with the rural scene in Iowa. It was appropriate that she should review this book, for its author was, like her, seriously concerned with mat-

[7] Suckow, *Carry-Over*, p. xii.

ters of style. She found in Wescott's novel "an exceptional sense of form and balance, poetic insight, and a kind of fine adequacy in form, characterization, speech, incident, style that is like the satisfying competency of technique which one feels in certain musicians."[8] She concluded, however, that "the vision underlying the book is not quite equal to its fine execution" (656).

Reduced to its essentials, *The Apple of the Eye* is an account of the conflict between the puritan and the pagan attitudes toward sex as this conflict takes place in the mind of an adolescent boy. The boy, Dan Strane, is at first under the influence of his mother, who teaches him that the body is a holy temple and that sexual relations outside marriage amount to a desecration of this temple; he must greet his wedding day with a clean body and a pure mind. But a young hired man, Mike Byron, has acquired another point of view at the university; he tells Dan that sex is natural and wholesome, evil only if it is used to hurt someone. Dan quickly adopts this liberal view, but when Mike's affair with Dan's cousin Rosalia results in her madness and death (in a fashion closely paralleling Ophelia's fate), he experiences a revulsion against it. Rosalia's father exonerates Mike and takes a liberal position close to that of the young man, so Dan is finally reconciled, in part at least, to their less rigid outlook toward sex. The real fault lies with Rosalia's mother, who has imposed upon her an idealistic and unworkable attitude, and the ultimate blame is placed on the mother's religion. The father, born in Germany, has doubts about America; he says, "But I see all the fine people, the people with brains—they all go to pieces. I guess it's the kind of religion they've got here."[9]

Although Wescott's first novel does not constitute an attack on the farm as such, it does take an extremely unfavorable view of the rural evangelical tradition which surrounds its characters, nearly all of whom are Methodists, Baptists, or Presbyterians. Their religion, like that of the Kaetterhenrys, is involved with their material concerns. In his later and better novel, *The Grandmothers* (1927), Wescott says that the religion of these people

[8] Ruth Suckow, "Mature Youth," *Nation*, CXIX (December 10, 1924), 654.
[9] Glenway Wescott, *The Apple of the Eye* (New York: Harper & Brothers, 1926), p. 275.

makes of Jesus "a compassionate attorney at the right hand of God the judge, and a fulfillment of the half-political prophecies of the Old Testament—whose jurisprudence of hygiene, family relations, patriotism, and commerce, its morality resembled."[10] Such a religion fetters their natural impulses, produces all manner of neuroses, and leads its adherents into monstrous hypocrisies. They worship the "God of clean and respectable living, innocent thought, and industry" (239).

The Grandmothers develops this and other themes more fully and more thoughtfully. Subtitled "A Family Portrait," it is a series of brief biographies of the people whose pictures Alwyn Tower, the boy who serves as the central intelligence, finds in an old family album. His grandparents, the Towers and the Duffs, came to Wisconsin in pioneer days, made farms in the wilderness, and raised large families whose lives are the subject of the novel. *The Grandmothers* might well be termed a "gallery of mangled souls," as Halford E. Luccock has called *Winesburg, Ohio*, for the range of personalities extends from the ludicrous to the horrifying, with emphasis on the wretched, the cruel, and the unbalanced. There is the woman with a psychopathic love of cleanliness, who leaves her coarse, untidy husband although she loves him; there is the adolescent boy who has a homosexual love for his older brother and allows himself to be killed when he learns that the brother loves a woman; there is the old man who tells stories "too senseless and too cruel even to be remembered in the daytime" (162–163) and who smiles after telling these stories, "as if he had ceased to see any difference between tragedy and comedy in what had happened so long ago" (161); and perhaps most awful of all, Alwyn's maternal grandparents, Ira and Ursula Duff, who live together hating each other with all the passion they are capable of feeling. They spend their lives finding petty ways of hurting each other; Ira, for example, tells people that his wife's mind is failing. Yet deeply pious in their behavior, they kneel each night side by side in prayer; a visitor to the house

heard Ira Duff's resonant, false voice, rising and falling in a heavy rhythm, and saw them, the sharp-tongued wife and her hated hus-

[10] Glenway Wescott, *The Grandmothers* (New York: Harper and Brothers, 1927), p. 240.

band, kneeling side by side in front of the sitting-room sofa, their
backs very straight, their eyes closed, like a bride and groom before
an invisible pastor [209].

The old man's prayer always includes the request: "And hold in
the hollow of thy hand the dear wife of my bosom" (339). No
wonder the past and future seem to Alwyn "years of miscon-
strued events, and unreasonable aversions, and useless ambitions,
and nightmares. . ." (15).

Ambition is one of the besetting sins of these people; allied
with their religion, it leads to their spiritual barrenness. Alwyn's
Uncle Leander is the only one not afflicted with the mania of
ambition, and when his adopted son Timothy gives promise of
not amounting to much, he is content. He sees in Timothy "one
pair of Tower eyes which refused to look into the future; one
flower not fertilized by hopeless ambition; one less regret to
wither on the family tree. No embarrassment, no vanity, no
resentment or covetousness or haste . . ." (129). The success the
Towers are dreaming of is conceived in urban terms. One of the
boys—Alwyn's father and uncles—should achieve such success and
fulfill their father's hopes. "Their father's life had been a long,
impatient prophecy, a prophecy of success at last for one of the
Towers, which Jim [a minister] alone bore the burden of having
to fulfill" (168). But Jim is perhaps the most unhappy of the
brothers, dominated by his wife (whom he calls a saint and who
bears him no children), her mother, and a sister-in-law.

The domination by women—especially mothers—is a major
theme in both books. In *The Apple of the Eye* young Dan, wavering between Puritanism and paganism, seeks a refuge: "There
was his mother to welcome him, when he had escaped from life:
the mother breasts, eternally warm and sweet—nourishment
shared and never fought for. . . ."[11] In *The Grandmothers* the
image is extended to the whole of America. According to Wescott,

It became the land of extreme youth. Middle age was merely a
struggle; old age was a time when failure could not be disguised,
or a time of success which did not satisfy. . . . The whole country
had one symbol: a very young man, always at the beginning of a

[11] Wescott, *The Apple of the Eye*, pp. 124–125.

career, always beside his mother. . . . America became a matri-archate.[12]

The title of the book is significant; it is not the grandfathers but their wives who determine the direction the country is to take by controlling the intellectual and emotional development of their children. The future of America is not hopeful. The descend-ants of the pioneers have been twisted and warped by their reli-gion and ambition, and little is to be expected of them. Wescott's view of the immigrants who are taking over the farms is even less sympathetic than Bromfield's; they are too hard and materialistic:

> Steadily they had bought fields, farms, and at last groups of farms. These determined fathers made their women and children work like serfs—the healthy young ones hurried into the fields, the unhealthy allowed to die, and more begotten. Their sons were not permitted to marry until their late twenties, or later still; then, broken to har-ness, they were put upon adjoining farms. There was no talk among them of letting the young go their own way [350–351].

Whether Wescott realized it or not, the grandchildren of these immigrants, now thoroughly Americanized, were to undergo the same process as the characters he portrays and leave the decaying farms to seek more congenial careers in the city.

If Wescott's indictment of American civilization in general seems to remove his novels from the classification of farm fiction, it should be pointed out that the materials of both are essentially the same as those utilized by other writers discussed here and the treatment of these materials not so dissimilar as the major themes might suggest. Some farm tasks are described in detail, as in the account of sheepshearing which occupies much of a chapter in *The Apple of the Eye*. Popular rural superstitions are mentioned in *The Grandmothers*; Alwyn's grandmother tells him, "In my day, if you had a sore throat, you tied your stocking, warm from your foot, around your neck; and if that didn't cure you, skunk oil was considered the best remedy" (153). Her husband "feared and despised doctors, and read all the patent-medicine advertise-ments in the newspapers, believing for a moment each flowery promise of an end to pain" (38). Anti-intellectualism appears in the earlier novel, when Dan's father sneers at him, in a moment

---

[12] Wescott, *The Grandmothers*, p. 28.

of anger: "Oh, you're clever! You're good at books. . . . But tell
me, young man, what's that good for? Will it give you a living?
That's another thing. You always hated to work. You always made
me feel like a slave-driver."[13] This is not typical, however, for
Wescott's farmers are comparatively cultivated people who do
not despise book learning. For this reason, there is little use of
characteristically rural speech in these novels; the characters
speak rather standard English, while the author employs a distinctly literary style in his passages of exposition and reflection,
which occupy proportionately far more space than in most farm
novels.

Glenway Wescott is clearly superior to the general run of
farm novelists in his style, in his characterization, and in the profundity of the themes he treats and the reflections he offers on
these themes. Furthermore, he has certain critical theories regarding his materials, some of which he has stated in a volume of short
stories entitled *Good-Bye Wisconsin* (1928). Although his portrayal of the area of his boyhood conforms to the usual standards
of regionalism, his own statements on the subject make him out
to be rather an anti-regionalist. After discussing the background
of his writings, he comes to a somewhat startling conclusion:

> So I decide that the novelist who is or wishes to be anything of a
> poet will avoid such problems as, for example, Wisconsin is now
> likely to suggest; and will try to contribute to the appetites which
> make themselves felt there rather than to portray the confusion in
> which they arise.[14]

And his attempts to define the Middle West end in the conviction
that "there is no Middle West. It is a certain climate, a certain
landscape; and beyond that, a state of mind of people born where
they do not like to live" (39). These remarks perhaps echo a reaction against the strident regionalism of the early 1920's, against
which Ruth Suckow had also reacted by the time she wrote the
preface to *Carry-Over*, a collection including *Country People* and
several short stories. Dayton Kohler has observed that "the Wisconsin of Glenway Wescott is more than a geographical region.

[13] Wescott, *The Apple of the Eye*, p. 286.
[14] Glenway Wescott, *Good-Bye Wisconsin* (New York: Harper & Brothers,
1928), p. 36.

. . . He sees it also as a symbol of narrowness because the old pioneer spirit has dwindled to the restlessness of discontent."[15] On the other hand, Fred B. Millett sees Wescott's view of Wisconsin life as "a subdued and almost nostalgic recovery of things past."[16] Whatever Wescott's theories and whatever interpretations his critics may place upon his works, his early novels of Wisconsin represent one of the major contributions to the body of farm fiction. It may be significant that Rölvaag, whose own methods and approach differ markedly from Wescott's, is said to have been an admirer of him.[17]

The three of Wescott's books mentioned in this study were published during the period when he lived as an expatriate in France. In the 1930's his attitude toward the United States underwent a change, and he returned to this country. His subsequent work, of which *Apartment in Athens* (1945) is best known, has not concerned itself with the Wisconsin farm scene and does not call for discussion here. It would seem, somewhat ironically, that his most significant writing was done during the period of his reaction against the subject of this writing—the time he was in Europe and writing about Wisconsin.

There is a considerable qualitative gap between Glenway Wescott's novels and the inferior but by no means negligible work of the Minnesota writer Lorna Doone Beers, whose first novel, *Prairie Fires* (1925), has been treated in Chapter V. In the earlier discussion it was observed that she failed to fuse successfully the love story and the fictionalized account of a social and political movement. This fault she eliminated from her later novels, *A Humble Lear* (1929) and *The Mad Stone* (1932), by abandoning any specific historical background and concentrating wholly on the psychological problems of her characters. The first, undoubtedly the better of the two, is a fairly adroit reworking of Shakespeare's theme, adapted to the circumstances of Blue Heron township, Hennepin County, Minnesota, in the later 1890's.

[15] Dayton Kohler, "Glenway Wescott: Legend Maker," *Bookman*, LXXIII (April 1931), 143.

[16] Fred B. Millett, *Contemporary American Authors* (New York: Harcourt, Brace & Co., 1940), p. 47.

[17] *Ibid.*, p. 555.

Adam Webb, an able, well-to-do farmer, is widowed after some
thirty years of frustrating marriage to Martha Stanton, an idealistic, puritanical, and spiritually frigid woman, excessively proud
of her New England antecedents and her experience as a Latin
teacher in a Vermont academy. Adam's two older children are as
different from his youngest as Goneril and Regan are from
Shakespeare's Cordelia. John, hard and grasping, marries a wife
of similar caliber; Chuck is easy-going and fond of pleasure, and
he mates with a woman who matches him in these respects. But
the youngest, inevitably named Cordelia, is selfless and devoted,
but her devotion is like her mother's, centered about duty rather
than love. Because of this and because of a tendency to suppress
her emotions, she is neglected by her father. Cordelia finds work
and a husband in Minneapolis, while her father is being gradually disillusioned by his sons and their wives, to each of whom
he has given a third of his farm. Finally, he builds himself a
shack in the woods, where Cordelia finds him, ill with pneu-
monia, and takes him to her home in the city to live out his days.

   Miss Beers gives much stress to "refinement" and "elegance,"
by which is meant a particularly sterile brand of cold intellectu-
ality characteristic of New England. Although Martha recognizes
before her death that her coarser-grained husband represents the
reality, there is no indication that the author rejects Martha's
values as altogether fake. The symbol for her values is derived
from a cartoon of the eighties "picturing the midwestern house-
wife on her knees before a scrub pail to which was lashed a volume of Emerson."[18] Martha has her silverware handed down
from the seventeenth century, her files of the *Atlantic Monthly*,
and her library of Horace, Cicero, and the rest of the Latin clas-
sics. Although her grandfather thought Byron a great poet, she
feels that "he dwelt too much on man's baser nature" (22). She
will never join other women in talking of their confinements, and
she winces when her husband's mother speaks of "thundermugs."
Cordelia shares the natures of both her parents, but it is clear
that the influence of her mother predominates, particularly when
she selects as a husband a bloodless philosophy professor so un-

[18] Lorna Doone Beers, *A Humble Lear* (New York: E. P. Dutton & Co.,
1929), p. 250.

versed in practical matters that he is unable to crack a boiled egg without making a mess. Cordelia's standards are necessarily urban, and her escape to the city is no mere temporary gesture. Once settled in the city, she vows that "she would never go back to Blue Heron, that she would in some way lift herself into just such a station of life as this, as her dear mother would want her to do" (260).

Characterization is Miss Beers' weak point. Adam is perhaps the best done, but his coldness toward Cordelia and his generosity toward his sons have the effect of producing the illusion of two characters rather than one. The sons are sketched only in outline, and Cordelia is only slightly better portrayed. The daughters-in-law are sharply depicted, although they verge on caricatures. As with the author's other books, the total product is uneven. Some scenes are maudlin, and the attempt to make Adam talk like Captain Ahab is foredoomed to failure. But there is one splendid scene in which Adam, about to build a house for himself, goes to the old sawmill where he bought the lumber to build his and Martha's first house. He finds that the mill has ceased operation because of low water and a declining market, and the proprietor, past seventy and a widower, is planning, like Adam, to start over again and build a mill at a more suitable site. The pathos of the two old men trying to recapture their youth, each knowing the futility of the other's dream but deluding himself, is clearly the best thing in the book.

The Mad Stone has little to say about farming, although the characters, impaled on their own neuroses, do most of their wriggling in a rural setting. The plot centers about the extramarital carrying-on between Ollie Hackett, sent by her husband to his parents in the country to separate her from a lover in the city, and Lewis Ludlow, a former Baptist minister who has become a sort of Nietzschean nihilist and is trying to write a book on the various interpretations of Jesus Christ down through the ages. Nothing much really happens, and everything turns out for the best in the end, but the emotional agonies of the main characters and their impact on others afford the reader a good deal of vicarious suffering. The title of the novel refers to a bit of rural folklore, the fantastic myth of the mad stone. A certain porous stone found occasionally in the heart of a deer is supposed to have diagnostic and curative powers in cases of real or suspected hydrophobia. A person bitten by a dog should place the stone on the wound; if it falls off, the dog was not mad, while if it stays on, it will draw out the poison. Lewis says we all need a mad stone to take the madness out of our hearts. His affair with Ollie serves some such function, for it purges him of his dawdling over a book he will never write.

As with *A Humble Lear*, the characters in *The Mad Stone* fall short of the degree of plausibility necessary to successful fiction. Besides that, it lacks the engrossing theme of the former book, and so it fails to produce much of an impact on the reader. Both books are weakened by the author's absurd ventures into the realm of formal philosophy, as when she tries to state Spinoza's philosophy in a sentence. Her strong point is her perceptiveness into the springs of human emotion, and this is seldom capitalized upon because of her inability to draw convincing characters.

In the same year that Miss Beers' first novel appeared, Martha Ostenso, a young Minnesota woman of Norwegian birth, attained sudden fame with the publication of *Wild Geese*, a highly colored, somewhat implausible story of brutal paternal domination of a frontier family in Manitoba. Her success in winning a $13,500 prize offered jointly by *Pictorial Review*, Dodd, Mead and Company, and the Famous Players-Lasky Corporation led Miss Ostenso to turn out eight novels in nine years, and several more later. Those which qualify most definitely as farm novels are discussed in the annotated bibliography at the end of this book. Although *Wild Geese* has merit, chiefly in its portrayal of the satanic Caleb Gare, who derives a sadistic pleasure from bullying his family, the novels that followed do not fulfill the promise many reviewers professed to see in the first one. Some improvement in technique is perceptible in the later novels, but they suffer from a progressive impoverishment of thematic material. The reader finds in them an annoying repetitiveness of situation; at least two novels repeat the patterns of the banker's daughter who marries a farmer, is disillusioned with farm life, and leaves her husband; the English professor who is a farmer by instinct and returns to the land; the daughter of a small farmer who is dazzled by a scion of a decadent family of landed gentry.

More important to this study, Miss Ostenso's novels display very few of the rural attitudes and beliefs being used here as criteria for evaluating farm fiction; those few which do appear seem synthetic, as though the author had determined to make her characters say and think what farmers are popularly supposed to say and think. Furthermore, the authentic farm figures are seldom made the center of attention in these novels. There is often a similarity to the nineteenth-century type of novel in which a genteel hero and heroine occupy the center of the stage; the chief characters are usually outsiders—the beautiful daughter of a gambler, a college teacher whose grandfather founded an estate in Minnesota, the dissolute son of a wealthy family who comes home to the farm where he was born—and a condescending attitude is often taken toward the genuine farm characters, especially the rustic philosopher with a Scandinavian accent who appears frequently. In short, the best that can be said for the work of Martha Ostenso is that it is an excellent example of popular fiction with an incidental farm background. But her books are not farm novels in the sense in which that term has been used here, inasmuch as they do not really reflect farm attitudes and beliefs or make any effort to deal with problems peculiar to agriculture.

In marked contrast to the fiction of Martha Ostenso are the strongly realized, carefully written novels of Leroy MacLeod, *The Years of Peace* (1932) and *The Crowded Hill* (1934). These two novels tell the story of Tyler Peck and the people around him in a farming community of southern Indiana in the years immediately following the Civil War. The central theme of the first book, which covers the period from 1865 to 1875, is the relationship between Tyler and his wife Evaline; the second book, which continues the story from 1876 to 1878, centers about the problems created by the presence of Tyler's Aunt Mary and her daughter Lucy in the same household with Tyler and his family. It would be inaccurate to speak of a "plot," in the conventional sense of the term, in MacLeod's novels. Like Corey's later trilogy of the

Mantz family, they chronicle a period in the lives of a number of people in a specific locality. Children are born, men die, technological changes occur, political campaigns are conducted, and the cycle of planting, harvesting, and plowing is repeated again and again.

Tyler proposed to Evaline in a moment of drunken bravado, and she accepted him because he was a good catch. Since their marriage each has tried to make the most of a situation from which there is no escape, but neither has told the other of his reasons for marrying. Marriage is a trial to Tyler, in his early twenties, for he feels that he is trapped. Children come with distressing frequency, and each one binds him more firmly to the bargain he has made. He has been cheated out of participation in the Civil War because of his marriage. When his brother Bernard, who has been in the war, decides to go west, Tyler is filled with envy. A few days later he is sitting beside the millpond, fishing: "He thought of Bernard again, and Bernard gone out West, and himself here, waiting for a fish to bite. As far as he could see, that was all his life would ever come to—just waiting and waiting for a fish to bite."[19]

Tyler has some consolations, however. His Uncle Lafe prefers him to his own son, Alan, who has turned out to be a drunkard and a deserter, and finally wills him the farm. But even Lafe's generosity is spoiled for Tyler, for just before the old man's death—too late to change the will—Uncle Lafe sees Tyler slip out of the house for an assignation with Minnie Scott, the widow of a man killed while helping Tyler haul hay. Tyler, a man of strong physical drives, is unable to endure the enforced continence during the later stages of Evaline's recurrent pregnancies, and he begins an affair with Minnie, only to break it off upon her husband's death. But Lafe does not know that Tyler has gone out to tell Minnie that the affair is all over, and he dies thinking that he has been deceived in his high opinion of the nephew who took the place of a son in his life. At the end of the novel Tyler and Evaline confess the secret that each has had during their years of married life—that neither married for love—and each

[19] Leroy MacLeod, *The Years of Peace* (New York: Century Co., 1932), p. 108.

concedes that he has come to love the other in spite of the inauspicious beginning.

The conflict between Aunt Mary and Evaline gives unity to the second novel. Aunt Mary, a Presbyterian, wants the children to join her church; but Evaline is Methodist and ultimately joins the Baptist church, since there is no Methodist church in the locality. Finally Aunt Mary and Lucy leave, and the conflict is resolved. During the course of the novel, Tyler has another extra-marital adventure, with a hired girl who gets married immediately afterward and after an appropriate interval bears a son who strongly resembles Tyler. He is also involved in local politics (as MacLeod himself was during his career as a farmer)[20] and is greatly troubled by hard times, which are in evidence chiefly in the form of low prices on farm products.

MacLeod's picture of a rural community in the 1860's and 1870's has a documentary vividness: the physical details of farming in this period, the slow decline of the "less-than-a-village" of Freedom when it is passed up by the railroads, the amusements and recreations of country people, the political caucuses and maneuvering for votes, the beliefs and practices of the people of this time and place. Language is carefully suited to the character. Tyler has had some college training, and all the central figures are possessed of a measure of culture, so their speech is not noticeably rustic. Tyler, born in Kentucky, occasionally slips into dialect forms like "you-all" and "like to" for "almost," but for the most part his speech is standard American English. Although some of the less well educated people speak a rustic dialect, there is no condescension shown toward them as in Miss Ostenso's novels. MacLeod defends some dialect forms, as when he mentions "punkins" and then explains in a footnote: "Punkins is the word. 'Pumpkin' is something townfolk eat. It usually tastes like squash."[21] Incidentally, this is about as near as these soberly written books ever come to humor, except in the stories told by their characters. Rural practices and superstitions receive due attention. Early potatoes are to be planted on Good Friday; and

[20] "Leroy MacLeod," *Wilson Bulletin for Librarians,* VII (September 1932), 78.

[21] MacLeod, *The Years of Peace,* p. 85.

a quid of chewing tobacco is used as a poultice on wounds. (Evaline first discovers that her husband chews when she finds him employing this somewhat unhygienic device.) The rural feeling of superiority to the town appears now and then, as when old Aaron Van Dine is telling Tyler about his children; he seems to have exhausted the topic, so Tyler asks him if he didn't have some other children. He replies, "Oh yes—*girls*. They's Abigail lives in St. Louis and Magdalen was in Louisville last I heard. I sorta lost track of 'em. City-ites is all they ever 'mounted to."[22]

Emotional states and conflicts are admirably presented in MacLeod's novels. Tyler's attitude toward his marriage is entirely convincing, as is his weakness for the physical attractions of women other than his wife. The conflict between Evaline and Aunt Mary is deftly handled despite the temptation to oversim-plify a situation of so frequent occurrence. The gradual estrange-ment of Tyler and his friend Lew Williamson, which starts with an election bet, is treated with the restraint and understanding that characterize MacLeod's writing throughout. Although Tyler is the central character through whose eyes most of the action is seen, Evaline's side of the marriage problem is sympathetically presented, especially in their disagreements over the children. Ella, the oldest, is mentally deficient, but nevertheless Evaline insists on keeping the girl in school until the teacher requests that she be withdrawn. Evaline's unwillingness to accept her daughter's feeble-mindedness is quite believable, and the whole issue is handled skillfully.

One criticism which might be leveled at MacLeod's novels is that very little happens in them. They are longer than any of the novels previously discussed in this chapter, and the pace is slow. In one respect the leisurely pace is an advantage: the reader does not feel hurried along as he does when reading a novel such as, for example, Garland's *Rose of Dutcher's Coolly*, in which too much happens too quickly. But if a novel is to move slowly, the reason must be that of giving cumulative power to the climax. Unfortunately, the effect in these novels is somewhat akin to that of the mountain being delivered of a mouse; in the

[22] Leroy MacLeod, *The Crowded Hill* (New York: Reynal & Hitchcock, 1934), p. 170.

second one particularly there is no real climax. Aunt Mary and Lucy just leave, as they should have done long before, and Tyler and Evaline go back to their labors. But this objection is of little weight in view of the vivid and satisfying treatment of the setting and the convincing portrayal of emotional conflicts. Leroy MacLeod's two novels represent a high artistic level in the realm of farm fiction.

In 1934 the publishing firm of Simon and Schuster brought out a first novel by a young woman of twenty-four, Josephine Johnson. The novel, *Now in November,* concerned the fortunes (uniformly bad) of a farm family in a rocky, sterile, drought-ridden area of Missouri. Besides being frowned upon by nature, the Haldmarnes are deeply in debt, and the eldest daughter, Kerrin, is highly emotional, neurotic, and anti-social; before the end of the novel she goes insane and kills herself. The burden of the book seems to be the futility of farming and, by extension, of all living, although there is a muted note of affirmation at the end. The hopelessness of the Haldmarnes' efforts is evident to the father, Arnold, but he goes on striving with dogged desperation. Human agencies are in part responsible for their plight, as the Haldmarnes discover when they try to sell milk and find that the law of supply and demand affords them little help:

> Milk was scarcer everywhere, but we didn't get much more at the dairy than before. Last year there had been too much, and all farmers had it. . . . This year nobody had very much, but the price didn't seem to change—not at the *back* door of the dairy anyway.[23]

There is much bitterness toward city people, especially those who keep insisting that farmers at least have enough to eat; even a family of five cannot consume all the milk produced on the farm, and they are unable to sell it for enough to buy the things they *can* consume. The economic trap he is in sometimes leads Arnold Haldmarne to voice expressions of desperate bitterness: "God! don't they *want* a man to farm? . . . Where they think corn's going to come from after they pry us off the land? They've got to eat, God knows!" (224).

This is not a proletarian novel, however, although Miss John-

[23] Josephine Johnson, *Now in November* (New York: Simon & Schuster, 1934), pp. 101–102.

son did venture into proletarian fiction in a few short stories; she recognizes that factors other than economics are involved in the family's problem. Marget, the daughter who serves as narrator, wonders how much of it was their own fault and reflects that "God—if you choose to say that the drouth is God—against us. The world against us, not deliberately perhaps, more in a selfish than malicious way, coming slowly to recognize that we are not enemies or ploughshares" (227). Nor is the novel specifically an attack on farming, for as Marget remarks, "We are not trapped any more than all other men. Any more than life itself is a trap" (226–227). There is no clearly defined social or economic theme here; the attention is centered upon the psychological problems of the characters.

The Haldmarne family is largely isolated from their neighbors, and each member is isolated from the others. Kerrin especially is increasingly cut off from her parents and sisters as the novel progresses, and the others seem to be unable to discuss her among themselves. When Grant Koven comes to work for Arnold, the two older daughters fall in love with him, while he falls in love with the third one, Merle. Most of the potentialities of such an uncomfortable situation are developed, against a background of harrowing drought and deepening hopelessness. The family is deprived of the income provided by Kerrin when she is forced to give up her teaching job because of her rapidly deteriorating mental condition. Then a fire results in the death of the mother and Kerrin's suicide. On this note the novel ends.

So much unmitigated misfortune might seem inevitably to result in melodrama, but Miss Johnson skillfully avoids that pitfall and creates a generally convincing piece of fiction. Perhaps the most noticeable feature of *Now in November* is the highly poetic language employed. Sometimes this appears in figurative expressions like the reference to Kerrin's "shrill black laugh" (106); at other times it appears in passages in which imagination and realistic detail are blended, such as the following bleak picture of the endless round of farm duties:

> The hope worn on indefinitely . . . the desire never fulfilled . . . four o'clock and the ice-grey mornings . . . the cows and dark . . . the cans enormous in the foggy lamplight . . . day come up cold

and windy . . . the endless cooking . . . the sour rim of pails. . . .
There seemed no answer, and the answer lay only in forgetting [38].

Such a style unavoidably makes for difficult reading at times, and
there is in the novel probably more vagueness than the author
intended, but in general the emotional force of such passages is
heightened rather than weakened by her technique. *Now in
November* achieves much of its distinction through the use of a
style not previously employed in farm fiction.

Two years after *Now in November* another Johnson published
a novel about farm life. Instead of a first attempt by a relatively
unknown young woman, however, this novel, *Spring Storm*
(1936), was the product of a man in his sixties, Dr. Alvin Johnson, a professor of economics at such universities as Nebraska,
Texas, Chicago, Stanford, and Cornell, editor and one of the
founders of the *New Republic,* director of the New School for
Social Research in New York City, and chief working editor of
the *Encyclopedia of the Social Sciences.*[24] Although lacking a
high imaginative gift, Alvin Johnson could write with the advantages of both a farm boyhood and a wealth of formal knowledge unavailable to the average farm novelist. Hence it would
be surprising if *Spring Storm* did not reflect a variety of rural
attitudes and beliefs.

The central theme, as might be expected of an autobiographical novel, is the emotional and intellectual maturation of a boy
in his middle teens. Julian Howard has come west with his
father, a former school teacher whose penchant for moving from
place to place has led him to buy a thousand-acre farm in northeastern Nebraska, near the Missouri River. Entirely ignorant
of farming and much less practical than his son, the elder Howard
is imposed upon and ridiculed by people in the locality and
soon finds himself losing money at an appalling rate of speed.
Unable to sell the farm for his purchase price, he is virtually
forced to stay on it and hope that conditions will improve. Julian
makes friends with a community of poor whites who live on river-
bottom land too valueless for the owners to bother them. Originally from Arkansas and Missouri, they profess a philosophy of

---

[24] Kunitz, *Twentieth Century Authors: First Supplement,* pp. 493–494.

anarchic individualism, but they actually form a tightly knit social organism, to which Julian is admitted on the strength of his friendship with Dut Bates, one of their number. But the "Benders" represent for Julian something comparable to what the valley of the Typees meant to Melville; life among them is pleasant and carefree, but it leads nowhere. His real maturation occurs as the result of an unsuccessful love affair with the young wife of Henry Millsbaugh, a middle-aged sensualist with a habit of getting periodically drunk. The affair is thwarting to Julian first because he is discovered and therefore unable to carry out his plan to escape with the girl, Elizabeth, and then later because he finds out that she is little more than a calculating adventuress, with no real love for him. At the end of the novel, he leaves for college, relieved to have come through the "spring storm" of his life comparatively uninjured.

Several of the standard themes of farm fiction appear in this novel. For example, there is the hostility between town and country. Julian learns early that town boys are young toughs; when he first visits the nearby village he is accosted by "one of the Dutchman's Bluff gang of young rowdies, already about ripe for the penitentiary."[25] And when he considers what his life would be like if he became a farmer, one of the unpleasant prospects is that on market days he would spend a few hours in town, "exposed to the flattery and disguised contempt of the man in a white collar who needed to conciliate his support or hold his custom" (276). When Dut sells wormy catfish to the grocers in town, he justifies himself on the grounds that they sell wormy flour and "clo'es that bust when ye breathe" (36).

When on the farm one must do as the farmers do. Julian cannot refuse to help Henry in threshing because "nobody can refuse to 'change work in threshing. It's the custom of the country" (231). Following the "custom of the country" includes speaking like the natives. Henry advises Julian early in the novel that he had better let the local people alone, because they don't take to him. Why? "Ye don't talk right. These people here have got the ignorantest language, but oh, my, if ye don't use it right they walk all over ye" (23). Of course, Julian's father is an object of

[25] Alvin Johnson, *Spring Storm* (New York: Alfred A. Knopf, 1936), p. 29.

scorn from the start as a "book-farmer" in a region where learning of any kind is held in small esteem. His impracticality is well illustrated by his response to Julian's insistence that a certain field should be disked rather than plowed, because if it was plowed, the grain would lodge. His father's interests are more philological than agricultural: "Queer use of the word 'lodge,' isn't it? Now, I wonder, is it a form surviving from some earlier speech, or is it a strained metaphor of recent origin?" (107). The characterization of the elder Howard never reaches the proportions of caricature, as in the case of Cooper's Dr. Obed Bat in *The Prairie*, but his idiosyncrasies afford some amusement to the local farmers.

Spring Storm is no paean of praise for life on the soil. Johnson himself had left the farm and sought an urban career, and Julian does likewise. When he is considering an elopement with Elizabeth, he reflects that it will mean being tied to a farm for the rest of his life—a dismal prospect:

> What it meant to him was an indefinite succession of laborious spring plowings, feverish harvests, tedious corn-huskings, and long, dreary winters given to chores and petty tasks. His associates would be farm hands, tenants, farmers; and their talk would be of the weather and the crops, with sometimes an obscene tale, moldy with age [276].

There is an odd vein of misogyny in Johnson's novel, explained, perhaps, by Julian's adolescence. Women are for the most part treated unkindly, and Julian's passion for Elizabeth even at its peak is never so attractive as his friendship with Dut Bates, who seems willing to make any sacrifice to help him. And at the end, as Julian is riding eastward on the train, he thinks he has learned a lesson: "Girls. He would avoid them throughout his future. Weeds. To him they could only be as weeds. He was through with that part of life. He would be free" (351). This may be only a natural reaction to such an experience as he has just been through, but it expresses a determination unusual in a seventeen-year-old boy.

Spring Storm illustrates what a mature man of high intelligence and wide learning could do with recollections of his boyhood, but it is not the most memorable fiction. The poor-

white community is too idyllic, few of the characters are individualized, and the machinery tends to creak in places. Nevertheless,
it is useful for our purposes because it provides a good picture
of a particular time and place and because it reflects several
widely prevalent rural attitudes.

Although the vogue of the farm novel seemed to be waning
by the late 1930's, the end of that decade saw the arrival of two
newcomers to the field. One, Paul Corey, has been discussed in
earlier chapters; the other was Herbert Krause, whose first novel,
Wind Without Rain (1939) is laid in the Pockerbrush country of
west-central Minnesota where he grew up. Krause's novel, like
Martha Ostenso's *Wild Geese*, centers about the domination of a
family by a tyrannical father. But Johan Vildvogel is three dimensional where Caleb Gare was only two dimensional; by giving
him a past to account for his harshness and a vein of tenderness
that emerges after the death of his wife, Krause has made Johan
a far more credible character than Caleb. Nevertheless, he is cruel
toward his family, particularly his youngest son Franz, whom he
long suspects of being not his son at all. Franz is sensitive, artistic,
passionate, and rebellious against his father's severity and the
regimen of the farm but unwilling to desert his mother. He plays
"Barcarolle" on a hand organ until the minister destroys the
roller, and he learns to play the violin from old Jens Lindegard,
who wills his fiddle to Franz upon his death. Another son,
Jephthah, crippled in a sledding accident caused by Franz, serves
as narrator and is not greatly developed as a character. His close
relationship to Franz presents a front against their father and
two brothers, Walter and Fritzie, who run away from home and
do not figure importantly in the story thereafter.

Throughout much of the novel Franz is in love with Liliem
Schoen but courted by Tinkla Bauer. Liliem, who captivates him
with a toss of her golden curls, is wavering, capricious, selfish, but
weak rather than vicious and a fit companion to Franz in her
sensitivity to beauty. Tinkla, in contrast, is buxom, cheerful,
unimaginative, but capable of a deep affection for Franz; she is
portrayed as "dependable Tinkla, solid as a ledge of stone; plenty
of common bread-and-milk sense in her, but blind to a curl of
ivy under her feet and deaf to the loneliness in a kildeer's cry.

. . ."[26] When Liliem's engagement to Jonas Bluber is announced, Franz rushes into marriage with Tinkla, but later, when Liliem breaks with Jonas, Franz manages clandestine meetings with her. His final disillusionment comes when he finds her in a more than compromising position with Jonas at a cheap night club to which Franz is helping a friend bring bootleg liquor. He strikes Jonas and rushes home, thinking he has committed murder. Recalling the fate of another youth who killed in a moment of passion, Franz thinks when the sheriff comes that he is about to be taken to prison. He leaps into a car and starts off, only to strike and kill his daughter, whose golden hair has reminded him of Liliem.

The tragedy in *Wind Without Rain* is not confined to the ending. Besides the tyranny of the father, which is the chief cause of the mother's death, there is the background of a hideous religion and a debt too large for the combined efforts of the family ever to throw off. The religious life of the community is securely in the control of Pastor Sunnenbaum, a clerical counterpart to Johan Vildvogel. Censorious, unsmiling, hard as nails, he represses his own passionate nature by savagely lashing his congregation for their sins and venting his wrath on erring members. When he is in the pulpit, he preaches in this vein:

> The seed of sin is woman, and the man who lies with her in secret is cursed. . . . Sinners, you are, that's what; all of you. Slimy as a rat crawling out of a spittoon; born in the dirt of your mother's womb, the lot of you, and going to Hell; tomorrow, maybe; or tonight; when you sit down to eat. No hope, unless you repent. . . . the grease of Hell is hot and smoking, ready to fry such as live so [85–86].

Minatory invective can scarcely go further. The worst of it is that his hearers, isolated as they are, believe what he says, even though they defy his will and hold dances the night before they come to sit and cringe under his scathing attacks. Johan, no hypocrite like Caleb Gare, accepts this religion and practices it; he opposes Franz's fiddle-playing and consents to it only because by playing at dances the boy can earn an occasional badly needed dollar.

The heightened and figurative style of *Wind Without Rain*

[26] Herbert Krause, *Wind Without Rain* (Indianapolis: Bobbs-Merrill Co., 1939), p. 286.

(reminiscent of Josephine Johnson's)[27] so occupied the attention of critics of the novel on its appearance that they neglected the very real merits of the book in their efforts to prove the fairly obvious point that the style often seems like an elaborate and artificial striving for effect. Such figures as the following are occasionally effective but are used so frequently as to call attention to themselves:

> quiet rained down with the shadows . . . Long Lake fretted in the cattails. . . . He let hours dribble on. . . . Remembering that night from this peak overlooking the valley of years . . . wind scattered the bright feathers of summer into the corner places. . . . We undid the spool of our daily jobs.[28]

But there is also an element of hard realism in Krause's descriptive passages, as in the following (31):

> The hours we put in riding milking stools, morning and night, endless with the patience of resignation; hours of lantern red and shadow gray slanting over the cows, and horned shapes moving on the walls . . . stink of horse wet, acrid and filling the throat, until smell became heavy on the tongue and left in the mouth a taste of manure . . . the heifer with the brush of her tail curled on her back like a snake . . . Franz crouched on his one-legged stool, dodging the hairy swishes and failing, no matter at what angle he crooked himself . . . endless.

Or in the fine description of Franz's wedding dance, typical of the festivities indulged in by the German farmers of Pockerbrush:

> Jollity echoed with the yells between these stout walls—the accordion man tweedling his bellows close to his ear; "Be damn' if she ain't got a leak!" . . . beer never growing flat in the bucket, so often was the ladle dipped . . . Mr. Dorset chanting, "Fiddle in the furrow and the corn rump-high" . . . two whiskered cronies tearfully slob-

---

[27] Compare, for example, the opening pages of *Now in November* and *Wind Without Rain*. This is how Miss Johnson's book begins: "Now in November I can see our years as a whole. . . . I can look back now and see the days as one looking down on things past, and they have more shape and meaning than before" (p. 3). The first page of *Wind Without Rain* contains this sentence: "I can look back now, quietly from this white interlude of peace, and see as one from a far hill how all our days were spent" (p. 11). The use of a narrator who is not the central character also constitutes a parallel between the two novels.

[28] Krause, *Wind Without Rain*, pp. 11, 19, 22, 37, 41, 48.

bering into one another's necks; "Hell of a good feller you are, Hank, you old son of a bull-kicker . . ." [302].

Krause's realism is evident even in such short passages as this: "Franz and I put our bread and lard in a Prince Albert tobacco box and black coffee in a sirup pail, and got ready to go on the path to school" (41). Krause has the power of characterizing a man with a few telling details: Sornas Tetzlauf, a rich farmer from across the valley, is described as a man with "a shifty glitter under his lids and ice in the way he talked. . . . A man few trusted and then only halfway." A hard driver, his motto is "Whip keeps 'em dancing."[29] Whatever the faults of Krause's style, *Wind Without Rain* owes much of its power—and its emotional impact is perhaps greater than that of any other farm novel of the past generation—to the fact that its author was a poet before he was a writer of fiction.

By 1939 a familiarity with farm tasks and farm speech and an ability to handle them effectively were essential parts of the equipment of any novelist who expected to write an acceptable tale of farm life, and Krause's command of these matters is at least as good as that of his contemporaries. He seems especially skilled at the representation of the folklore brought over from Germany. A typical scene shows

> Grandma Katzenhoft squeaking in her rocker . . . spinning off stories of the old country as she knitted the hank of yarn . . . stories about the man with hooves under the gaming table; the minister's wife ripped to pieces by ghosts; the maid who called up the Devil; the E-string . . . the E-string [72].

A tornado is predicted when old Ma Morton says she has seen a cross in the fog; she is also charged with "lacin' a feller 'cause he didn't bury a cat. Brings awful bad luck . . . 'specially if it's black" (172). She says that Franz's fiddle "stinks after *hexerei*; stops the blood, like a cross made upside down—" (186). Some common rural attitudes appear in the novel, like Johan Vild-vogel's suspicion of education; Jephthah says, "Father had no patience with the waste of time in getting book schooling. . ." (43). In the Pockerbrush country such suspicion may be well

[29] *Ibid.*, pp. 169, 191, 192.

founded, considering what is told of the district school, where unfamiliar words form the bulk of the spelling curriculum: "long-legged monsters like 'asafoetida' and 'latitudinarian' which Old Lafferty called 'terms familiar in every home' " (44).

It is significant that Krause's *Wind Without Rain* and Corey's *Three Miles Square* should have appeared in the same year, for in a sense they represent the culmination of two types of farm novel, which, at the risk of considerable oversimplification, may be termed romantic and realistic. Similarities between *Wind Without Rain* and Martha Ostenso's *Wild Geese* (in theme) and Josephine Johnson's *Now in November* (in style) have been pointed out. These novels and many others, including those by Lorna Doone Beers, Frederick's *Druida*, and Wescott's *The Grandmothers*, may be called romantic in that they emphasize exceptional characters (usually maladjusted), involve love stories, tend to sentimentalize their material in varying degrees, and in some cases are written in a poetic style. By contrast, Corey's novels represent another tradition, going back at least to Ruth Suckow's *Country People* and including also Leroy MacLeod's work in the early 1930's, characterized by a stress on average people living average lives, absence of a formal plot structure, restrained and sometimes under-written treatment of emotion, and an objective, reportorial, and rather flat style. The oversimplification here involves mainly the terminology, for of course all the novels mentioned are "realistic" in their selection of details, in keeping with one of the literary conventions of the twentieth century. The two types here defined are in fact clearly discernible in farm fiction since 1920, however difficult it may be to fit a particular novel into one or the other category.

Perhaps never wholly distinct, the two types seem to have been combined in Krause's second novel, *The Thresher* (1946). Although it would be inaccurate to say that this book sums up the farm novel, many of the themes found in earlier works and most of the characteristics of farmers and farm life that have been used to measure the genuineness of a piece of farm fiction are brought together here. This is not surprising, considering that Krause had behind him a half-century of experimentation and development since Garland published *Rose of Dutcher's*

Coolly, but it is none the less significant. Consequently, there may be some value in enumerating the varied strands which are united in Krause's long novel.

The central theme may be defined as the material growth and spiritual decline of Johnny Black. Simultaneously, the novel treats the ominous beginning of his material decline, which culminates in his death. The story begins soon after the death of Johnny's mother, when he is nine years old. He is placed in the hands of Uncle Herm and Aunt Phrena, his mother's sister, who run a farm in the Pockerbrush country. Uncle Herm loves the boy and is loved in return, but Phrena alienates him by her soggy solicitude and incessant nagging. The presence of Kurt, her son by an earlier marriage, does not add to the harmony of the household. But what troubles Johnny most are the frequent veiled references to his father, Albert Schwartz, who, as Johnny eventually learns, was a "wild one," with a weakness for women. Schwartz died in a brawl, after ruining the life of Johnny's mother. Bitterness toward the father whom he does not remember, coupled with the suspicion that the father's nature has descended to the son, leads Johnny to change his name from Schwartz to Black.

The occasion for this change is Johnny's coming of age when his signature is added to that of Uncle Herm's on the purchase of a threshing rig. Johnny has been fascinated since his arrival on the farm by everything associated with the yearly ritual of threshing grain. Called upon in emergencies to work, he shows his mettle and is soon a better thresherman than Uncle Herm. When Uncle Herm is injured, Johnny becomes boss of the rig, although not yet twenty. He runs the enterprise with a savage energy that wins the respect if not the affection of his crew. The rest of the novel is an account of the gradual expansion of Johnny's threshing business until he has three rigs in operation and dominates the whole area. In reaching this eminence, however, he indirectly causes the death of his friend Snoose and blasts the hope of his sweetheart, Lilice Rose.

Johnny's love story plays a prominent part in the novel. Lilice is not a church member, and so Pastor Steuber (virtually a repeat performance of Pastor Sunnenbaum in *Wind Without Rain*) re-

fuses to marry them, even when he learns that Lilice is pregnant.
Therefore they are married by a justice of the peace, to the scandal of the community. Their married life is not a happy one, for
there is a continuing struggle between Lilice and the threshing
business for Johnny's primary affection. In addition, Lilice is
conscience-stricken over their "sin," which seems especially sinis-
ter because she is outside the church. When their first child dies
and another develops ichthyosis, she regards her misfortunes as
divine punishment, and her mind begins to weaken. Pastor
Steuber is chiefly responsible for this notion, and Brother Erdman's "slop religion" (revivalistic preaching) is of no help to her.
When Steuber dies and is replaced by a man of liberal tendencies, Gabriel Ewig, her obsession with her sinfulness begins to
dissipate. But just as complete recovery seems to have been
achieved, Johnny is killed in the threshing accident she has
always expected.

Despite the variety of thematic material present in *The
Thresher*, it is fundamentally a psychological study. The sense
of insecurity engendered by Phrena's (and others') remarks about
his father forces Johnny to find compensation in gaining the respect and even fear of his neighbors, a goal he achieves by becoming a thresherman and driving his crew hard. Snoose's death, for
which Johnny is blamed by himself and others, seems also to
require expiation. Lilice's behavior toward him when she denies
him her bed likewise calls for compensation. Together these factors drive out of Johnny's make-up whatever gentleness originally
resided there. As he thinks just before his death, "There were
folks who wasted half an hour over the crags of a sunset. He
couldn't do that; hadn't been able to. He was too busy."[30] The
similarity to the theme of *Dust* is obvious; like Martin Wade,
Johnny Black has squeezed all the love and beauty out of his life
in his single-minded quest for power and material gain. But the
matter is much more adroitly handled in *The Thresher* than in
the earlier novel; the motivation for Johnny's monomania and
the consequences of this drive are more fully portrayed, and the
story therefore carries greater conviction.

[30] Herbert Krause, *The Thresher* (Indianapolis: Bobbs-Merrill Co., 1946),
p. 537.

Other themes prominent in earlier novels also have their place in *The Thresher*. Like Rölvaag's *Giants in the Earth*, it treats of a woman obsessed by a belief in her sinfulness and unable to share her husband's enthusiasms, losing her grip on her sanity but being at least partially restored through the agency of an understanding clergyman. Lilice's feelings and behavior, however, do not quite carry the conviction that Beret's do; her hostility toward Johnny's occupation is made believable, since her father has been crippled in an accident involving machinery, but her sense of desperation over being outside the church does not seem entirely plausible. Also like *Giants in the Earth*, Krause's novel deals with the problems faced by a national group trying to adapt itself to the American social environment. Pockerbrush is a German community, and religious instruction is entirely in German, but contacts with other immigrant groups and with "Yankees" are beginning to erode away the national identity and separateness of the Germans. The process is, of course, staunchly resisted by many. When Johnny suggests including Mr. Muri and other Scandinavians in his threshing run, Alb Hukelpoke comments sarcastically, "Get 'em all in. Kitten, cat and tom. Mr. Edgely, too. Yankee and Dutchman and Norskie. It's a good mixture" (341). When among the Germans, Edgely makes fun of the Norwegian names, but Uncle Herm knows that he speaks of the Germans in the same manner when he is away from them. The loss of national identity is most evident in the matter of names. Uncle Herm has changed his last name from Bhaerwulff to Barewolf to prevent misspelling by Yankees; in the same way Tjöstöl Skjelle becomes Chester Shelley and another Norwegian with the unfortunate name of Aas becomes Blackstone. Kurt, progressive in most matters, tends to be conservative here; citing Mr. Muri, who favors racial continuity, he remarks, "Like he says, the old must make the new stronger and richer. You can't do that by throwing it away. You can't throw your grandpa aside and forget him" (292).

The conflict between conservatism and progressivisim, which has been noted in the novels of Paul Corey and elsewhere, comes in for a good deal of treatment in *The Thresher*. Much attention is given to the technological changes in threshing. Johnny learns the business by working with a horse-powered outfit, but when he acquires his own rig, it is powered by a steam engine—a traction engine at that and not a stationary engine hauled from place to place by horses. Later the self-feeder type of separator comes into use, followed by the wind-blower, which further reduces the amount of work that must be done by men. Johnny keeps pace with these developments, but when tractors begin to replace steam engines, he refuses to go along with the innovation and becomes, before his death, a sort of reactionary whose failure to accept the fact of change undermines his status in the community. An even more serious threat to his position is the shift from wheat raising to diversified farming. A series of good years, coupled with high prices, leads the farmers to concentrate almost wholly on wheat, and Johnny capitalizes on this one-crop economy; his high-speed operations make it possible for them to get their grain to market in better condition than when it had to lie in the stacks through the fall rains. But when drought comes, the advantages of having cattle and hogs become more evident, and the base on which Johnny's standing in the community rests begins to slip from beneath him.

The shift in the farm economy does not take place without resistance. Even Uncle Herm, who is in most respects a shrewd man, laughs at the idea that wheat exhausts the soil: "That's a crazy notion. Ground is ground. It'll last as long as we will" (288). He is equally suspicious of new inventions, such as the cream separator, of which he has heard reports. He says, "The next thing you knew, some smart aleck would rig up the cow so that a farmer needn't do more than stand by and shosh her; cream would leak out of one set of teats and milk out of another" (161). This attitude grows partly out of hostility to the town, partly out of anti-intellectualism. The neighbors hoot with merriment when they hear that Dunkel has acquired a pedigreed bull—a bull with a baptismal certificate, they say. When Kurt Barewolf remarks that he would like to attend a farmers' institute, Mr. Marchen asks, "What you want there? . . . Listen to a college perfesser who don't know which end of a cow gives milk?" (343). The rest of the neighbors agree with him about Kurt: "That Kurt Barewolf, he thinks he's gonna farm by reading a book. . . . Ya, he'll find the manure don't fly out of the horse-barn window. . . . Kurt, he better fix his north fence before his heifers get into my cornfield again. . ." (400).

But there are exceptions. Matt Dornover announces that he is taking down his rail fences and putting up wire. And Mr. Dunkel, though conservative in some ways, stands up for the new kind of agriculture. The contrast between the two attitudes is illustrated by Uncle Herm's remarks about the characters of Dunkel and his archenemy, Old Geppert:

> That Dunkel, he cradles his wheat and uses oxen, sure. But he's sproutful of notions. He wants to change things, like that road on the town line. But Geppert now—when Geppert puts down a post for a fence, he wants it to stay there [49].

The rivalry between these two reaches a climax in a cradling match which ends tragically when Dunkel runs upon his small daughter in the grain and kills her.

The economic problems faced by the farmers also receive attention in *The Thresher*. There are mortgages held by the bank and complaints over unfair treatment by elevator companies. But the farmers of the Pockerbrush country are far from united on a solution to their problems. Nussbaum thinks "we oughta have farmers in the wagon seat, that's what, and tell those pants warmers in St. Paul a thing or two. Oughta own the elevators and stores" (86). But he is reminded that previous attempts by farmers to operate grain elevators have resulted in failure. The Farmers' Alliance is mentioned, but Uncle Herm is skeptical: "Seems like all they want is the gover'ment to run things. Well, I don't want a gover'ment feller telling me how to plant my spuds nor how to nut my pigs either" (126). Kurt speaks the language of Corey's Ed Crosby: "Folks have got to get together. There must be co-operation. This cutting each other's throat, it belongs way back in the dark ages. We've got to co-operate—" (445). But Johnny Black is not interested in cooperation; he wants to run things to suit himself.

All the distinguishing features of the farm novel are present in *The Thresher*. The language of the characters is reproduced with satisfying fidelity, including the rhythms of German speech as the pastor utters it while lashing his congregation collectively or grinding repentance and humiliation out of individual members. Threshing works its way into the vocabulary of the people who practice it; the language acquires such figures of speech as "he had a family big as a thrashing crew. . . . I cooked me supper enough for a bunch of thrashers" (465). Folklore, both native and introduced, has its place in the lives of these people. Old Man Fleischer claims to see the Crooked Ones in the woods on hot, sultry days, and Torsten Torgrimson tells of Huldrekall he has seen in Norway. Various signs are believed in as indications of coming events; rain in a new grave means that another grave will soon be dug. Farmers predict the kind of season to come by several devices. If the mice have long tails, there will be a good crop; if their tails are short, the grain will also be short. One can thrust a weed stalk into an anthill; if the ants swarm over it clear to the end, a good season is in prospect, while if they crawl only half way, there will be only a half-crop.

The Thresher is in many respects a better book than *Wind Without Rain*. The stylistic tricks of the earlier book are no longer so much in evidence, although there is plenty of figurative language:

> The empty ladder of the railroad track lifted into the skyline. . . . Uncle Herm's neighbors these were, folding their talk and ways stripwise into the growing matter of Johnny's thought. . . . laid her tongue in soggy twists upon her household. . . . a moment of laughter lifted wildly in the night. . . . Once she unearthed the bone of the idea, she worried it like a teething puppy.[31]

There is perhaps less emotional power in Krause's second novel, although the handling of Snoose's death and its effect on Johnny is as fine as anything in its predecessor. A good deal of symbolism is used, some of it spelled out for the reader, such as the central pattern in which the thresher represents time. But the chief significance of *The Thresher* for the present purpose is that it illustrates, probably better than any other book, what farm fiction had become after fifty years of existence.

Farm novels of this type did not end with Krause, however. Although the output since 1946 has greatly diminished, the few that have appeared show a technical competence that places them

[31] *Ibid.*, pp. 12, 17, 30, 47, 100.

abreast of recent trends in general American writing. Two novels of the past few years deserve at least passing mention as examples of continued artistic development in farm fiction: Gordon Webber's *What End But Love* (1959) and Curtis Harnack's *Love and Be Silent* (1962).

Almost devoid of plot in the conventional sense, *What End But Love* employs a complex structure to explore the relationships among the numerous members of a Michigan family. On Memorial Day, 1934, the children, brothers, sister, and other relatives of old Hollister Zenas (Holly) Hobart gather at his farm home as they do each year. All are concerned over the rumors that Holly, long a widower, is threatening to marry a woman in her twenties and has torn up a lease he had previously signed turning over his land to an auto company in nearby Flint. These issues, which sharply divide the relatives, are resolved at the end of the novel by Holly's death as a result of overexertion while helping put out a fire in the barn.

The significance of the novel lies not in the simple plot but in what the reader learns about each of the characters through his thoughts and words on the way to the gathering. Holly's relatives represent a wide range of occupational and educational levels, from his sons Randall, Methodist minister and Phi Beta Kappa, and Ripley, auto executive, to his niece Dee, whose husband, Jim Tady, combines pig farming and garbage collecting and might fit well into an Erskine Caldwell piece, and Julian, actually Holly's illegitimate son, who has virtually resigned from the human race and leads a semisavage existence, living at times in a nest in a tree. Most of them feel that they have taken a wrong turn somewhere and wasted much of their lives, but no one finds an answer, except in the terms suggested by the title of the book. The members of the Hobart family have typically been stubborn and hot-tempered, and these qualities have led to clashes and breaches never healed; others have lived lives of self-sacrifice and have not been adequately rewarded.

Besides this exploration of human relationships, *What End But Love* offers a contribution to the rural-urban dialogue by showing how industrialization and urbanization are encroaching upon the rural world. Not only will the family farm be taken over for industrial purposes, but all of Holly's sons except Randall have been seized by the auto industry. The juggernaut keeps right on rolling, with no solution suggested in the novel. Actually, the book is barely on the periphery of farm fiction, for nearly all the characters are city folk now; even Holly has turned the farm work over to a couple who run it on shares. But in its analysis of the urbanization process it makes a significant contribution to the chronicle of the decay of rural America.

Curtis Harnack's *Love and Be Silent* contains more about farm life and has more plot but may nonetheless represent a slighter performance in the realm of farm fiction. It is mainly a book about marriage—specifically about the respective marriages of Robert Schneider, an Iowa farmer, and his sister Alma. Robert marries his childhood sweetheart, Donna Schmidt, who is never quite sure, before or after the event, whether she really wanted to marry him. Despite difficulties, they manage to arrive at a reasonably satisfactory relationship and look, to outsiders, like an ideally mated couple. Alma is not so fortunate. Left motherless early, she has to run the household until her father's death when she is nearly thirty. Then in her haste to find a normal place in life, she rushes into marriage with a weak and unstable young man, Roger Larkin, who is at least four years her junior. The rest of the book is an account of her attempt to make Roger approximate her ideal of him, or at least to keep him from running away whenever the going gets rough. Robert is no help to her, for he has opposed her marriage to Roger from the first and continues to interfere and frighten Roger away whenever an opportunity presents itself.

The novel's central theme—the complexities of human relationships—is at once its strongest point and its weakest. Although the characterization is effective, there are unresolved ambiguities in both Robert and Alma which make some of their actions hard for the reader to accept. The two marriages are subtly intertwined; Robert and Alma each think they comprehend and can solve the other's marriage problems, yet Robert, at least, only complicates matters by his interference. The reader is left with some doubt as to whether either of these two main characters is entirely plausible.

Although a good deal of the novel takes place in cities or towns, the farm occupies the center of the stage enough of the time to provide a basis for some evaluations of Harnack's skill in treating this subject. As with most farm novels written since 1930, farm tasks are given careful attention, though not so much as by Corey or Krause. There is just enough of this kind of background detail to lend the proper ring of authenticity to the book, never so much as to make it seem that the author is trying to write social history. The North Dakota "ranch" on which Alma and Roger spend the first year of their marriage contending with drought, loneliness, desolation, and Roger's ineptitude is described in graphic detail of a type not calculated to further the promotional activities of the Greater North Dakota Association. As with nearly all works of serious fiction published in the past thirty years, the speech of the characters is handled skillfully, and considerable attention is given to sex, as befits a book about marriage.

All in all, Harnack's novel is a good one though not a great one. In its choice of a theme it is to a degree self-limiting. Although set mostly in the 1930's, little is said about drought (except in North Dakota), almost nothing about the economic problems of farming during the depression. It would have been better if it had displayed some recognition that farmers and their wives in that period of history would have had concerns other than those treated so deftly by the author of *Love and Be Silent*.

The books discussed in this chapter constitute only a small proportion of the total output of this type of farm fiction; only the most significant or most representative of them have been selected. Even the relatively small number treated here, however, show a definite progression toward greater technical competence. A product of the later 1930's, mediocre by comparison to the best general fiction of that period, might, for example, be technically superior to such an early work as Mrs. Munger's *The Wind Before the Dawn*, published in 1912. But a similar advance in craftsmanship has been evident in other fiction as well, with the result that the farm novel has continued to lag behind the best of contemporary non-farm fiction. It should be stressed, however, that if no farm novels of the 1930's can be classified with the best of

American fiction, the reasons are not altogether internal. As will be explained in greater detail in the next chapter, external factors, such as the decline in the number of people directly connected with farming, have had much to do with the estimates placed by the critics and by the reading public on farm fiction. To some extent it may also be that the choice of themes adopted by the novelists discussed in this chapter—individual emotional problems and conflicts—rendered their books less significant than some of those written about a subject such as the pioneer experience. Whatever reservations must be made, the fact is that fiction of considerable distinction was written on these themes, as evidenced particularly by the work of Ruth Suckow, Glenway Wescott, Leroy MacLeod, Josephine Johnson, and Herbert Krause.

VII.

The Farm Novel in Perspective

IF THE foregoing chapters have demonstrated anything, it is that a coherent body of fiction exists in the United States dealing with farm life truthfully, perceptively, and significantly. Nearly all the writers whose novels have been discussed display a high degree of familiarity with the physical details of farm life, although some—particularly women novelists like Martha Ostenso and Lorna Doone Beers—tend to give little attention to this aspect of their materials. There has been a progressive development in the direction of greater emphasis upon such details. Novels written during the 1920's tend to concentrate on the plot and provide the reader with only a bare minimum of factual background. On the other hand, more recent writers like Corey, Krause, and Feikema make such extensive use of this kind of detail that they have been accused of overloading their novels with it; the objection is that most readers are not familiar enough with farm life to sense the significance of these details and are likely to be more bored than impressed.

The use of the vernacular has become an all but universally accepted technique of the writers of farm fiction. The only differences are the purely technical ones involved in rendering dialect, and in this matter present-day novelists avoid both the extremes of allowing all the characters to speak an undifferentiated kind of English and of representing the peculiarities of pronunciation so carefully as to make the dialogue almost incomprehensible to the reader.

It is in the fidelity with which farm fiction portrays characteristically rural attitudes that it shows the greatest variety. Although there has been a marked improvement in this respect since the early farm novel, even the books which appeared in the decade of the 1930's display striking differences. Some writers, such as Martha Ostenso and Phil Stong, seem to make no particular effort to present these attitudes, or when they do their attempts have the hollow ring of concessions to convention: farmers are supposed to think in a certain way, and so they must be represented as thinking in that way. People like Paul Corey are very careful that the thoughts expressed by their characters are the kind of thoughts those characters would have and express. Evaluation of the novelist's skill in this respect, although necessarily based to some extent on the critic's own notions of what farmers think and believe, is not entirely subjective. There is such a thing as consistency within a character, and if a novelist portrays a character who displays this kind of consistency in expressing his attitudes, then one can place a good deal of reliance on that writer's insight into character. If the same novelist displays a high degree of familiarity with the physical details of farm life, it can with reasonable safety be assumed that his representation of rural attitudes is also accurate. This is true of Corey; it is true of Krause; it is largely true of Feikema. It appears to be true also of MacLeod, but since he deals with a period nearly a century past, his skill is more difficult to estimate. The case is the same with novelists like Rölvaag, who write of the immigrant and of an earlier period. One is inclined to trust Rölvaag's handling of his characters' attitudes, but there is no way of arriving at even the modest approach to certainty that is possible with those who write of the present and recent past.

Farm fiction seems, as a whole, to give about equal weight to and to treat with equal skill the various attitudes specified in Chapter I as being characteristic of rural people. Perhaps the town-country hostility receives slightly more attention than the others, but the difference is probably not significant. Such differences as there are in the frequency of their appearance may be indicative of their relative importance in rural thought patterns. If so, this fact might suggest something concerning the value of literature in defining as well as reflecting conditions in the rural world. Be this as it may, the accuracy with which the novels examined here do in fact reflect such attitudes, as well as the skill with which they reproduce the physical details of farm life and the speech of farm people, would seem to justify designating the middle western farm novel as a literary genre.

Because a strictly chronological pattern has not been followed in the preceding chapters, the development of farm fiction since Hamlin Garland has been necessarily somewhat obscured by other features of the materials. One task which remains, therefore, is to review the history of the middle western farm novel, to note the stages through which it has passed, and, if possible, to account for these stages.

It was pointed out in earlier chapters that although farm life received attention from several nineteenth-century writers, middle western farm fiction as it has been defined here had its beginnings in the work of Joseph Kirkland and Hamlin Garland, just before the turn of the century. One of the first facts to strike the investigator is that almost no one followed Garland's lead in the years immediately after his initial efforts. Joy Allison's *Billow Prairie*, a very minor work of fiction dealing only superficially with farm life, appeared in 1892, the year after *Main-Travelled Roads*, but the former novel, really a Sunday-school tract with a farm setting, represents nothing that could be termed a follow-up of Garland's work. Much the same may be said of Opie Read's *Yankee from the West* (1898), which places a group of highly improbable characters in a farm situation where they speak a stage-rustic dialect and do no physical work, unless an occasional brawl may be considered work. In fact, except for such romances of the cattle country as *The Plow-Woman* (1906) and *The Homesteaders* (1909) and one or two other minor works, Garland remained virtually the only farm novelist for two decades after the publication of *Main-Travelled Roads*.

The second decade of the century saw a slight increase in the number of farm novels produced. Dell H. Munger's *The Wind Before the Dawn* (1912), Willa Cather's early novels of Nebraska pioneer life, and a few less distinguished efforts in the same direction represented the beginnings of a large-scale flowering of farm fiction. This efflorescence came after 1920, and for the next generation a flood of farm novels rolled off the presses of the major publishing houses and several minor ones. 1925 was an especially productive year, for at least eight farm novels appeared in that year alone; but there were other years when almost as many were published. The boom continued into the early 1940's and then collapsed with surprising suddenness. The following table, based upon the publication dates of 137 books (including three volumes of short stories) which have some claim to being called farm fiction, gives an indication of the number appearing in each five-year period from 1891 to 1960. It is worth noting how large a proportion of the earliest novels were written by Garland.

1891–1895	6 (5 by Garland)	1926–1930	14
1896–1900	1	1931–1935	23
1901–1905	0	1936–1940	26
1906–1910	3 (1 by Garland)	1941–1945	16
1911–1915	3	1946–1950	7
1916–1920	5	1951–1955	4
1921–1925	17	1956–1960	12

Although these figures are admittedly selective, based chiefly on works of fiction listed in *Book Review Digest*, they probably account for most of the books on middle western farm life published during this period. Whether the sharp increase in the number of farm novels in the period 1956–1960 betokens a revival of the genre or is merely the result of coincidence cannot be determined until enough time has elapsed to permit the plotting of a trend, if there is one. On the basis of the trend illustrated by the previous five-year periods, however, it seems unlikely that the farm novel is going to experience any major resurgence of popularity.

The methods of classification used by *Book Review Digest* also cast some light on the rise and decline of farm fiction. Beginning with 1917, this periodical provided a subcategory called "Farm Life" under the larger heading of "Fiction." (Prior to that time there had been a section called "Farm Life" which included both fiction and nonfiction.) Thenceforth the "Farm Life" subcategory increased in size from year to year, until the Cumulated Index covering the five years 1932–1936 included sixty entries, of which twenty-one were middle western.[1] The number declined

---

[1] *Book Review Digest*, XXXII (1936), 1254–1255. It should be mentioned that these listings include books with foreign settings; in the 1936 volume there were twenty of them, most of them English. By no means all of the farm novels treated in this study are listed by *Book Review Digest* under the heading of "Farm Life." Some are listed under "Frontier and Pioneer Life" or "Locality."

thereafter, until in 1952 there were only four entries, in 1953 two, and in 1954 one; in 1955 the "Farm Life" classification was omitted. (Phil Stong's *Blizzard*, published that year, was listed under "Iowa" in the "Locality" subcategory.) In 1956 the classification was reinstated, with six entries. But in 1957 the number of entries had fallen to two; for the next three years only one entry appeared each year, increased in 1961 to two. In 1962 there were two entries, plus a third in a new subcategory, "Farm Tenancy." Except for the surprising spurt in 1956, therefore, there has apparently been no increase in the number of farm novels published during the past decade.

One who examines such statistics as these may question why the farm novel developed when it did and why it subsequently declined in numbers. The answers can be sought in literary, economic, and social terms. If we look first at the relatively sudden burst of farm-novel activity in the 1920's and try to analyze the phenomenon in literary terms, certain facts become apparent at once. This remarkable development of the farm novel coincided with one of the periodic manifestations of middle western regional consciousness, a movement which was reflected in other arts as well as literature, as illustrated by the Benton-Wood-Curry school of painting, and which included such writers of farm fiction as Herbert Quick, John T. Frederick, and Ruth Suckow. Although Miss Suckow later wrote that the regional aspect of her work had been overemphasized,[2] her early novels are probably best understood in regional terms. Quick was outspoken concerning the suitability of Iowa background and history as materials for fiction, and Frederick was one of the interpreters of Miss Suckow's regionalism as well as a conscious regionalist in his own writing. Since the Middle West, at least that portion of it lying west of Chicago, was predominantly rural (according to the Census Bureau's definition of the term) in the 1920's, novels dealing with farm life might reflect regional peculiarities more effectively than novels treating of city and small-town life. As Fred B. Millett has pointed out, "the concept of regionalism is almost always associated with rural rather than with urban America."[3] His

[2] Suckow, *Carry-Over*, p. vii.
[3] Millett, *Contemporary American Authors*, p. 38.

observation is true not merely of the Middle West but of all sections of the country, including the urbanized Northeast. And so it is not surprising to find a large number of farm novels among the middle western regional fiction of this decade. The self-conscious seriousness and determination of those who participated in this movement was sometimes the subject of amused comment by easterners, as when a writer for the *Forum* said in 1924: "There is feverish literary activity in the region of the Mississippi Valley. Countless novels are being published, magazines founded, prizes awarded, in an attempt to establish a distinctive *genre*. And a stupendous monotony has been achieved."[4]

Middle western regional consciousness of course goes back to a point earlier than the 1920's. Garland had been its spokesman in the 1890's. After a period of inactivity, a revival began which may be traced back as far as the establishment of Harriet Monroe's magazine *Poetry* in Chicago in 1912. Of greater consequence to the development of the farm novel was the appearance, in 1915, of John T. Frederick's regional literary magazine, the *Midland*, previously mentioned in connection with Frederick. In the first issue the editor expressed a regional purpose when he termed it "merely a modest attempt to encourage the making of literature in the Middle West." Already renowned for material accomplishments, the region had always turned elsewhere for a market for its literary and artistic productions. He hoped that by providing a market for such products, the *Midland* would help retain more of its writers and artists. In this way the region would gain in variety and perhaps "civilization itself might be with us a somewhat swifter process. . . ."[5]

Three years after its foundation there appeared in the *Midland* an article by L. H. Bailey calling for a literature dealing with agriculture. With an eagerness to establish historical continuity reminiscent of those Medieval historians who always be-

---

[4] Weare Holbrook, "The Corn Belt Renaissance," *Forum*, LXXII (July 1924), 118. Likewise, when Thomas Boyd's novel *Samuel Drummond* appeared in 1925, the *New York Times Book Review* headlined its review "Thomas Boyd Joins the Rush Back to the Farm" (August 30, 1925, p. 8).

[5] John T. Frederick, "First Person Plural," *The Midland*, I (January 1915), 1.

gan with the Creation, the author of this article finds the earliest rural literature in the Bible. He notes that there has been a falling-off in recent millennia, however, and expresses the hope that a revived interest in rural life as the subject of literature will lead to something

> more than a flavor or than any inviting series of suggestions and illustrations, much more than metaphor and simile and comparisons, more than rural allusions; this literature will be of the essence of the open country, founded in its experience. . . .[6]

He concedes that such works will probably not be written by working farmers, "but they must be the work of those who are born to the environment and driven by the motive" (104). He concludes, however, that we are not yet ready "for a bold artistic literature that shall express the marrow of rural civilization," for we are still analyzing country life and applying newly discovered facts, which we must assimilate before there can be artistic creation (105). Bailey's article is interesting chiefly because it indicates that there was in 1918 a realization of the literary possibilities of farm life and the inherent dignity of rural themes as the subject of serious literature.

Although middle western regional consciousness developed later in painting than in fiction, one of the best expressions of the spirit that animated all aspects of the movement appears in a manifesto published by Grant Wood in 1935. Significantly titled *Revolt Against the City*, his statement of purposes and aims is a defense of regionalism in general and of middle western regionalism in particular. It speaks of the "present revolt against the domination exercised over art and letters and over much of our thinking and living by Eastern capitals of finance and politics," and attributes this revolt to the discovery that the East and the cities have always been more colonial, more subject to European influence, while the interior of the country, and especially the rural areas, have been more distinctively American.[7] The depres-

---

[6] L. H. Bailey, "Can Agriculture Function in Literature?", *The Midland*, IV (May–June 1918), 103–104.

[7] Grant Wood, *Revolt Against the City* (Iowa City: Clio Press, 1935), pp. 16–17.

sion, says Wood, has sent people back to the land, where they have rediscovered some of the frontier virtues.

For our present purpose, the most important statements in Wood's essay are those relating to the suitability of the farmer and farm life as subjects for artistic treatment. He says, "Central and dominant in our Midwestern scene is the farmer," character-ized by independence, individualism, and conservatism (29). The fact that the farmer is not himself vocal makes him the richest kind of material for the writer or the artist. "Serious, sympathetic handling of farmer-material offers a great field for the careful worker. The life of the farmer, engaged in a constant conflict with natural forces, is essentially dramatic" (33). As possible themes to be used by the writer or artist he mentions the nomadic movements of cattlemen in various states, the great dust storms, the floods, the milk strikes, the violent protests against foreclo-sures, and "the sacrifices forced upon once prosperous families— all these elements and many more are colorful, significant, and intensely dramatic" (34).

Wood's remarks, made after the farm novel had enjoyed more than a decade of popularity, are less valuable as prophecies of future achievements than as statements of accomplished facts. But in this essay he explains some of the causes for the movement of which he was a part and points out the important contribu-tion made by the farm novel to that movement.

The rise and decline of the farm novel are also attributable in some degree to economic factors. The prevalence of farm fic-tion in the 1920's and 1930's can probably be accounted for to some extent by the depressed state of agriculture in those decades. Just as novels of social criticism were popular in the last three decades of the nineteenth century, a period of painful adjustment to an industrial economy, and just as proletarian literature flour-ished in the depression period of the 1930's, so farm fiction has tended to proliferate in periods of agrarian discontent. Garland's earliest productions were the result of a reforming zeal which hoped to better the lot of the middle western farmer in a period of agricultural depression, the Populist era of the 1890's. In the first two decades of the twentieth century, the farmer was com-paratively well off; and, as we have seen, there was very little farm fiction published during that period. After World War I, however, American agriculture entered upon a prolonged depression, which was not relieved until the coming of the next world conflict.[8] During these two decades the farm novel flourished as never before or since. True, there were many farm novels published after 1939, including some of the few that can in any sense be termed proletarian fiction. But their appearance then may be taken as another example of the truism that literature lags somewhat behind actual conditions, even when its object is the betterment of those conditions. Steinbeck's *The Grapes of Wrath*, for example, appeared in 1939, well after the events it describes had taken place.

A more serious objection to this theory of the economic influence on the farm novel is the fact that has been pointed out earlier, that very few of these novels have much to say about economic conditions or display any interest in social reform. About all that can be said in defense against the objection is that the prevalence of farm fiction in a period of agricultural depression reflected a widespread interest in the farmer, due at least in part to the distressed state of agriculture. The farmer's plight itself was perhaps not a subject of extensive discussion in fiction, but at least his existence was recognized by the increase in fictional treatment of farm life.

When we attempt to analyze the social factors underlying the growth of the farm novel in the 1920's and 1930's, we are on even more tentative ground, for here we are dealing with the question of who reads novels. It seems safe to assume that an increase in the number of books representing a particular genre reflects an increased reader interest in such books. Such a process is likely to work both ways and to be temporarily self-perpetuating; an increased public demand produces an increased output, and this in turn increases the demand—up to a point at least. The question we must ask, knowing that any answer will be only conjectural, is, who were and are the readers of farm novels? Probably few farmers would be numbered among them, although farmers'

[8] For the most thorough recent discussion of this period in American agriculture see Saloutos and Hicks, *Agricultural Discontent in the Middle West 1900–1939*, especially pp. 87 ff.

wives might be somewhat more likely prospects. Most readers of farm novels, however, may be assumed to be urban, including under that term all people not living on farms. It seems unlikely that such novels would appeal greatly to people whose urban roots extended back for more than a generation or two and who had had no first-hand contact with farm life. This is evidenced by the rather flippant attitude frequently taken by reviewers for the *New Yorker*, perhaps the most distinctively urban periodical in America. About Krause's *The Thresher* a reviewer writing in this magazine said, after praising the book for its technical merits, "Still, it is hard to believe that anybody wants to know as much about threshing wheat as he is bent on telling."[9] Essentially the same attitude was taken toward Feikema's *This Is the Year*, which the reviewer thought gave altogether too much attention to the weather and to the details of farm life.[10] The point is that of course the *New Yorker's* readers would tend to see in even the best-written of farm novels much ado about nothing—nothing very interesting at least.

If it is conceded that neither the farmer himself nor the strictly urban reader would figure importantly in the audience of the farm novel, then the conclusion follows that farm fiction is read mostly by people who know something about farm life, either because they live in small towns and are in close touch with the farm or because they have themselves lived on farms in their youth. Since the inhabitant of the small town tends to adopt a rather supercilious attitude toward farmers and farming and to pride himself on his ignorance of farm matters, there is reason to believe that the most important body of readers of farm fiction consists of those city dwellers who have known some early association with farm life and feel a certain amount of nostalgia for the scene of their youthful experiences. This supposition was apparently recognized by a reviewer of Josephine Donovan's *Black Soil* who said, "Any piece of fiction which evokes the prairie and farm life with competent realism is certain of a reading in these days when many a harried city dweller turns a

[9] *New Yorker*, XXII (January 18, 1947), 93.
[10] *New Yorker*, XXIII (March 29, 1947), 101.

nostalgic eye toward the disappearing country life of his youth."[11]

In order to bring this hypothesis down from the realm of pure conjecture, it might be well to examine some of the causes for the farm-to-town migration and to determine when this movement was most extensive. Three principal reasons may be cited as responsible for the farm boy's desire to leave the farm. The first might be termed economic pressure. With the gradual transition from subsistence to commercial agriculture, the family-type farm became increasingly uneconomical. That is to say, as the nineteenth century passed, the individual farm became incapable of supporting a large number of sons and their wives and children, and subdividing the land only compounded the problem. The result in many cases was that most of the sons would go farther west and take up farms of their own. This was practicable so long as such farms were to be had, but once the supply of economically valuable land had been exhausted or seriously depleted, the surplus sons and daughters were likely to seek employment in towns and cities, where the growth of industry provided something of a chance for them to make a living. The theory of the West as a safety valve for urban laborers in times of depression has been largely exploded, but there is little reason to doubt that it often did serve such a function for the surplus farm population in the older states. When the frontier was gone, the city tended to take its place as an outlet, and as a result, the movement from farm to city increased near the end of the nineteenth century.

Another cause for the movement of the young from the farm to the city was a revolt against patriarchal authority. The persistence of parental domination in farm families has been noted in several novels and seems to have been an actual condition much more prevalent in the country than in the town. So long as the presence of available land provided a means of escape, the farm boy or girl in rebellion against such domination could go farther west and remain in the occupation to which he was born. For after all, farming was and is a type of skilled labor, and the farm youth possessed the training necessary to farming, while he lacked the skills required for any kind of urban employment.

[11] *New York Times Book Review*, October 5, 1930, p. 6.

The pattern is illustrated in fiction by Walter J. Muilenburg's *Prairie* (1925), discussed in Chapter III, in which an Iowa farm boy rebels against his father's moral strictness, marries in defiance of the father's wishes, and then goes to Nebraska, where cheap land is still available. But when the frontier had disappeared as a practical outlet, young people who ran away from home to escape the stern regimen imposed upon them by their parents were likely to go to the cities and take what work was available there.

Still a third factor to be considered in accounting for this mass movement is a temperamental dislike of farm work or a distaste for the social, cultural, and intellectual deprivations of farm life. Undoubtedly this factor has been operative throughout American history and was not materially affected by the disappearance of the frontier. But the coming of rapid communication and transportation, by placing the farm youth in greater contact with urban life and by making that life more accessible, probably increased the tendency of young people to leave the farm rather than stay and endure what they saw no escape from. Furthermore, the spread of universal education tended to reduce the gap between young people born on the farm and those born in towns and thus facilitated the individual's adaptation to city life. So long as the farm boy had to face the stigma of being regarded as a "greenhorn" or "yokel" when he moved to the city, he might well hesitate before making the jump; but when the cultural disparity between him and the town boy diminished, he would be more inclined to take the chance.

Let us imagine a specific instance of the kind of movement that has just been described and see what the effect, if widespread enough, would be on the taste for fiction. Let us visualize a farm boy reaching maturity about 1890 or slightly later and, for one or a combination of these three reasons, wishing to break with the home farm. The opportunities for escape provided by vast expanses of western lands to be had at very little expense are no longer available to him, and so instead of remaining a farmer he migrates to the city and finds a job somewhere near the bottom rung of the occupational ladder there. Or, in the improbable event that he has acquired some education before leaving the farm, he may, like Garland, break onto the ladder well above the foot. In any case, he is probably busy establishing himself economically during the next thirty years and has little time to interest himself in things cultural. But by 1920 or 1925 such a farm boy, if he has been capable, industrious, and fortunate, may have achieved an economic status that permits him some leisure time, which he—or, more probably, his wife—may devote in part to reading novels. The kind of fiction he would prefer would naturally be that which reflects his own experiences, especially those of his childhood and youth, now invested with a nostalgic haze. Here is a ready-made audience for a literary form just then emerging, and it would be surprising if this form should not burgeon for a time. But after a generation is past, this ex-farm boy would have been replaced by his own sons and daughters, who have no first-hand contact with farm life and little interest in it and who therefore would tend to find the farm novel much less appealing than their parents did.

But what about the continuing stream of farm-to-city migration in the twentieth century? Here, it would seem, would be the materials of a permanent audience for farm fiction. The fact is, however, that this migration has been greatly reduced in recent decades, mainly because the source from which it flowed has dwindled (both because of a decline in the number of farmers and because of a decline in the size of families), possibly also because as the cultural gap between farm and city life has narrowed, especially in the area of material well-being, the farm has seemed more attractive to young people, and a larger proportion of them may have chosen to stay with agriculture.

Reduced to its simplest terms, then, the theory offered here holds that the apparent popularity of the farm novel between 1920 and 1945 was due in part to the existence during that time of a larger number of people with both farm background and leisure time than before or since. The chief difficulty with such a theory is that it is virtually impossible to document. In the first place, there is no way of proving that people of farm background are any more avid readers of farm fiction than anyone else. As a matter of fact, the appearance of a considerable body of English fiction dealing with farm life during the same period might tend to cast doubt upon this notion. The prevalence of such fiction in a highly urban society such as that of England might, however, be explained on the basis of a greater interest in such subjects as folklore than in America, a greater consciousness of locality and regional differences, and perhaps a greater awareness of the need for each geographical and occupational group to be familiar with other groups.

It would be equally difficult to show when the migration of middle western farm youth to the cities was at its peak, whether any significant number of such people ever attained an economic status that would enable them to devote leisure time to reading novels, and whether, if they did, they displayed any interest in fiction. Gross population statistics are not particularly helpful in determining movements of this kind involving a specific section of the country. Even such information as is available for the country as a whole on the movement of people from the farm to the city does not tell us how many of these people were middle westerners; and statistics on the growth of middle western cities and the decline of the middle western farm population do not tell us how much of the urban increase came from other portions of the country or what proportion of those who gave up farming in this region went elsewhere and resumed farming there. The census figures do show that the rate of urbanization in the United States was about twice as rapid between 1890 and 1920 as it has been since 1920.[12] This fact, although it tends to support the theory under discussion, is based upon statistics so general as to be almost meaningless in terms of the specific situation being considered here.

Fortunately, the theory is not obliged to bear the whole burden of accounting for the popularity of the farm novel between 1920 and 1945 and its subsequent eclipse. The order of importance of the three factors considered here—the literary, the eco-

[12] Carl C. Taylor et al., Rural Life in the United States, p. 219. In 1890 the American population was 35.1 per cent urban, and in 1920 it was 51.2 per cent urban—an increase of 16.1 per cent. In 1947 it was estimated to be 59.1 per cent urban—an increase of only 7.9 per cent. But those figures tend to mask the fact that as the population increased, the rate of urbanization, in percentage, would naturally decline.

nomic, and the social—probably corresponds to the order in which they have been discussed, with the social causes being the least significant. Furthermore, no effort is being made to exclude the possibility of other influences which have not been treated here. Sheer momentum perhaps accounts for much of the output in the 1930's; the success of a few novels led other writers, many of whom possessed little talent, to draw upon their experiences to produce novels superficially like those which had met with a good reception from readers and critics. In time the resulting flood of mediocre fiction would bring its own extinction, and this is in part what happened in the 1940's, when war stories, historical novels, and other forms of fiction found greater favor in the popular taste than the farm novel.

The discussion so far has been concerned exclusively with the audience of the farm novel. Something needs to be said of the authors themselves. Here the theory just described would have to be greatly modified if it were to be seriously advanced as an explanation for the vogue of the farm novel in the 1920's and 1930's, for in general the writers of the novels that appeared in these decades were not late nineteenth-century migrants to the city but comparatively young people whose arrival in the city occurred much later than that of the audience postulated in the preceding paragraphs. Except for a few authors, like Herbert Quick and Alvin Johnson, who did most of their important work in late middle age, the leading farm novelists were in their twenties and thirties when they wrote their books. Consequently, the social theory discussed above appears to have little utility in attempting to account for the authors' choice of farm life as a subject for their writings. It should be pointed out, however, that the novelists whose books have been treated in the preceding chapters and about whom biographical information is available had, with the exception of Haldeman-Julius, some personal acquaintance with farm life, whether as a result of a farm childhood or through some later attempt at farming. Comparatively few earlier writers (Garland would be an obvious exception) could claim such background. By 1900 literature had long since ceased to be the monopoly of a Brahmin group in New England, if it ever was that, but it continued to be dominated by practitioners with urban backgrounds. Perhaps improved educational facilities in rural areas may be given partial credit for increasing the number of farm-to-city migrants after 1900 who were not merely literate but somewhat literary as well. In the final analysis, however, the changing composition of the audience, with the effects such change would necessarily have on tastes, probably had more to do with increasing the output of farm fiction than any increased proportion of potential novelists with rural backgrounds.

The popularity of novels about pioneering life in the early years of the farm novel vogue also needs to be explained. From Willa Cather's *O Pioneers!* through Herbert Quick, O. E. Rölvaag, and a host of lesser writers, this subject held the interest of farm novelists until about the mid-1930's, when an increased interest in the contemporary scene came to supersede it. Some of the reasons for the popularity of fiction about pioneering are obvious. The conquest of the continent has long seemed to many Americans the greatest achievement of the national genius, and it had been reflected in fiction long before the process was concluded. (John T. Frederick calls it "the most dramatic event in human history."[13]) As the frontier advanced westward, easterners displayed a continuing interest in a drama that was going on in regions far removed from their own established communities. And when there was no longer a frontier, the whole nation embraced this interest. As might be expected, the greatest interest was in the more recent frontier; hence many novels dealt with the settlement of the Great Plains: the Boyles' *The Homesteaders*, Garland's *Moccasin Ranch*, Cather's *O Pioneers!*, Rölvaag's *Giants in the Earth*, Rose Wilder Lane's tales of the Dakota prairie country, and Kramer's *Marginal Land*. Many of them were part and parcel of the earlier tradition of western romance and only incidentally farm novels. The best of them, of course, go beyond the limitations of this tradition, but the weaker ones are close to the Wild West thrillers of the nineteenth century. The difference between *Moccasin Ranch* and Garland's later romantic stories of the Rockies is principally a matter of longitude.

The decline of the novel of pioneering can probably be ac-

---

[13] Frederick, "The Farm in Iowa Fiction," p. 127.

counted for mainly by the fact that by the later 1930's even the latest phases of the pioneering experience had receded into the remote past, so far as the actual experience of living Americans was concerned. The coming of the depression and its attendant social, economic, and cultural changes had diverted popular attention to new topics by then, and the fiction of the period somewhat tardily reflected this shift in interest. Novels about pioneering are by no means extinct (as evidenced by the appearance in 1956 of Breneman's *The Land They Possessed*), nor are they likely to become so in the immediate future, but the day of their greatest appeal is almost certainly past.

The discussion so far in this chapter has perhaps placed undue emphasis on the mere quantitative output of the farm novel, as though the importance of the genre in different decades were to be judged solely on the basis of the number of novels published. To some extent quantity alone is a valid criterion, inasmuch as the general artistic level of farm fiction has not been high, and therefore comparative statistics on output do afford a useful rule of thumb for determining when the farm novel was at its peak. In the final analysis, however, other standards must be taken into account, as in other art forms; it would be manifestly unjust, for example, to compare the English drama of the Elizabethan period with that of the early nineteenth century purely on the basis of the number of plays written. Throughout the present investigation qualitative differences among farm novels have been pointed out. Because of the attention which has already been given to these differences, only a few generalizations need be added here.

Looking at the entire body of farm fiction in the twentieth century, it would seem that individual high points of artistic skill were reached in the work of Willa Cather and Rölvaag relatively early in the history of the genre. Miss Cather's two novels that most clearly fall into the category of farm fiction appeared in 1913 and 1918, while *Giants in the Earth* was first published, in Norwegian, in 1924 and 1925. Another peak seems to have been reached at the end of the 1930's and during the following decade, represented principally in the work of Paul Corey and Herbert Krause. The achievement of these later writers consists more in the attainment of a high degree of technical skill, based upon what was by that time a long tradition, than in any notable individual power based upon the exceptional insights of artistic genius. The achievements of Miss Cather and of Rölvaag transcended the farm-novel form; that of Corey and Krause remained emphatically within it but gave it a technical perfection it had not attained in the hands of earlier writers, some skilled, some not, on whose collective achievements they drew. In effect, therefore, the answer to the question of who has done the best work in the farm-novel field depends on how broadly we define the farm novel. If we include (as has been done in this book) all those novels which deal with farm life in the Middle West, Miss Cather and Rölvaag must be considered the finest practitioners of the genre; if, however, we define it more narrowly, restricting it to those novels which most completely reflect all aspects of farm life, Corey and Krause seem to represent the highest development of the form.

Only the very finest of farm novels can be placed in a class with the leading fiction of their time. *Giants in the Earth* and Miss Cather's two novels about Nebraska farm life are almost the only examples that can be cited; and it can be argued that *O Pioneers!* and *My Ántonia* do not constitute their author's best work. Most farm fiction has been eminently "popular" in the sense that it was written to sell. Hence there has been a tendency to follow successful formulas rather than to experiment. Sometimes, however, experimentation has paid off, at least in terms of prize awards. Glenway Wescott's *The Grandmothers* might be termed experimental, in that it departed from the customary plot structure, and it won a publisher's prize. Likewise Josephine Johnson's *Now in November* and Krause's *Wind Without Rain* represented stylistic experiments, and they won prizes, the former the Pulitzer award, the latter the Friends of American Writers award. But all too often farm novelists have followed formulas that were stale in Garland's day, and the result has been the kind of stereotyped light fiction represented by Dora Aydelotte's *Long Furrows* (1935) and *Full Harvest* (1939), Elizabeth Corbett's *Faye's Folly* (1941), Loula Grace Erdman's *The Years of the Locust* (1947) and *The Short Summer* (1958), and, at its sentimental worst, Mae Foster Jay's *The Orchard Fence* (1935).

Even if it could be shown that the best farm fiction has a technical finish comparable to that of the better American novels generally, that would not be enough to place it on a par with these non-farm novels, for there is the matter of content to consider. One commentator states categorically that "the criticism occasionally heard, that rural fiction is sentimental and is not tackling hard country problems, is not justified."[14] But the fact is that the average farm novel has tended to be sentimental and has avoided the "hard country problems" or treated them so superficially as to have made no contribution to their diagnosis or solution. Some novels, as we have seen, have come to grips with contemporary issues and have treated them in a realistic and significant manner; Paul Corey's work is perhaps the best illustration of that kind of fiction. But this type of novel is rarely if ever distinguished stylistically by anything more than straight technical competence, and hence it fails to move the reader while it informs him. In no middle western farm novel written in English is there the combination of stylistic power and realistic treatment of significant material that makes for the very greatest fiction.

Only a few characters, such as Ántonia Shimerda, Per Hansa, and possibly Jacob Vandemark, stand out as memorable figures among the hundreds who come and go on the canvases of the middle western farm novel. Corey, with all his ability to make his characters believable, has not created one who can be ranked with these, and somehow Krause's Johnny Black fails to achieve the individuality that his author undoubtedly intended for him. The ignorant, stubborn, and yet thoroughly human Pier Frixen in Feikema's *This Is the Year* perhaps comes closer to the stuff of real character portrayal than any other personality in recent farm fiction. In part, the deficiency of the farm novel in this respect is a reflection of the tendency of modern fiction in general to subordinate the individual to the group and to be more concerned about types than about individuals. But it is chiefly due, especially in the earlier decades of the farm novel, to the inability of most of the writers to create memorable characters. Here as in other respects the fact is that the highest talent among

[14] Sherman, "The Development of American Rural Fiction," p. 75.

American novelists has not gone into the writing of farm fiction.

Mention has been made from time to time in this book of such literary movements as realism and naturalism, and the term "romantic" has occasionally been applied to the farm novels discussed. Some general remarks on the subject of literary fashions seem called for, in order to relate the farm novel to the main body of American fiction. Despite Garland's emphasis on "veritism," as exemplified in such early works as *Main-Travelled Roads*, his imitators and many other writers in the first two or three decades of the twentieth century tended to adopt a romantic approach to their subject matter. Halford E. Luccock, writing in 1934, professed to find a stock attitude of "homesick piety" in literature about farm life written prior to and for a few years after World War I. He regarded Herbert Quick as being mostly in this romantic tradition, which produced a reaction of extreme soberness in the work of Martha Ostenso and Ruth Suckow.[15] John T. Flanagan, in an important article written in 1942, took much the same view of farm fiction published up to the middle 1920's. The novels of Willa Cather, in Flanagan's opinion, represented the finest achievement in the romantic school, which ended with *Giants in the Earth*, just as an earlier romantic treatment of the farmer may be said to have come to an end with the publication of *Main-Travelled Roads*.[16]

Romanticism in the realm of farm fiction did not die in the 1920's, however, at least not if we use the term "romantic" as it has been used in Chapter VI of this book. Some of Miss Ostenso's novels, those by Lorna Doone Beers, and Krause's *Wind Without Rain* have all been characterized as romantic in tone and subject. But unquestionably other novels, such as those of MacLeod and Corey, are predominantly realistic, and a realistic use of detail has been evident in practically all farm fiction of the past thirty years or more. Unless we except the rural idylls of Phil Stong and some extremely trivial works, there has been nothing that could be termed "escape literature" in the realm of farm fiction; nor has there been any development of fantasy akin to Cabell's

[15] Halford E. Luccock, *Contemporary American Literature and Religion* (Chicago and New York: Willett, Clark & Co., 1934), pp. 93–98.

[16] Flanagan, "The Middle Western Farm Novel," pp. 116–117.

Jurgen. Most farm novels have been matter-of-fact, down to earth, concerned chiefly with the accurate portrayal of farm life. Even when the characters selected have resembled those of romantic fiction, the background has been presented realistically.

Virtually all of the farm novels discussed here were published subsequent to the American appearance of the school termed "naturalism," and so they might reasonably be expected to show the influence of that movement. Except for Garland's earliest work, however, none of the farm fiction produced before 1920 can be called naturalistic, if by naturalistic writing one means that which displays the characteristics specified by Parrington: objectivity, amorality, frankness, determinism, pessimism in the selection of details, and pessimism in the selection of characters. The first evidence of this approach in farm fiction appears in Haldeman-Julius' *Dust* (1921), and the applicability of the term "naturalistic" to this novel is debatable. G. D. Eaton's *Backfurrow* (1925) is a much better example, while Walter J. Muilenburg's *Prairie*, published the same year, also contains naturalistic features.

Possibly a better term to apply to these novels and to the later work of Leroy MacLeod and Paul Corey is "post-naturalistic realism." They tend to display some of the characteristics of naturalism but not all or even a majority of them. Objectivity and frankness are generally found in these novels; they reveal perhaps as much amorality as do such admittedly naturalistic works as Norris' *The Octopus* or Dreiser's *An American Tragedy*. Some appear to reflect a philosophy of determinism, while others place a heavy burden of individual responsibility on their characters. The practice in this investigation has been to apply the term "naturalistic" only to those novels displaying more or less of a deterministic attitude on the part of the author. Some writers, such as Eaton, seem to choose their details and characters so as to produce a gloomy view of life, but a pessimistic outlook is not restricted to authors otherwise in the naturalistic tradition. Wescott and Krause, for instance, tend to center their attention on the maladjusted and neurotic types which Parrington found in Sherwood Anderson and regarded as indications of the naturalistic technique; yet both authors display other qualities that entitle them to be called "romantic" and have been so dealt with in previous chapters. All this may only underscore the point that naturalism is a slippery term, both easy and difficult to apply to particular novels, depending on what evidence one cites to prove his case.[17]

One thing is obvious: the writers of farm fiction do not group themselves neatly into schools. Rather, they tend to reflect, somewhat tardily, the movements and schools prevalent among the writers of non-farm fiction. In some instances, authors can be classified on the basis of resemblance to other writers generally considered naturalists or realists or romanticists; in other cases, their novels can be placed in appropriate categories according to the degree to which they illustrate the chief principles of naturalism; in a few rare instances, such as that of Sophus Keith Winther, the author's open avowal of a belief in determinism may simplify the problem of classification.[18] But in many cases, novelists cut across conventional lines of demarcation and can be discussed as naturalists in some respects and romanticists in others. Thus Holger Cahill, in a novel titled *The Shadow of My Hand* (1956), combines a romantic, even melodramatic, plot with extremely naturalistic detail.

It may be profitable, by way of illustration, to trace one naturalistic trait through the entire period covered by this study and see what stages it has passed through. Presumably as a result of the naturalistic influence, American fiction has become increasingly frank in its treatment of sex in the twentieth century. In the two decades around the turn of the century, Crane, Norris, and Dreiser treated sex with a reticence that contrasts sharply with the later handling of the subject by Hemingway, Farrell, Steinbeck, and others. Frankness became considerably more pro-

[17] The problem of applying this and other terms to individual novelists is further complicated by the tendency of critics and biographers to use these terms in a variety of ways. Fred B. Millett, for instance, calls Willa Cather a "genteel realist" and Edna Ferber a "sentimental realist." (Millett, *Contemporary American Authors*, pp. 25–26.) Such categories as these, though useful once their meaning is agreed upon, require explanations on the part of the person using them and perhaps some reorientation on the part of the reader.

[18] Desmond Powell, "Sophus Winther: The Grimsen Trilogy," *American Scandinavian Review*, XXXVI (June 1948), 146.

nouneed in the 1920's and reached at least a temporary plateau in the 1930's with the appearance in novels of the four-letter Anglo-Saxon words heretofore proscribed.

As with other naturalistic traits, the farm novel lagged slightly behind the general body of fiction in the matter of frankness, though not far. Garland's treatment of sex in *Rose of Dutcher's Coolly* is said to have drawn objections from some critics, but today it seems innocuous enough. Not until the 1920's did farm fiction begin to give a conspicuous place to sex, in such novels as Eaton's *Backfurrow* and Wescott's *The Grandmothers*. Rölvaag seems to have expected criticism of his treatment of sex in *Peder Victorious*,[19] but there is nothing about this novel, published in 1929, that strikes the reader of the 1960's as particularly daring. Sex comes in for a good deal of attention in Leroy Mac-Leod's novels in the early 1930's, but it is only with the appearance of Paul Corey's trilogy at the end of the decade that frankness in farm fiction can be said to have reached the level of Farrell's earlier works or Steinbeck's *The Grapes of Wrath* (1939). Krause gives the subject less attention in *Wind Without Rain* than Corey does in *Three Miles Square* (both 1939), but by the time of *The Thresher* (1946), he has clearly come up with the procession. Feikema's *This Is the Year* (1947), strongly naturalistic in tone, carries the process about as far as it has been carried by non-farm novelists. And Cahill's *The Shadow of My Hand* admits even the subject of homosexuality, treated in the argot of the hobo fraternity.

As might be expected, many novelists have refused to follow the dominant trend. Except for Martha Ostenso and Lorna Doone Beers, who treat sex frequently but with much restraint, the women novelists of the period under consideration are characterized by an almost Victorian reticence. This is true of Ruth Suckow (in her distinctively farm fiction), Edna Ferber, Rose Wilder Lane, Josephine Donovan, Josephine Johnson, and especially Bess Streeter Aldrich, with whom it is a matter of deliberate policy. Some of the men, even as late as Horace Kramer, whose *Marginal Land* appeared in 1939, give the appearance of a similar reticence, while others, such as Sterling North and Phil Stong,

[19] Jorgenson and Solum, *Ole Edvart Rölvaag*, p. 381.

both of whom wrote in the early 1930's, display much greater frankness, and David McLaughlin, whose *Lightning Before Dawn* appeared in 1938, permits his handling of sex to border on obscenity.

Other naturalistic traits are more difficult to trace from decade to decade, partly because in some cases the general pattern in American fiction is not one of simple progression in one direction. Determinism, for example, seems less attractive now than it did in 1900. In fact, the strict mechanical determinism that Dreiser seems to endorse in *The Financier* (1912) had largely gone out of fashion by the time the farm novel developed as a significant literary genre and hence can hardly be said to be reflected at all in farm fiction. It is true, however, that the characteristics of naturalism which have survived in the body of American fiction do appear in many farm novels, along with romantic features that persist from a time antedating the arrival of naturalism in the United States.

Whether the waning of the vogue of the farm novel in the late 1940's and early 1950's represents a permanent trend or only a temporary one remains to be seen. One long-time student of farm fiction, writing during World War II, pointed out that the "intensification of the war interest means a time of peace for rural literature," but concluded that after this fallow period it would revive, better than ever.[20] The evidence indicates, however, that farm fiction will never regain the popularity it had in the 1930's. With the continuing decline in the number of people engaged in farming, the potential reading public of the farm novel will presumably also decrease in numbers, and as an art form it will lose much of its appeal. It is unlikely that it will ever develop into the romantic, nostalgic sort of thing represented by the treatment of the Indian in some of the imitators of Cooper, for this would be in conflict with modern literary tastes. Anyone aspiring to success in the realm of farm fiction in the future may have to reckon with the possibility of his work being read by a higher proportion of actual farmers than ever before, since labor-saving machinery and modern farming techniques are

[20] Caroline B. Sherman, "Rural Literature Faces Peace," *South Atlantic Quarterly*, XLII (January 1943), 59, 71.

constantly increasing the leisure time of those who remain on the soil. In such an event, two types of novels would seem to have the greatest appeal: the kind that gives realistic and perceptive treatment to the problems of human relationships and the sort that deals with economic problems peculiar to agriculture. The former type will probably be distinguished from other novels dealing with the same subject only by its rural setting, since the cultural gap separating farm and city people is constantly narrowing, and consequently human relationships are likely to present in the future much the same problems on the farm as in the city. Thus Harnack's *Love and Be Silent* (1962) is perhaps representative of one direction that farm fiction seems to be taking. The second type mentioned need not be proletarian fiction, but it will come under the heading of fiction of social criticism. As such it will necessarily have to appeal to a public of urban people as well as farmers if it is to eventuate in social action, and so it is likely to include the most artistically satisfying kind of farm fiction. Mrs. Hudson's *The Bones of Plenty* (1962) may be a suggestion of things to come in this type of novel. The old theme of escape and return is not likely to receive much further attention, since the experience of a dwindling number of Americans will include a conflict over the desirability or undesirability of farming as a career.

Perhaps the chief service performed by the farm novel during the years of its greatest popularity was that suggested by Paul Corey at the end of his trilogy: to help enable all of the people to know intimately all sections of the country, to the end that social and economic conditions may be improved. By describing middle western farm life to the rest of the nation, these novels helped promote understanding among sections and among occupations. If the farm novel of the future can continue this function, it will justify its existence.

APPENDIX

AN ANNOTATED BIBLIOGRAPHY OF
MIDDLE WESTERN FARM FICTION, 1891–1962

The following list of middle western farm novels aims at some measure of completeness, although undoubtedly some novels have been overlooked in the compilation. The principal sources of information are the listings of *Book Review Digest* and John T. Flanagan, "A Bibliography of Middle Western Farm Novels," *Minnesota History*, XXIII (June 1942), 156–158. Some of these books are so trivial that subjecting them to serious criticism may seem like breaking butterflies on a wheel, but even the slightest of them reflect in some degree either a familiarity with farm life or a notion of what the reading public expected of farm fiction.

ALDRICH, BESS STREETER. *A Lantern in Her Hand*. New York and London: D. Appleton & Co., 1930. (Original copyright 1928, same publisher.) Life story of Abbie Deal, who comes west to Iowa as a child, marries, and goes on to Nebraska, where she raises a family and takes part in the development of the country in the period following the Civil War. Sentimental. Contains a good account of the early stages of community growth, but neglects its later development. Shows typical attitude toward pioneering: success crowns the pioneers' efforts, individually and collectively.

ALDRICH, BESS STREETER. *Song of Years*. New York and London: D. Appleton-Century Co., 1939. (Published serially in 1938.) Fictionalized account of the settlement and growth of the Waterloo-Cedar Falls, Iowa, area, centered about the affairs of Josiah Martin, leader in local and state politics, and his family of seven daughters. Detailed and convincing picture of settlement and early history of the locality. Sentimental in its treatment of the love plot. Little reference to farming.

ALLISON, JOY [pseudonym of Mary A. Cragin]. *Billow Prairie*. Chicago: Congregational Sunday-School & Publishing Society, 1892. Sunday-school tract with a farm setting. Family of nine come west to Kansas, meet with hardship and (temporary) failure. Wife deeply religious, husband not, works on Sunday and dies of exposure as a result. Sunday-school is formed by itinerant missionary and all major characters join. All marriageable characters are paired off by the end of the novel. Perseverence and prayer make even the hard soil of Kansas yield richly. Setting sketchy, characterization poor, style undistinguished, moralization oppressive.

AYDELOTTE, DORA. *Long Furrows*. New York: D. Appleton-Century Co., 1935. The story of a farm family in Shelby County, Illinois, in the 1890's, mostly as seen through the eyes of the eldest daughter, a girl in her teens. In the course of the story, she experiences the usual incidents of farm life, box socials at school, baptism, and finally marriage. A fair picture of life of the period among the congregation of a rural Methodist church.

AYDELOTTE, DORA. *Full Harvest*. New York: D. Appleton-Century Co., 1939. Further experiences of the same family. The mother persuades the father to move to town for the sake of the younger children. Adjustment is difficult, and when financial reverses compel them to sell their house and return to the farm, everyone is glad to do so. Both novels stress the life of this particular family without much attention to daily farm routine or to economic conditions. The point of view is feminine in both novels, and a great deal is said about matters of housework, social activities, and the like. Nothing about the style of either book raises it above the commonplace.

BAYLEY, MARJORIE. *In Friends We Trust*. New York: Coward-McCann, 1938. Improbable but engaging tale of Johnny Hincks, a lonely old widower, who invites four bums from the hobo jungle to live with him on his Nebraska farm. In the four months covered by the novel, the four become involved in Johnny's affairs, and two of them undertake to help him save his farm from the clutches of the local banker. These two, Rogers Ingen, a onetime New York banker, and a woman of doubtful antecedents named Jess, also provide most of the love interest and marry at the end. Dialogue realistic, characterization uneven. Not much about specifically rural activities or problems.

BEERS, LORNA DOONE [Mrs. C. R. Chambers]. *Prairie Fires*. New York: E. P. Dutton & Co., 1925. Fictionalized account of the formation of the Nonpartisan League in North Dakota 1912–1916, unsuccessfully fused with love story of Christine Erickson, daughter of farmer active in League work, and Christian Lövstad, small-town banker and hence archfoe of farmers. League is successful, but Christine is disillusioned by her Torvald Helmer–like husband. She resists opportunity for extramarital liaison with Benjamin Paul, erratic agricultural college instructor, however, and dutifully sticks by her husband. Better in its treatment of the historical background than in its handling of love plot.

BEERS, LORNA DOONE. *A Humble Lear.* New York: E. P. Dutton & Co., 1929. Reworking of Shakespeare's theme in setting of Blue Heron township, Hennepin County, Minnesota, about 1890. After the death of his wife, Adam Webb divides his land between his sons, neglecting his daughter Cordelia because her love for him has been inadequately expressed and seems the product of duty rather than spontaneous. Disillusioned by his sons and their wives, he is finally made happy by Cordelia. Characterization uneven, treatment of subject generally restrained and realistic. Some fine scenes.

BEERS, LORNA DOONE. *The Mad Stone.* New York: E. P. Dutton & Co., 1932. Interlude in the lives of Lewis Ludlow, ex-Baptist minister, now Nietzschean nihilist, working on book about historical interpretations of Jesus, and Ollie Hackett, erring wife sent by her husband to his parents to remove her from temptation. After a brief affair, she returns to her husband and Ludlow returns to his wife, renounces his book, and decides to study some branch of science and make contribution there. Neurotics themselves, they accentuate neurotic tendencies in those about them. Characters improbable because of extreme maladjustment, style competent. Little about farm life.

BELLAMANN, HENRY. *Floods of Spring.* New York: Simon & Schuster, 1942. Peter Kettring, son of Philadelphia minister, wearies of world of books, marries Pennsylvania Dutch girl and buys farm in Missouri, where he isolates himself. Alienation from one son and death of another and of his wife (in a spring flood) lead him finally to reconsider his determination to discard civilization and start from the bottom. Well conceived and well written, if unspectacular, this novel shows close familiarity with farm life and with Pennsylvania Dutch speech and literature.

BLAKE, ELEANOR [Mrs. B. K. Pratt]. *Seedtime and Harvest.* New York: G. P. Putnam's Sons, 1935. Novel about the successive pregnancies of Else (Jacobson) Martison, starting before her marriage and continuing to the end of the book, nineteen years later. The daughter of Norwegian immigrants to a primitive section of Michigan, Else is bored with farm life and has hopes of escaping. Before her marriage and frequently thereafter, she dreams of joining a sister in

California, but each time her plans are frustrated by pregnancy. Eventually she abandons the notion and settles into a stolidity almost like that of her husband. Perhaps the dream of escape will be realized in her daughter Bergit. The theme of seedtime and harvest is so prominent that Else becomes little more than a fertility symbol. Fairly skillful treatment of the changing status of the farm woman.

BOYD, THOMAS A. *Samuel Drummond.* New York: Charles Scribner's Sons, 1925. Life story of an Ohio farmer in the middle and later nineteenth century. Samuel marries a girl chosen by his parents but defies his father's wishes by joining the Union army in the Civil War, mainly to escape criticism from neighbors, who regard the Drummonds as Copperheads. Upon his return, he finds his farm neglected. From this point on, his fortunes decline as a combination of bad luck and bad management push him ever deeper into debt, finally into bankruptcy and premature retirement. Samuel, a very unheroic hero, cloddish, indecisive, passive, contentedly ignorant, cuts a sorry figure against a background only thinly sketched.

BOYLES, KATE and VIRGIL D. *The Homesteaders.* Chicago: A. C. McClurg & Co., 1909. Conventional western romance played against background of conflict between cattlemen and homesteaders in trans-Missouri region of Dakota Territory. Josephine and John Calhoun ("Jack") Carroll, brother and sister, leave Virginia and attempt farming but encounter resistance of cattlemen. One of these, Tom Burrington, falls in love with Josephine and protects her, but Jack is killed by improbably wicked villain. Standard setting for love stories. Generally undistinguished, novel has one good feature: realistic and colorful description of Wild West celebration on Indian reservation.

BRENEMAN, MARY WORTHY [pseud. of Mary Worthy Thurston and Muriel Breneman]. *The Land They Possessed.* New York: Macmillan Co., 1956. This novel deals with pioneering in northern South Dakota in the last two decades of the nineteenth century, centered about the family of John Ward, whose daughter Michal is the central intelligence. The plot revolves about Michal's growing up, against a background of townsite-booms, blizzards, drought, and prairie fires. A major theme is the relationship between the Wards, self-consciously "Anglo-Saxon" and snobbish (except for Michal), and the Russo-Germans whose success as farmers is resented by the Wards. When, at the end of the novel, Michal elopes with Karl Gross, her father disowns her. Despite stock furniture of the pioneering saga, the treatment of the theme is superior to most novels of its type, though inferior to Cather and Rölvaag. Details and dialogue are realistic, plot and view of pioneering, romantic.

BROMFIELD, LOUIS. *The Farm.* New York and London: Harper & Brothers, 1933. Volume of reminiscences and genealogical information centered about people and forces that have gone to produce Johnny Willingdon, the central character. Covers more than a century, multitude of characters. Unified by fierce hostility toward commercialism and nostalgia for pre-industrial America. Difficult reading, because of multiplicity of characters, this novel is valuable as re-creation of history, as seen by author, but his interpretation must be qualified if balanced view is to be arrived at.

BROMFIELD, LOUIS. *The Wild Country.* New York: Harper & Brothers, 1948. Eighteenth-century tale of seduction and revenge placed in setting of baronial estate of Judge Stillcombe in Missouri in twentieth century. Henry Benson has married reformed streetwalker, originally seduced by Wayne Torrance, protégé of the Judge. When Torrance tries to repeat the performance, she pushes him off a cliff. Melodramatic, not to be compared with *The Farm.*

CAHILL, HOLGER. *The Shadow of My Hand.* New York: Harcourt, Brace & Co., 1956. Cameron Johnson, veteran of World War II and Korea, returns to his home town of Buffalo Coulee, N. Dak., to re-establish contact with his past and his native soil. He takes a job on the large Red River Valley farm of John Durham, hoping to stay on as a renter, falls in love with Millie Shaw, Durham's sister-in-law, and finds the course of love anything but smooth because of Durham's proprietary interest in Millie and his insane jealousy of any man who looks at her. When Durham learns of Cam's relationship with her, he tries to kill the young man, only to be killed in the ensuing fight. Despite this melodramatic plot and a tendency toward talkiness, this is a strong novel, with skillfully managed dialogue, some memorable characterization, and a well-realized theme—the relationship between man and the earth that he exploits.

CANNON, CORNELIA. *Red Rust.* Boston: Little, Brown & Co., 1928. Account of development of rust-resistant strain of wheat by Matts Swenson, son of Swedish immigrants to Minnesota. Underrated because of his taste for reading and his inaptitude for farm work, Matts marries a widow much his senior after her tyrannical husband has been killed, nearly falls in love with his stepdaughter, is shot by his epileptic stepson, and dies just as his strain of wheat is proved successful. Often sentimental and melodramatic, its characters wooden, its final tragedy unmotivated, the novel attains some merit through the development of its theme: man's ability to alter nature to his own purposes.

CATHER, WILLA. *O Pioneers!* Boston: Houghton Mifflin Co., 1937. (Originally published 1913.) Novel of Nebraska farm life centered about Alexandra Bergson, daughter of Swedish immigrants. Capable, imaginative, determined to succeed, she operates the farm after the death of her father, comes through years of drought to success. Illicit love affair between her brother Emil and Marie Shabata ends in killing of both by Marie's husband, darkens Alexandra's life. She forgives her brother's murderer and at end of novel decides to marry Carl Linstrum, artist son of another immigrant family who were forced out in the dry years. A truly distinguished farm novel.

CATHER, WILLA. *My Ántonia.* Boston: Houghton Mifflin Co., 1937. (Originally published in 1918.) Life history of Ántonia Shimerda, daughter of Bohemian immigrants to Nebraska in 1870's, as seen by Jim Burden, who spends part of his youth with his grandparents near the Shimerdas. Ántonia grows up on the farm inured to hard work, has experience as a servant girl in town, undergoes a disillusioning love affair, finally marries a man of her own group and fulfills her destiny as a farm wife and mother. On a par with, and perhaps superior to, *O Pioneers!, My Ántonia* is one of the few great farm novels.

CATHER, WILLA. *One of Ours.* New York: Alfred A. Knopf, 1922. Life story of Claude Wheeler, a Nebraska farm boy who, after years of drifting, finds a meaning and purpose in life as a soldier in World War I, only to be killed in the closing days of the war. Raised on a farm, Claude goes away to college but drops out when called home to operate the family farm. Here he blunders into an unsuccessful marriage, which collapses when his wife goes to China as a missionary. He then enlists, and the rest of the novel is concerned with his military career and the broadening of his character through association with Europeans. A slighter novel than *O Pioneers!* and *My Ántonia,* vitiated by its idealistic view of war, *One of Ours* nonetheless contains subtle characterization and some exploration of the complexities of human relationships.

COATES, GRACE STONE. *Black Cherries.* New York: Alfred A. Knopf, 1931. A farm novel only incidentally and for part of its course, this book deals with the theme of a tyrannical father and the effects of his tyranny on the children. Henry Von S— reveres the memory of his first wife but is hostile toward their children and toward his second wife but indulgent toward his children by the latter. Given to speculation, he loses his Kansas farm after a hailstorm destroys the crop into which he has sunk his resources, makes and loses a fortune in the city, and winds up the bitter inmate of an old soldiers' home, abandoned by all his children except Genevieve, who is the central intelligence. Most of the story is told from the point of view of a child, and the language is suggestive rather than expository.

COOK, FANNIE. *Boot-Heel Doctor.* New York: Dodd, Mead & Co., 1941. Fictionalized account of flood in Missouri "boot-heel" section, followed by sharecropper demonstration along highways in protest against attempts by landowners to reduce them to level of day laborers. Actual events took place in 1938–1939. Novel is centered about personality of Dr. Joel Gregory, associated by birth and social standing with the landowners but sympathetic to sharecroppers. Reuben Fielding, Negro farmer and minister, is leader of demonstration, despite anti-Negro feeling among whites of all social classes. Nearest approach to proletarian fiction in the middle western farm novel. Style competent, reproduction of local speech and mores good.

CORBETT, ELIZABETH FRANCES. *Faye's Folly.* New York: D. Appleton-Century Co., 1941. Sentimental love story with a farm setting. Sheba Faye, seventeen when the novel begins in 1864, falls in love with Jim Warner, husband of her best friend, Rose, who is carrying on a dalliance with Pierce Bigelow, a Copperhead, while Jim is in the Union army. After many vicissitudes, Rose and Pierce run off together, Jim gets a divorce, and he and Sheba finally marry. Except for Sheba, the major characters are somewhat improbable: her father, who dies midway through the book, is too perfect, Bigelow is a stereotyped villain, the Dobbin-like Jim is too noble for complete credulity, and Rose is too frivolous to be entirely acceptable as Sheba's best friend. Little treatment of farm life, no exploration of important issues.

COREY, PAUL. *Three Miles Square.* Indianapolis and New York: Bobbs-Merrill Co., 1939. First volume in Mantz trilogy. Mrs. Mantz, just widowed, decides to keep the farm, plans to have oldest son run it until he is twenty-one, then go to school and turn farm over to next son, and so forth. Andrew is the hero, for he runs the farm despite Wolmar's and Verney's wishes to move to town. Otto, still a child, learns about Socialism from a cook on a dredge crew. Taken by itself, this novel is incomplete, for its issues are unresolved at the end, to be carried further in the other two novels. Corey's strongest point is his convincingly realistic handling of details and character. His novels may be charged with a lack of emotional power.

COREY, PAUL. *The Road Returns*. Indianapolis and New York: Bobbs-Merrill Co., 1940. Covers the period 1917–1923 in the lives of the Mantz family. Wolmar and Otto run the farm, while Andrew studies architecture, then is drafted. Upon his return from the war, he has lost interest in school, and Mrs. Mantz sells the farm. Wolmar works in a garage, sets up his own. Otto attends high school, saves money to go to college. In the post-war depression, the buyer of the farm is unable to meet his payments, and it comes back to the Mantzes. Good treatment of the anti-German hysteria in 1918 and the influenza epidemic after the war.

COREY, PAUL. *County Seat*. Indianapolis and New York: Bobbs-Merrill Co., 1941. Third in the Mantz family trilogy. Andrew, who has occupied the center of attention in the first two novels, slips into the background after the collapse of the contracting firm in which he is a partner. Wolmar, operating a garage (the "successful" member of the family), keeps going, although slipping ever deeper into debt. Otto, the youngest son, at the State University of Iowa, has a sordid affair with a home-town girl, gets a job in Chicago, loses it in the depression of 1929, and finally comes home to take over the family farm. The trilogy ends on a note of reconciliation to the soil. Heavily documented with realistic detail, written in a straightforward, rather flat style, these books constitute important contributions to the farm novel.

COREY, PAUL. *Acres of Antaeus*. New York: Henry Holt & Co., 1946. A somewhat propagandistic novel about the efforts of large corporations to supplant the small independent farmer. Jim Buckly, needing work during the depression, takes a job with Midwest Farms. Although refusing to pass judgment on the ends or means of his employer, Jim is forced into a difficult situation when he marries a girl whose father is being forced off the home farm by the insurance company backing Midwest Farms. Novel ends with a change in management in Midwest, promising cooperation with the small farmer, and with a resolution to Jim's domestic difficulties. The basic problem remains, however, and so the novel is unsatisfying in terms of its apparent purpose. Displays the same literary qualities as Corey's other novels.

CROY, HOMER. *R.F.D. No. 3*. New York and London: Harper & Brothers, 1924. Josie Decker, daughter of northwest Missouri farmer, enters a beauty contest and allows her head to be turned. Backing out of marriage to a local farmer on her wedding day, she runs off with silo salesman, Floyd Krock, comes home unmarried, deserted, and pregnant, finally agrees to marry Bushness Higbee, well-to-do widower who has been pursuing her for some time. This alliance resembles that of Zury Prouder and Anne Sparrow in Kirkland's *Zury*. Better than average popular novel of farm life, this book gives a good picture of the 1920's in a rural area.

DEJONG, DAVID CORNEL. *Light Sons and Dark*. New York and London: Harper & Brothers, 1940. A depressing and rather melodramatic tale of family disharmony, drought, debt, and general misery. Seen from the point of view of Joel Davis, the youngest son, the story is mostly about Ben, the eldest, who has returned to the family after a disillusioning try at marriage and now lives in increasing desperation on run-down farm inefficiently managed by their bumbling father. One son, Sutton, has left the farm and is now a rumrunner, married to a neighborhood slut named Ruby. The other two, Bruce and Marius, are unsympathetically portrayed, especially the former, who is thoroughly bad. The novel ends with Ben killing himself, Joel hitchhiking to New England in search of a job, and the parents and Marius moving to town. In its stress on the characters' inability to communicate with one another, this book resembles *Winesburg, Ohio*, to which it is otherwise far inferior.

DONOVAN, JOSEPHINE. *Black Soil*. Boston: Stratford Co., 1930. Account of pioneering in northwestern Iowa by Irish, German, and Dutch groups. Tim and Nell Connor, their children, and an adopted child, Sheila, endure the standard quota of blizzards, prairie fires, locust plagues, and economic difficulties but achieve success when the railroad establishes a town on their land. A few realistic touches, some melodrama. Unlike most farm novels, *Black Soil* treats Catholic community, seen from the inside.

DORRANCE, WARD ALLISON. *Sundowners*. New York: Charles Scribner's Sons, 1942. Sensitively told narrative about the first eighteen or nineteen years of a boy's life. Noel Fauquier Deslauriers lives with his maternal grandfather, Joseph Shelley, on a diminished estate called Saukston overlooking the Missouri River not far from Jefferson City, Mo. Instead of a conventional plot, the novel is made up of a series of anecdotes, reminiscent of *Death Comes for the Archbishop*, each illustrative of some phase of the history and culture of the region. Among the best are those told by Mary Corncob, descendant of Osages and Shawnees. Exposition is handled by means of incremental revelation; the reader learns as Noel does. Except for Joseph's change of character after his second marriage, characterization is consistent, if not strongly effective. Noel himself is largely passive and ineffectual. Best is perhaps Edward Ratcliff, hunter and occasional farmer.

DOWNING, JOHN HYATT. *The Harvest Is Late.* New York: Hampton Publishing Co., 1944. Study of conflict between farming and town life. Peter Oliver worked up from farm hand to owner of Sundown, then allowed his wife to persuade him to become banker in small South Dakota town of Acadia. She wants him to sell farm, but he refuses. In depression of 1920–1921 he mortgages farm to avoid having to foreclose on farmers. Then bank fails, and he loses everything, becomes section hand on railroad. His wife leaves him, but old friends buy back Sundown and give it to him. In middle age, he has found his real occupation. Extramarital affair with Dr. Lydia Brayden is handled with restraint. Peter resembles Silas Lapham, both in his general integrity and in his occasional lapses from strict rectitude.

EATON, GEOFFREY DELL. *Backfurrow.* New York: G. P. Putnam's Sons, 1925. Grim, naturalistic treatment of Michigan farm life in first quarter of twentieth century. Ralph Dutton, of illegitimate birth, grows up in harsh rural environment, escapes to Detroit but is forced by economic pressures to return to the country. Gradually saving money, he is about ready to leave for the city again when he becomes involved with Ellen Tupper, marries her, and becomes a farmer for life. He suffers a succession of misfortunes, including illness, debt, and crop failure, ends up resigned to a hopeless fate. Structurally faulty, with large unassimilated chunks of exposition, this novel is significant as the strongest attack on the farm in the whole body of farm fiction. Paralleling Frederick's *Green Bush* (q.v.), published the same year, in many factual details, it arrives at opposite resolution.

ENGLE, PAUL. *Always the Land.* New York: Random House, 1941. A love story with overtones of social criticism, set against a background of horse racing in the Cedar Rapids, Iowa, area. Joe Meyer runs a farm and stables in cooperation with his grandfather, Jay, although they take opposite views on such matters as government aid to farmers. Jay has support in his conservatism from Henry Hope, an old horseman who works briefly at the Meyer farm, but when Henry dies, at the end of the novel, the prospect is that Joe, who has fallen in love with Jerrie Holmes, another racing enthusiast and daughter of an old enemy of Jay's, will win out in the controversy. Characterization and dialogue good, representation of rural attitudes accurate, main plot not memorable.

ERDMAN, LOULA GRACE. *The Years of the Locust.* New York: Dodd, Mead & Co., 1947. Third of thirteen novels turned out by this author between 1944 and 1960, covers the three days following the death of old Dade Kenzie, well-to-do Missouri farmer and clan patriarch. As the news of his death reaches his relatives and friends, it starts a train of recollections, especially in his children, who have scattered and are besieged by various troubles. The funeral brings them all together and leads to the solution of most of their problems. Good treatment of varied types within a family. Characterization is uneven. Best is that of Harlan, a farm boy turned novelist, who is a sensitive artist but petty in his personal behavior. There is little about the details of farm life, since most of the characters have left the farm.

ERDMAN, LOULA GRACE. *The Short Summer.* New York: Dodd, Mead & Co., 1958. Two months in the summer of 1914 in the lives of the Will Gregory family, centered about the romance of Margie, eighteen, and Scott Montgomery, distant relative of Will's sister-in-law. Each chapter concerns a social gathering—a chautauqua, a W.C.T.U. meeting, a threshing, a band concert, etc. The histories of several characters are woven into the main plot. Again, solutions to problems are found, and the novel ends happily for most of the characters. Competently written light fiction.

ERICKSON, HOWARD. *Son of Earth.* New York: Dial Press, 1933. Unsuccessful blend of naturalism and sentimentalism. Tolf Luvversen, brought to Iowa from Denmark as a child, grows up under the tyranny of a stepfather, works as farm hand for Danish farmers and, later, for native Americans. Ambitious to become like the "English," i.e., English-speaking Americans, he falls in love with a shallow American girl who treats him with contempt and finally marries someone else. Tolf is shattered by this experience, rapidly becomes a drunken bum, but is finally rehabilitated by marriage to daughter of one of the Danish farmers he worked for. She dominates him, however, through her ownership of the farm, and he lives on as little more than a hired hand. He hopes that his children will realize his ambitions. Characters are largely caricatures, dialogue is wooden, and many events (such as Tolf's reaction to his unhappy love affair) are overdrawn. Time is 1895–1920.

FALSTAFF, JAKE [pseud. of Herman Fetzer]. *Come Back to Wayne County.* Boston: Houghton Mifflin Co., 1942. A collection of sketches, originally published separately, centered about Lemuel Hayden, a New York boy who spends a summer (or perhaps several) in Wayne County, Ohio, mostly at the farm of Ora Weiler, who is married to

Lemuel's cousin. Some of the stories have touches of local color ("Mushrat Geer," about a trapper and hunter who provides fish illegally to a road house), but many of the rambling anecdotes are pointless, the characters two-dimensional, and the philosophizing amateurish. Melodrama enters with the story "Pete Gurdy's Rig," about a man noted for his unsociability who unexpectedly appears, alone, at a pioneers' picnic, then goes home and hangs himself. Later it is learned that he has killed his wife two weeks before.

FEIKEMA, FEIKE [Frederick F. Manfred]. *This Is the Year.* Garden City, N.Y.: Doubleday & Co., 1947. Enormously detailed account of the period 1916–1936 in the life of Pier Frixen, son of Frisian immigrants in extreme northwestern Iowa. Pier marries, takes over the family farm, and prospers for a time. He mistreats both his wife and his land, however, and in the 1920's he begins to have trouble, culminating in the death of his wife during a miscarriage and the loss of his farm to the local bank. A conservation tract as well as a story of human character, this novel ranks as one of the most significant farm novels in recent years. Characterization of Pier is convincing and consistent, use of Frisian legend and language is effective, and use of detail is good, if somewhat overabundant.

FERBER, EDNA. *So Big.* New York: Grosset & Dunlap, 1924. Life history of Selina Peake DeJong and of her son Dirk, nicknamed "So Big." Daughter of a professional gambler, Selina is thrown on her own resources when he dies. She tries teaching school in the High Prairie truck-farming district near Chicago and there marries a stolid Dutch farmer, who later dies and leaves her with a small son on whom she fixes all her hopes. She educates Dirk and sees him materially successful, but it is clear that he is superficial and lacks her qualities of character. Largely an attack on American materialism in the 1920's (Dirk is a bond salesman), this novel has little to say about typical farm life, although Selina remains a truck farmer all her life. Except for a shift from Selina to Dirk midway in the book, *So Big* has no conspicuous technical faults and carries its message effectively.

FERNALD, HELEN CLARK. *Plow the Dew Under.* New York: Longmans, Green & Co., 1952. A simply written story, intended for juvenile readers, about Crimean immigrants to Kansas. Ilya Palevsky runs away from his Mennonite community, works in town and learns English, later goes to Kansas City and becomes part owner of a bakery specializing in hard-wheat crackers. At the end of the novel he returns to the Gnadenau settlement to marry his childhood sweetheart. Although American freedom of opportunity is glorified, the author does not ignore the intolerance shown toward immigrants. The solidarity of the Mennonite group is well described.

FIELDS, JONATHAN. *The Memoirs of Dunstan Barr*. New York: Coward-McCann, 1959. A slow-moving family chronicle centered about the career of Dunstan Barr, twenty when the novel begins in 1890. A farmer by inclination, heir to the seven-hundred-acre Barr estate in Illinois, he is obliged by circumstances to devote most of his life to banking. The novel recounts his three love affairs, the third ending in marriage to Mary Howard, and the divergent careers of his two brothers and four sisters, his four children, and numerous other relatives and friends. Wealthy, educated, thoroughly civilized, the Barr family none the less experiences its share of tragedy. The tone of the novel is subdued, the style leisurely and somewhat old-fashioned.

FRANK, ARMIN. *The Flesh of Kings*. Garden City, N.Y.: Doubleday & Co., 1958. A tale of hatred and violence, told in a heightened style, about the feud between the Diskos, southwestern Ohio farmers, and the Spicers, their shiftless, degenerate neighbors. Coit Disko, partially paralyzed in an automobile crash that killed his wife, and his sons Harper and Rancell are the central figures. Regarded by the townsfolk of Zion as half-civilized, they retaliate with contempt and gradually isolate themselves. Even participation by the sons in the Korean War does nothing to break down this isolation. In a horrifying climax, both sons and two of the Spicers are killed. An impressive novel, despite overwriting and a perilously close approach to melodrama.

FREDERICK, JOHN T. *Druida*. New York: Alfred A. Knopf, 1923. The childhood and youth of Druida Horsfall, daughter of Mrs. Oscar Horsfall and a mysterious hired man named Ed Brown, who worked briefly on the Horsfall farm in west-central Minnesota. Druida is intelligent and sensitive, and she is apparently unaffected by her miserable childhood under the tyranny of her brutal "father," Oscar, and the alternating love and mistreatment of her neurotic mother. A fortuitous meeting with an English instructor at the nearby normal school leads her to do the preparatory work necessary for entrance into that school. There she assimilates all the place has to offer, innocently gets herself expelled and the instructor dismissed, and finally decides to marry Bud Madsen, a neighbor boy who is about to take up land in Montana. The plot contains many improbabilities, and the treatment of Druida's relationships with men tends to be melodramatic, but the novel is a fairly successful statement of the desirability of an active rather than a passive life and a defense of farm life as opposed to town life.

FREDERICK, JOHN T. *Green Bush.* New York: Alfred A. Knopf, 1925. Another and stronger defense of farm life. The central character, Frank Thompson, grows up in a Lake Huron town where his father combines newspaper publishing with small-scale farming, against the wishes of the mother, who, after the father's death, deprives the son of both farm and paper and obliges him to continue his academic training at the state university. But he marries and returns to Green Bush after his mother's death, to begin farming again and to go on editing the newspaper. Seriously injured, he nevertheless retains his faith in the land. A far better novel than *Druida*, *Green Bush* is both an affirmation of the reconciliation-to-the-soil theme and a penetrating treatment of maternal domination and its effects on children.

GARLAND, HAMLIN. *Main-Travelled Roads.* Boston: Arena Publishing Co., 1891. Consisting originally of six Mississippi Valley stories (later enlarged), laid chiefly in Iowa and Wisconsin, this book may be regarded as the starting point of middle western farm fiction. Best-known story is "Under the Lion's Paw," a powerful object lesson on the evils of unearned increment in land. Timothy Haskins, defeated in Kansas by drought and grasshoppers, buys a farm in Iowa at an agreed-upon price to be paid at the end of a specified time. When that time comes, the owner asks not only the original price but the added valuation produced by Haskins' improvements. Less known, but perhaps equally good is "Up the Coulé" (Garland's spelling), in which a farm boy, long absent in the city, returns to the family farm a success, to find the members of his family still in poverty, his brother resentful of his success. The existing state of affairs, Garland seems to say, offers no solution to such problems. The other stories, "A Branch Road," "Among the Corn-Rows," "The Return of a Private," and "Mrs. Ripley's Trip," all have merits of their own and an authentic flavor similar to those outlined.

GARLAND, HAMLIN. *Jason Edwards: An Average Man.* Boston: Arena Publishing Co., 1892. Attempt to show that the farm is no longer an escape for surplus urban population. Jason Edwards, a Boston foundry worker living in chronic poverty, flees to Boomtown, South Dakota, where he buys a farm. A succession of bad years causes him to lose the farm, and he is saved from the poor house only by the intervention of a prosperous son-in-law, Walter Reeves, who has been pursuing Edwards' daughter throughout the novel and who now takes the whole family to a New Hampshire farm. Good picture of conditions in a frontier community and also of conditions in Boston slum areas. Plot contains numerous points of doubtful plausibility, such as Reeves' relatively disinterested guardianship of the Edwards family.

GARLAND, HAMLIN. *Prairie Folks*. New York and London: Harper & Brothers, 1892. Collection of eleven stories written about the same time as those in *Main-Travelled Roads* but generally inferior to them. Best perhaps are "Lucretia Burns," a portrait of a farm woman, overworked and lonely, who rebels against her husband, and "Daddy Deering," a good character sketch of a hard-driving old man who loses his place as favorite fiddler at dances when tastes change; weakened by melodramatic ending. Some, like "Elder Pill," are overly didactic; others, like "Drifting Crane," are romantic; still others, like "A Day of Grace," are trivial.

GARLAND, HAMLIN. *A Spoil of Office*. Boston: Arena Publishing Co., 1892. The outstanding contemporary treatment in fiction of the Populist movement. Bradley Talcott, a farm boy with no strong political leanings, discovers that he has forensic talent, comes under the influence of political leaders in his Iowa locality, and soon becomes active in politics, first as an Independent Republican, then as a Democrat, and finally, as a member of the People's Party. More effective as propaganda than as literature, yet the novel has good features, such as the treatment of Bradley's disillusionment with political officeholders, both in Des Moines and later in Washington.

GARLAND, HAMLIN. *Rose of Dutcher's Coolly*. New York: Macmillan Co., 1899. (Originally published in 1895.) Early example of the success-story type of farm novel in which the central character leaves the farm and achieves success in the city. Rose Dutcher resembles Frederick's Druida in that she is intelligent and sensitive and is discovered by a teacher who persuades her to go to college, in this case the state university. Here she develops tastes and interests that render a return to the farm unsatisfying. She goes to Chicago, makes friends among influential people, and finally marries an urban newspaperman fifteen years her senior. The narrowness of farm life is not so evident here as in *Main-Travelled Roads*, but it is still the chief characteristic of that life to Garland. Rose's rise to fame and social success is too swift for complete plausibility, and her personality is greatly idealized.

GARLAND, HAMLIN. *Moccasin Ranch*. New York and London: Harper & Brothers, 1909. A romantic novelette about the first years of settlement on the Dakota prairie. Willard Burke and his wife Blanche take up land, but the ordeal of a prairie winter is too much for Blanche, already wearied of her husband's ineffectualness, and she begins an affair with Jim Rivers, part owner of a store. When she becomes pregnant, Rivers attempts to take her away but is stopped by his partner, Ed Bailey, who acts in the interests of the proprieties. At the end, however, Bailey, awed by the complexities of the situation, withdraws his objections, and they leave. Garland's picture of life on the prairie is excellent, presumably drawn from personal experience, and redeems an otherwise unimportant novel from failure.

GATES, ELEANOR. *The Plow Woman.* New York: McClure, Phillips & Co., 1906. A Texas family consisting of a father and two daughters come to the Missouri River region of Dakota Territory to attempt farming. The father has been disabled in a railroad accident, and the work must be done by the daughters. The elder, Dallas (the "Plow Woman"), is the mainstay of the family. A love triangle involving a misunderstanding like that in *The Rise of Silas Lapham* figures importantly in this story of Indian troubles, Wild West heroism, and paternal tyranny. The setting is convincing, but neither the characterization nor the plot rises above mediocrity.

GREW, DAVID. *Migration.* New York: Charles Scribner's Sons, 1928. A highly romantic novel, full of *Sturm und Drang,* centered about a preposterous love story. Stacey Conrill, whose father has a farm near Devils Lake, N. Dak., leaves home when his father sells Blossom, the boy's pony, to punish him for his involvement in an adventure that has led to the burning of a neighbor's shanty. Taken in by his grandparents, Stacey soon begins having rendezvous with Marcia Stoner, a restless neighbor girl. When he takes her to a circus, she promptly joins the troup, to return three years later and lead Stacey a merry chase before finally agreeing to marry him. The style, including the dialogue, is stilted, the characterization is neither consistent nor convincing, and there is little treatment of farming except for an account of Stacey's experiences with a threshing rig. But the description of the prairie is often good, and there is an evident familiarity with the locale.

GROVE, FREDERICK PHILIP. *Our Daily Bread.* New York: Macmillan Co., 1928. Sober, cheerless treatment of the theme of the second generation's failure to maintain the high standards of character and industry of the pioneers. John and Martha Elliot, pioneers on the Saskatchewan prairie, see the failure of their hopes for their children, as each one shows himself unable to keep up the proud traditions of his parents. Old John farms well and refuses to go into debt, but his children farm carelessly and accumulate debts which soon well-nigh bury them. In his old age he wanders homeless from one child to another, unwanted everywhere, disillusioned by everything he sees in the modern world. A strong indictment of modern materialism and the abandonment of simplicity and integrity, the novel has only one serious fault: it overdocuments its case.

HALDEMAN-JULIUS, EMMANUEL and MARCET. *Dust*. New York: Brentano's, 1921. A study of values and of the dangers inherent in false valuations. Martin Wade, brought to Kansas as a child by his pioneer parents, has learned by experience that hard work is the only key to success and that success is to be measured in material terms. His marriage to Rose Conroy is thus doomed to failure, for Martin considers her merely a part of his equipment for the attainment of greater prosperity. He alienates his son, who soon dies in a mining explosion, and he himself dies in middle age, all his successes turned to dust. Style is simple and straightforward, characterization limited to two characters but successful in those cases.

HARNACK, CURTIS. *Love and Be Silent*. New York: Harcourt, Brace & World, 1962. Story of human relationships in a rural setting. Robert Schneider and his sister Alma each marry after their father's death, neither altogether satisfactorily. Robert and his wife Donna finally reach an adjustment to each other on the home place, but Alma's marriage to the unstable Roger Larkin brings unhappiness to both of them, for he is inclined to disappear when things get bad, sometimes for years at a time. Robert's repeated interference in Alma's marriage aggravates the situation. Although the scene is Iowa in the 1930's and 1940's, not much attention is given to farm problems of that period. A skillfully told story, with the technical finish to be expected of fiction written in the 1960's.

HARRIS, GARRARD. *The Treasure of the Land*. New York: Harper & Brothers, 1917. A tract on scientific farming and community improvement cast in novel form. Alice Warren, bored with farm life and on the verge of leaving for the city, is persuaded by Cynthia Allen, a new teacher, to stay and join with her in an effort to better the neighborhood. After a few initial failures, Miss Allen's program gets under way. Tomato clubs for the girls, corn clubs for the boys, and relief for the monotony of the farm wife's existence provide the means for rehabilitating the community. The novel has so many stereotypes and contrived situations, the propaganda is so blatant, and the farmer's problem is so grossly oversimplified that it is hard to take the book seriously. Self-help and individual effort, stimulated by competition, will solve all problems. The contrast between farm and city life is pointed up so frequently and in such extreme terms as to be more ludicrous than convincing.

HART, MILDRED. *Dead Woman's Shoes*. New York: Thomas Y. Crowell Co., 1932. A short novel covering a year in the life of Virgie Benson, an orphan of eighteen, who hires out to Henry Armstrong, a stolid, well-to-do widower still mourning his first wife's death. At first indifferent to Henry, Virgie later begins a somewhat awkward campaign to become his second wife. Their relationship makes no progress until one night when a thunderstorm brings them together. In a scene reminiscent of *Zury*, Henry enters Virgie's room to comfort her (she has a terror of storms), and his passions run away with him. A few months later, when she reveals that she is pregnant, they are married, but it is not until after the birth of their child and Virgie's attempted suicide that Henry decides he loves her. Neither the characterization nor the style redeems this novel from triviality, nor is there any attempt to describe the details of farm life or to treat the problems of agriculture.

HAYES, CHARLES EDWARD. *The Four Winds*. New York: Macmillan Co., 1942. A harsh story of farm poverty and ruin in an Irish Catholic community in Kansas—almost a rural *Studs Lonigan*. Told in the first person by sixteen-year-old Eugene Hardin, it tells of the declining fortunes of the Hardin family. The father, a bitter, ineffectual man, falls from owner to renter to farm hand and finally to laborer on a road crew, and his family accompanies him in this decline. Except for Gene, the family is no asset: the mother is pious and futile, Dugan is cruel, hypocritical, selfish, and crooked, Patricia is preoccupied with a birthmark on her face, and Rob is moody, in poor health, and at odds with Dugan. Many of the other characters in this novel of violence and brutality are vicious, and their religion seems to do nothing to mitigate their viciousness. The language of the narrator is appropriate to a boy who has not finished high school, as is the dialogue of the other characters. Although the plight of the farmer is depicted in dismal colors, neither causes nor solutions are given much attention.

HUDSON, LOIS PHILLIPS. *The Bones of Plenty*. Boston: Little, Brown & Co., 1962. A distinguished farm novel dealing with a fifteen-month period in the early 1930's in central North Dakota. George A. Custer, his wife Rachel, and their two children rent a farm adjacent to that of Rachel's father, Will Shepard, but successive years of drought and low prices push them ever deeper into debt. When Will, who has helped them, dies, George tries to get a loan from his landlord, fails, and tears up his lease. At the end of the novel they are about to leave for the West Coast. The author points out in a concluding note that for a large part of the farm population the depression has never ended, but she offers no clear-cut solution. Will, at times her spokesman, is only bewildered by the problem, and George is too ignorant of economics and too suspicious of all attempts to help the farmer to have any workable answers. The author's style is effective, the speech of the characters authentic. The characterization is convincing, even though most of the story is presented from the point of view of the child Lucy.

JACKSON, DONALD DEAN. *Archer Pilgrim.* New York: Dodd, Mead & Co., 1942. Skillful treatment of farm-versus-town theme, in an Iowa setting in the period 1920–1937. Archer Pilgrim grows up on a farm and likes it, but his parents, his girl, and a friend persuade him to go to college. After less than a year of half-hearted effort, he is advised to leave school. An attempt at operating a garage ends when his father is about to lose the farm; Archer, now married, takes over the farm, only to be deserted by his wife, who hates farm life. But he stays, contented at last with what he is doing. Good observation and recording of detail compensate for an unsatisfying plot and the use of a hackneyed (by 1942) theme. Written by an Iowa State College student.

JAY, MAE FOSTER. *The Orchard Fence.* Boston: W. A. Wilde Co., 1935. A paean of praise to the wholesomeness of farm life as opposed to the corruption of city life. Andrea Churchill, eighteen when the novel begins (later 1920's), loves the farm so much that when she goes to college, she studies agriculture. Called home by the crash of 1929 and her father's illness, she runs the farm almost single-handedly. Her childhood playmate from the next farm, Neil McNeil, has meanwhile achieved success as a writer for pulp magazines and has seemingly been lost to the city. As any reader can foresee from the start, Neil finally comes home to marry Andrea so that their farms can be united and the orchard fence, erroneously thought to mark the boundary, can be theirs in common. Light fiction of a type popular in the 1930's.

JOHNSON, ALVIN. *Spring Storm.* New York: Alfred A. Knopf, 1936. Based on the childhood recollections of a man in his sixties, this novel treats of the attempts at farming in northeastern Nebraska of Julian

Howard and his impractical father. At ease with the "Benders," a colony of poor whites who live along the river, Julian has an unfortunate affair with the young wife of a middle-aged neighbor and decides to return to the East and have no more to do with women or farming. Weak as to plot, and not overly successful in characterization, this novel is significant chiefly for the number of rural attitudes it reveals. The author was not only familiar with farm life but trained in the disciplines which enabled him to understand what he saw.

JOHNSON, JOSEPHINE. *Now in November.* New York: Simon & Schuster, 1934. Grim and depressing story of Missouri farm life, written in a highly poetic and figurative style. Arnold Haldmarne, his wife and three daughters are oppressed by debt, harassed by drought, and beset by emotional problems. Kerrin, the eldest, isolates herself more and more from the others and before the end of the novel goes insane. She and the narrator, another daughter, fall in love with Grant Koven, a hired man, who in turn falls in love with a third daughter. Their situation grows steadily worse as the novel progresses, ending in the death of the mother and the suicide of Kerrin. Despite the possibilities of melodrama in such a plot, this novel is not melodramatic. A Pulitzer prize winner, written by a young woman of twenty-four, it achieves a surprising measure of impressiveness, considering its brevity, chiefly because of the author's style.

KEMP, HARRY. *Mabel Tarner.* New York: Lee Furman, 1936. A story about the first twenty years of a girl's life. Born to a somewhat over-serious father and a mother resentful of her existence, Mabel grows up to be surprisingly normal. She goes to the district school, participates in neighborhood activities, develops a childhood attachment to Jimmy Tyrell (whom she eventually marries), and is idolized by the hired man, Jed Hoskins, who also wants to marry her. If Mabel's own life is uneventful, melodrama is provided by Ozdas Treffer's bank robbery and subsequent suicide to evade punishment for killing the man whose daughter he has wronged. This novel suffers from a certain meretriciousness; stylistic and other tricks are attempted; sex gets plenty of attention, but deference is paid to the proprieties by having all irregularities duly punished.

KRAMER, HORACE. *Marginal Land.* Philadelphia: J. B. Lippincott Co., 1939. Factual treatment of the attempts to cultivate land beyond the line of sufficient rainfall. Deluded by the talk of land agents and his father's experience farther east, Steve Randall tries to raise wheat on the prairies of central South Dakota. Beaten by drought, he has to fall back on cattle raising, which his friend Simon Peter Voorhees tells him is the only way of farming in this country. Steve is further handicapped by a wife unsuited to prairie life who later divorces him. Kramer's style is undistinguished, at times slovenly, but he has humor and something to say.

KRAUSE, HERBERT. *Wind Without Rain*. Indianapolis and New York: Bobbs-Merrill Co., 1939. Best treatment in farm fiction of the popular theme of patriarchal domination of a family. Johan Vildvogel rules his family with absolute authority and is especially demanding of Franz, the central figure, a sensitive, talented, passionate youngster with musical inclinations that are all but completely repressed by the father. A love affair between Franz and Liliem Schoen produces only unhappiness, and he marries Tinkla Bauer, without, however, losing his love for Liliem. The persistence of this futile passion is indirectly responsible for Franz's killing his daughter in the final scene of the novel. Neither so monumental nor so polished as *The Thresher* (q.v.), *Wind Without Rain* has merits of its own, chiefly an emotional quality that makes it one of the most moving of farm novels. Its figurative style, sometimes verging on an affectation, which made it the subject of both excessive praise and harsh criticism on its appearance, probably accounts for much of its power.

KRAUSE, HERBERT. *The Thresher*. Indianapolis and New York: Bobbs-Merrill Co., 1946. An attempt to accord to the business of threshing the definitive treatment given whaling by Melville, together with a love story in some respects paralleling that of Beret and Per Hansa in *Giants in the Earth* (q.v.). Johnny Black, who changed his name from Schwartz to symbolize the severance of his life from that of his infamous father, becomes the thresherman of the Pockerbrush country in west-central Minnesota, against the wishes of his wife, whose father has been crippled in an accident involving machinery. Their married life is tempestuous and unhappy, starting with a hurry-up marriage and ending with Johnny's death in the accident his wife has always feared. Successful or not in his attempt to memorialize threshing and to make the thresher the symbol of time, Krause has created one of the most impressive (and one of the longest) farm novels thus far, one which sums up tendencies in the genre extending back for at least two decades.

LANE, ROSE WILDER. *Let the Hurricane Roar*. New York: Longmans, Green & Co., 1933. One of two treatments by Mrs. Lane of the pioneering venture in South Dakota. A young couple homestead on the prairie and meet with great difficulties, especially economic ones, but survive them all and look to the future with hope. The brevity of this book makes it impossible for the characters to be developed as fully as in *Free Land* (q.v.), and so they tend to be types rather than individuals. (Significantly, they are not given last names.) The title comes from the first line of a hymn expressing hope.

LANE, ROSE WILDER. *Free Land.* New York: Longmans, Green & Co., 1938. Second and more detailed treatment by Mrs. Lane of pioneering in South Dakota, *Free Land* concerns the experiences of David and Mary Beaton, who undergo the hardships invariably recounted in novels dealing with this subject and are narrowly saved from defeat by a timely gift of two thousand dollars from his father. Fortune alternately smiles and frowns upon them, but the novel ends on a note of hope. Despite some romantically conceived incidents and mediocre writing, the novel carries conviction as an authentic account of a period and a process.

LOVELL, E. W. *Legacy.* New York: W. W. Norton & Co., 1934. An account of the gradual decay and distintegration of a French family, descendants of the *voyageurs*, in the Green Bay area of Wisconsin. The grandfather, who upholds the old ways against modern pressures, dies in the course of the novel. His sons are unable to maintain the standards he has passed on to them, but his legacy finds fruitful soil in his grandson, who presumably represents the author. By the end of the novel the expanding city of Green Bay has virtually destroyed the rural world into which the boy was born, and he, now a professor of history at the state university, resolves to memorialize the traditions of his family in a serious historical work. In its air of nostalgia and regret this novel resembles Bromfield's *The Farm* but is less penetrating.

MCLAUGHLIN, DAVID. *Lightning Before Dawn.* Indianapolis: Bobbs-Merrill Co., 1938. Reen Dorr, daughter of town drunkard, becomes pregnant by Steve Bierce, and is saved from shame, when Steve disappears, by marrying Lance Janssen, neighboring farmer. Although it is strictly a marriage of convenience, Reen and Lance eventually fall in love. Then Steve returns and resumes his pursuit of Reen. When he vanishes, Reen and Lance each think the other has killed him; but the murderer turns out to be Steve's feeble-minded brother Jim, who has a crush on Reen. A melodramatic plot filled with with improbabilities and contrived situations, an undistinguished style, inconsistent characterization, and an emphasis on sex that approaches the obscene make for a novel whose faults outweigh its merits.

MacLEOD, LEROY. *The Years of Peace.* New York: Century Co., 1932. Account of the career of Tyler Peck, his wife Evaline, and their children, relatives, and friends in a southern Indiana rural community in the period 1865–1875. Discontented with his seemingly empty life, Tyler constantly seeks adventure, usually of a sexual kind in illicit channels. To Uncle Lafe Ferguson, however, he is superior to Lafe's own son and is willed the farm by Uncle Lafe. Details of farm life and of community activity make this novel a valuable historical treatment of the period. Little occurs to make it emotionally moving, but such things as the decline of the "less-than-a-village" Freedom are chronicled with minute fidelity. The style is straightforward and factual, with attention to detail. Each chapter is prefaced with a running commentary on wars going on in the world, in contrast to the Indiana countryside in these "years of peace." MacLeod's novels anticipate the techniques of Paul Corey and Feike Feikema in the following decade.

MacLEOD, LEROY. *The Crowded Hill.* New York: Reynal & Hitchcock, 1934. Continuation of *The Years of Peace* covering the years 1876–1878 in the lives of Tyler Peck and his family. Tyler's Aunt Mary and his Cousin Lucy live with him and his family, as specified in Uncle Lafe's will, but the situation becomes increasingly uncomfortable as Evaline and Aunt Mary quarrel over the religious training of the children. Tyler's friendship with Lew Williamson is broken by an election bet, he has an affair with Josie Finkle, a servant girl, and finally Aunt Mary and Lucy leave the household. Good picture of rural life in the period. Attempt to catch the flavor of the times by the use of a device comparable to Dos Passos' "Newsreels" not so successful as in Dos Passos. Realistic detail in abundance is MacLeod's strong point.

MARTIN, GEORGE VICTOR. *For Our Vines Have Tender Grapes.* New York: Wilfred Funk, 1940. (Republished as *Our Vines Have Tender Grapes.* New York: Grosset and Dunlap, 1945.) Less a story than a depiction of a way of life. Set in a Norwegian community in Wisconsin, such plot as exists attempts merely to present a set of characters, their relationships, and their values. Central theme is the conflict between town and country. "Editor" has come back to Benson Junction from Chicago, disillusioned with city life and partial to the simplicity and wholesomeness of country life. Viola Johnson, with whom he falls in love, feels otherwise, but their differences are reconciled. Central intelligence is a nine-year-old girl, but this point of view is not consistently maintained, and the issues are oversimplified. Lightweight but entertaining.

MONTROSS, LYNN. *East of Eden.* New York: Harper & Brothers, 1925. Illinois counterpart of Beers' *Prairie Fires* (q.v., above), centered about attempt of farmers, led by Fred Derring, to set up grain growers' association and to gain representation on the Chicago Board of Trade. Outmaneuvered in his political efforts and finally repudiated by the farmers themselves, who think he has enriched himself at their expense, Derring is finally ruined and kills himself by running his car head-on into that of his archenemy, Tom Nicholson, local grain elevator man. Contains love story, unrelated to main plot, between Derring's daughter Lou, through whose eyes much of the action is seen, and Milt Bowen, local delinquent, who disappears before the book ends. Both narrative strands are inferior to those of *Prairie Fires*, and characterization of Derring never quite jells.

MOXLEY, VERNA [Mrs. Paul Melvin Smith]. *Wind 'til Sundown.* Caldwell, Ida.: Caxton Printers, 1954. Badly written story about twentieth-century pioneering on former Indian reservation lands in South Dakota. A Michigan couple, John and Anne Holland, occupy a shabby, vermin-infested cabin and endure the hardships of drought, hail, blizzards, loneliness, and even a contaminated water supply. Aided by an improbable Englishman who lives on a neighboring ranch, they somehow survive and sink their roots into the prairie. Despite plenty of realistic detail, this novel is rendered ineffective by stylistic faults, inept characterization, and the author's apparent belief that a novel must have a love triangle, whatever the cost in plausibility. Indians are treated condescendingly.

MUILENBURG, WALTER J. *Prairie.* New York: Viking Press, 1925. Fairly skillful treatment of two frequent themes: the pioneering experience on the Great Plains and rebellion against parental domination. Elias Vaughn, disowned by his father for marrying against the latter's wishes, goes to Nebraska and there contends with the usual hazards of Plains agriculture. After years of hardship and failure, he finally achieves a measure of prosperity, but the ordeal kills his wife. When he has alienated his son, at the novel's end, the wheel has come full circle. Unsparing realism in the portrayal of the difficulties of pioneer life. Novel is weakened by stiff characterization and too much action for the length of the book.

MUNGER, DELL H. *The Wind Before the Dawn.* Garden City, N.Y.: Doubleday, Page & Co., 1912. Perceptive study of masculine domination of wives and an appeal for a solution through financial independence for women. Elizabeth Farnshaw sees her mother tyrannized by a brutal husband but falls into the trap when she marries John Hunter, who appears to her as more cultured than other men she meets on the Kansas prairie. Intending no injustice, he dominates her in the belief that such domination is necessary for women. She escapes through the gift of half of John's property when his business partner dies and leaves his interest to her. The particular solution suggested may be objected to as unconvincing and melodramatic, but the author's insight into the problem partially offsets slovenly writing and structural weaknesses in the novel.

NORTH, STERLING. *Plowing on Sunday*. New York: Macmillan Co., 1934. Detailed character sketch of Stanley "Stud" Brailsford, epitome of virility. Stud has been faithful to his wife since marriage, but when a pretty young girl joins the household his fortitude is tested, especially when he ascertains that she is not, as he at first suspected, a daughter by some premarital liaison. It is not Stud, however, but his son Peter who will carry on the family line with Early Ann, as Stud realizes at the end of the novel. His own masculinity is paralleled by that of his prize animals, a stallion, a bull, and a boar. Characterizations of a spinster busybody and a hired man are entertaining but tend toward caricature. Some attempt at description of the southern Wisconsin countryside, but the emphasis is on the characters.

NORTH, STERLING. *So Dear to My Heart*. New York: Doubleday & Co., 1947. Rustic idyll of childhood in southern Indiana about 1900. A boy brought up by his strict, religious grandmother wishes to exhibit his black lamb at the county fair but is obliged to use all his resources and those of his friends to win her over to the scheme, since she believes that fairs and towns are sinful. When the boy is lost in the woods while in search of his lamb, the grandmother resolves that if he returns safely, she will allow him to have his wish. He returns, everyone goes to the fair, and the story ends happily. A slight novel, the authenticity of its picture of rural life suspect (the locale seems incredibly isolated for 1900), it has nevertheless been extremely popular.

OSTENSO, MARTHA. *Wild Geese*. New York: Dodd, Mead & Co., 1925. First of a long series of novels by Miss Ostenso. Lind Archer, a young outsider, comes to a remote frontier district (presumably in Manitoba) to teach school. While boarding at the Caleb Gare home, she sees how Gare dominates his wife and children. Unknown to her, the weapon he uses is the threat of exposure, for his wife has had an illegitimate child before her marriage. This child, now grown and unaware of his origin, also appears in the locality, and he and Lind fall in love. Caleb's control over his eldest daughter, Judith, wavers when she tries to run away in order to marry Sven Sandbo, but it does not break until Caleb himself dies in the muskeg, trying to save his flax crop from a fire in the nearby woods. An impressive first novel, despite annoying stylistic tricks and a tendency toward overdramatization of materials.

OSTENSO, MARTHA. *The Dark Dawn*. New York: Dodd, Mead & Co., 1926. Second novel by Miss Ostenso, much less impressive than *Wild Geese*. Lucian Dorrit marries Hattie Murker, much older than he, and is thereafter dominated by her. After the birth of a son who dies, Lucian becomes interested in a neighbor girl, Karen Strand, and ceases to have much to do with his wife. When he threatens to move to the attic, she throws herself into a rock quarry and is crippled for life. A weak heart brings about her death before long, however, and Lucian and Karen head for the city. Aside from some attempt to describe the locale (northwestern Minnesota), there is little but plot in this novel. The characters are not memorable, and there is no ideological content to give significance to the book.

OSTENSO, MARTHA. *The Mad Carews*. New York: Dodd, Mead & Co., 1927. Elsa Bowers, daughter of a poor Minnesota farmer, grows up hating and yet being fascinated by the wealthy, dissolute Carew family who live in splendor on a large estate nearby. Bayliss Carew pursues her for several years and finally wins her hand in marriage. By marrying him she virtually isolates herself from her own family and others in the locality. Furthermore, she is tormented by (unjustified) doubts of his faithfulness to her. When the Carews are ruined by oil speculation, Elsa and Bayliss are able to start anew on a farm given them by her father. Essentially the same criticisms can be made of this novel as were made of *The Dark Dawn*, although it is a more polished job.

OSTENSO, MARTHA. *There's Always Another Year*. New York: Dodd, Mead & Co., 1933. Silver Grenoble, daughter of gambler "Gentleman Jim" Grenoble, killed in a Chicago brawl, flees to her Aunt Sophronia Willard's farm near Heron River, Minnesota. Here she falls in love with her aunt's stepson, Roddy Willard, who is in love with Corinne Meader, the local banker's daughter, and marries her. Corinne despises farm life, however, and begins playing around with Gerald Lucas, operator of a night club. When Gerald is obliged to skip the country, Corinne goes with him, to divorce Roddy, who by this time is in love with Silver. All Miss Ostenso's tricks are in this one.

OSTENSO, MARTHA. *The Stone Field.* New York: Dodd, Mead & Co., 1937. Like *The Mad Carews* (q.v., above) in that the heroine, Jobina Porte, is a country girl intrigued by a wealthy family whose scions are at best unstable of temperament. Attracted to Royce Hilyard, she has to wait until he has tired of his wife to marry him. The portrayal of an insane hermit, Phineas Baggott, is good, and the novel contains a valuable plea for conservation of forest resources, but there is too much violence—four major characters die violently—for complete plausibility. The high-color characteristic of Miss Ostenso's novels is all too evident in this one.

OSTENSO, MARTHA. *The Mandrake Root.* New York: Dodd, Mead & Co., 1938. Eric Stene, English instructor at Anders College, resigns under pressure and returns to the farm where he grew up, founded by his grandfather, a Norwegian immigrant. A young couple, Andrew and Lydie Clarence, now rent it. Andrew, uneducated but intelligent and deeply religious, appeals to Eric and they become friends. But Lydie, disturbed over her childlessness, resolves to make use of Eric as a "mandrake root." The attempt is successful, but when Andrew learns of it, he kills himself. Eric then leaves the farm. Superior to most of Miss Ostenso's earlier novels and probably the most sophisticated of them, this novel suffers from the same defects as the rest, if to a lesser degree.

OSTENSO, MARTHA. *A Man Had Tall Sons.* New York: Dodd, Mead & Co., 1958. Story of conflicts arising when Luke Darr, fifty-two, brings home a twenty-five-year-old wife. His three grown sons still revere the memory of their free-thinking, strong-willed mother. Luke's efforts to assert his mastery of the household lead to deterioration of the family until the suicide of Mark, the youngest son, brings the others to their senses. Luke and his wife Bess are reconciled, and Luke comes to recognize that his sons have the right to live lives of their own. The novel is competently written, although the farm background is subordinated to the plot. The scene is southern Minnesota.

OYEN, HENRY. *Big Flat.* New York: George H. Doran Co., 1919. Story of the struggle between Martin Calkins, ambitious young farmer, and the Starin paper company, which recognizes the agricultural potential of a tract of cutover timber land in Wisconsin and wishes to buy out Martin and other farmers. By a combination of shrewdness and good luck, Martin and the farmers' cooperative that he organizes emerge victorious over the "octopus," which has the cards heavily stacked in its favor. Well stocked with stereotyped characters and situations, encumbered with an obtrusive antiurban philosophy and several "racial" prejudices (some attributable to the date of writing—World War I), and undistinguished by any noticeable skill at local color, this novel belongs, with many others, in the subliterary category of farm fiction.

POUND, ARTHUR. *Once a Wilderness.* New York: Reynal & Hitchcock, 1934. Family chronicle of Mark clan, owners of Mark section in central Michigan. John Mark, widowed patriarch of the family, directs the affairs of his children and grandchildren. In this novel he goes to England to find a breed of dairy cattle that can be crossed with his own, settles the problems connected with his illegitimate daughter and her illegitimate son, and carries Mark section through a series of financial storms. A multitude of Marks, of both English and American branches, appear in the novel, including several named John, but old John Mark so dominates the picture that his relatives hardly matter. An attitude of *noblesse oblige* characterizes the Mark family, who consider themselves and are considered by others superior to their neighbors. John Mark is one of the best individualized figures in modern farm fiction.

POUND, ARTHUR. *Second Growth.* New York: Reynal & Hitchcock, 1935. A continuation of *Once a Wilderness* (q.v., above) with greater emphasis on the children and grandchildren of John Mark, who gradually sinks into senility and finally dies as the novel progresses. Because of this shift of emphasis, *Second Growth* is weaker than its predecessor. A daughter, long consigned to spinsterhood, finally marries a Michigan State College professor (later president); one son is killed in a cave-in; another has marital troubles; a grandson starts an auto-parts factory, gains and loses a fortune, and starts on the road up with his grandfather's help; and another grandson (the illegitimate one) gains fame as an artist. Too many stories of too many Marks are told, and the genealogical chart at the end of the novel must be consulted at frequent intervals if the reader is to follow the numerous strands of the plot.

QUICK, HERBERT. *The Fairview Idea.* Indianapolis: Bobbs-Merrill Co., 1919. Essentially a tract on corn-belt agriculture, presented in fictionalized form. Told in the first person by Abner Dunham, an Iowa farmer, it describes how the community of Fairview organized to preserve its identity and rural culture. Drift to the cities by youth is halted by starting a consolidated school where practical skills are taught. The back-to-the-land movement is discussed, and recommendations are made to city folk intending to try farming. Little narrative stream, almost no attempt to individualize characters, little description, no dramatic conflict.

QUICK, HERBERT. *Vandemark's Folly*. New York: A. L. Burt & Co., 1922. Life story of Jacob Vandemark, one of the few memorable figures in farm fiction. Jacob comes west as a boy in his teens, extorts a grant of land out of his stepfather in Madison, drives to Iowa with a herd of cattle and the necessary implements for pioneer life, and settles on his land in Monterey County, where he grows up with the country. His romance with Virginia Royall, culminating in marriage at the end of the novel, provides the necessary love element expected by Quick's readers. Perhaps the best thing in the novel is the description of the Iowa scene in presettlement days, especially the picture Quick gives of the Old Ridge Road from Dubuque westward. His characterization, except for Jacob, is not exceptional, and the plot shows decidedly melodramatic features, doubtless derived from Quick's early reading, described in *One Man's Life*.

QUICK, HERBERT. *The Hawkeye*. New York: A. L. Burt & Co., 1923. The life story of Fremont McConkey, born on a farm near Monterey Center, Iowa, in the early years of settlement. He develops literary interests, becomes active in local politics, teaches school, elopes with the town girl whose father's protégé he is, and after a reconciliation with the father, becomes deputy county clerk. Identified with the corrupt "court house ring" then and later when he is county clerk, he falls when they are thrown out of office, although he is personally innocent of any wrongdoing. Meanwhile, his wife has died, and after making a blundering proposal to her sister, he marries another sister. As the novel ends, he is editor of a newspaper in Lithopolis. The chief merit of this novel is its use of Iowa history as background for the action: the lynching of the Bushyager gang, the corruption in county government (personified in Roswell Upright), and the growth of the community.

QUICK, HERBERT. *The Invisible Woman*. Indianapolis: Bobbs-Merrill Co., 1924. Centered about the career of Christina Thorkelson, daughter of Magnus Thorkelson of *Vandemark's Folly* (q.v., above), this novel takes place mostly in the town of Monterey Center and hence has little claim to being called a farm novel. Much attention is given to the litigation following the death of J. Buckner Gowdy, villain of the earlier novel, and the efforts of his illegitimate son to obtain his rightful share of the estate. Everything turns out for the best, and

Christina marries the man she has served as secretary for years. This is the weakest of Quick's three novels about Iowa history, although it contains good character portrayal and effective use of background material.

READ, OPIE. *A Yankee from the West.* New York: Rand McNally & Co., 1898. Only by courtesy can this be called a farm novel, for its chief character, Milford Newton, although supposedly operating a farm, actually does no farm work in the course of the novel and spends most of his time at the boardinghouse of the farm's owner, Mrs. Stuvic. Here he falls in love with Gunhild Strand, and eventually marries her, after a series of absurdly melodramatic adventures. The characters are types or nonentities, the plot is implausible, the background is totally neglected, the dialogue is a stage-rustic kind of speech, and the novel as a whole is trivial.

RÖLVAAG, OLE EDVART. *Giants in the Earth.* New York and London: Harper & Brothers, 1927. (Originally published in Norwegian, in Oslo, in 1924 and 1925.) In the opinion of John T. Flanagan, the greatest farm novel thus far produced. Per Hansa, his wife Beret, and their family and friends trek westward from Fillmore County, Minnesota, to the Dakota prairies, where they set up a colony and begin breaking the prairie sod. Per Hansa is enthusiastic from the start, but Beret is oppressed by constant fear, which increases in intensity until her mind fails. When her son is born normally, she gradually recovers her faculties, but then she slips into religious fanaticism and persuades the dying Hans Olsa to ask Per Hansa to go for a minister through the blizzard. Although Per Hansa knows this means certain death, he starts out. His body is found the next spring, beside a haystack, facing west. In characterization, in portrayal of the pioneers' experience, in its treatment of the setting, this novel is a superior achievement by any standards and has been used in this study as a touchstone by which to measure other novels dealing with the pioneering theme.

RÖLVAAG, OLE EDVART. *Peder Victorious.* New York and London: Harper & Brothers, 1929. Continuation of *Giants in the Earth* (q.v.), covers the boyhood and youth of Per Hansa's and Beret's son. As he grows up in the American environment, he loses interest in Norwegian culture and the Norwegian language, thus becoming alienated from his mother. Their conflict centers in the church, the school, and the home. Peder becomes the favorite of an English-speaking pastor and a rabidly American teacher and falls in love with the Irish Catholic Susie Doheny. Beret allows him to marry Susie only because she believes Per Hansa has come to her in a dream and asked her to permit the marriage. If this novel appears to mark a falling off from the high level of *Giants in the Earth*, it may be, as Rölvaag said, because the pioneering experience occurred only once. The same technical skill is evident here as in the earlier novel, but there is no character with the appeal of Per Hansa. Beret herself is strongly and consistently drawn.

Rölvaag, Ole Edvart. *Pure Gold*. New York and London: Harper & Brothers, 1930. A case study in the history of materialism. Louis (Lars) and Lizzie (Lisbet) Houglum begin hoarding money, continue the process through the years until they have $72,000 stuffed in boxes and corners around their farm. Yet they freeze to death because they are unwilling to spend money for fuel. In their monomania for gold they have destroyed all their ability to appreciate other values, just as they have cut themselves off from their cultural heritage by Americanizing their names. Not on a level with Rölvaag's novels about Beret Holm, this book has evidences of greatness, as in the treatment of anti-German sentiment misdirected against Louis and Lizzie during World War I.

Rölvaag, Ole Edvart. *Their Fathers' God*. New York: Harper & Brothers, 1931. Third in the series about the Holm family, concerned chiefly with the marriage of Peder and Susie. Not primarily an attack on mixed marriages, this novel traces the deterioration of the marriage as the participants' awareness of the differences in their cultural origins increases. Their child is first baptized secretly by Beret in the Lutheran faith, later baptized by Susie in the Catholic faith; in neither case does Peder know of the act. After Beret's death, Peder becomes active in local politics, on the side opposed to that of Susie's relatives. This brings a final estrangement when Peder, angered by something an opponent has said about him, destroys his wife's crucifix and devotional equipment, and she leaves with the child. Rölvaag's powers of characterization are still excellent, although both Peder and Susie are portrayed as slightly too emotional and impulsive for complete credibility. An earnest book, representing some of its author's most serious thinking, *Their Fathers' God* lacks the engrossing theme of *Giants in the Earth* and so must rank as an inferior book.

Saltzman, [Katherine] Eleanor. *Ever Tomorrow*. New York: Coward McCann, 1936. Life story of Joe Mueller in the period 1875–1931. He takes over operation of the family farm in southern Iowa upon his mother's death, marries a neighbor girl, Ada Martin, and raises three children, one of whom (Joe's favorite) dies before reaching maturity. Since the other children do not take to farming, the farm is rented. But when Carl, the son, loses his Des Moines job in the depression of 1929, he and his wife, a city girl with a real interest in farming, return to the country. Finally, Joe and Ada join Carl, by then a widower, on the home farm. Written in subdued tones, with no peaks of emotional tension, this novel displays a fine delicacy, especially in regard to its handling of the inner feelings of its characters.

SALTZMAN, [KATHERINE] ELEANOR. *Stuart's Hill.* New York: Bernard Ackerman, 1945. Although chiefly an account of the history of a rural church, this novelette concerns people nearly all of whom are farmers and so qualifies as farm fiction. James Stuart is born as the church on Stuart's Hill is being built, and his early life centers about the structure. After serving its people for many years, the church gradually declines, until it is no longer used and is finally sold to a farmer who plans to make a barn of it. The funeral of James' father is the last event in the church; before it can be dismantled, it burns, probably set on fire by a member of the congregation who opposed its sale. Restraint and tenderness are the characteristics of this book, written in a style strongly influenced by the Psalms.

SANDBURG, HELGA [Mrs. Arthur D. Golby]. *Measure My Love.* New York: McDowell, Oblensky, 1959. Another story of a strong-minded woman and a weak-willed man. Faith Summers at twenty-seven disappoints her father by marrying Buddy Bain. They rent a farm and manage, largely through Faith's planning and work, to keep going, although Buddy secretly borrows from Faith's father, a successful orchard man. The marriage disintegrates when Faith learns of Buddy's infidelities with her sister Lacy. After a quarrel he goes out to saw some trees down and is killed when one falls on him. The novel ends with Faith in possession of the farm (the owner, a childless widow, has deeded it to her) and faces the problem of supporting her two small sons. Characters and locale, Michigan dune country, well portrayed.

SEAGER, ALLAN. *Hilda Manning.* New York: Simon & Schuster, 1956. On the periphery of farm fiction, this novel deals with the attractive young wife of Acel Manning, forty-six, who has stopped farming after a heart attack but still lives on the farm. She knows (but he does not) that he is dying of cancer, and when her sister demands $5,000 in blackmail (Hilda has an illegitimate son who has been cared for by the sister), Hilda slips a dose of arsenic into Acel's coffee. His death is attributed to another heart attack, and Hilda is never prosecuted, although one of the men whose proposals of marriage she has rejected, Sam Larned, starts an investigation which dies out. She and Sam eventually marry. Except for the improbability of this conclusion, the novel is a rather polished performance, with good, if somewhat cynical, characterization and the technical finish usually found in recent fiction.

SIMONSEN, SIGURD JAY. *The Clodhopper*. New York: Fortuny's, 1940. Rambling narrative about Danish immigrants to Minnesota and the lives of one or two of their children. Jens Hansen and Nels Petersen break the tough prairie sod, sow crops of wheat and corn, bring wives over from Denmark, and raise families in the new world. Whatever merits the book has appear in the passages describing the social and religious life of these people and their adjustments to American conditions. Later the center of attention shifts to Jens' son, who becomes a telegraph operator at various railroad depots in Minnesota and the Dakotas. This part of the book reads like a railroad timetable but is less informative. The writing is consistently bad, the characterization wooden, and the book arrives nowhere.

SIMONSEN, SIGURD JAY. *The Mongrels*. New York: Diana Press, 1946. Herman Schultz comes to Sandville, Minn., in 1885, buys a farm in the pine country from John Ford. Most of the novel recounts the development of the community up to about 1900, then hurriedly rushes through the next thirty-five years. Despite such potential for fiction as a religious revival, a county fair, the coming of the railroad, threshing, glimpses of the rural school, and the effects of the depression of 1929, the execrable writing, stereotyped characters, and lack of any coherent plot structure prevent the effective utilization of this material. The "mongrels" are the new race produced by the intermarriage of the Germans, Scandinavians, English, Irish, Russo-Poles, and Bulgarians who have settled in the northern Minnesota locality.

SIMONSEN, SIGURD JAY. *The Plodders*. New York: Vantage Press, 1952. Another unsuccessful attempt to give fictional treatment to a Danish-Norwegian community in Minnesota. Covering the period 1932–1945, this book is centered about Martin Nielsen and his sons and neighbors. Of his three sons, only Viggo stays on the farm, and he is killed in World War II. Collectively, Simonsen's books represent the lowest level of farm fiction. An illiterate style, wooden characterization, obtrusive and sophomoric moralization, and a lack of anything that could be called narrative technique make these books seem more like volumes of reminiscences, haphazardly recorded, than like novels.

SINCLAIR, HAROLD. *American Years.* New York: Doubleday, Doran & Co., 1938. Not properly a farm novel at all, but rather fictionalized history dealing with Illinois in the first half of the nineteenth century. Towns and counties are founded, and a multitude of characters come and go, some of whom are real historical figures, such as Abraham Lincoln. A few of these remain in view long enough to be developed, but most of them merely pass by. There is a sense of authenticity in the account of the daily lives and concerns of these small town Illinois people and interesting sidelights on history, such as the slow development of a plow that would cut the tough prairie sod and the earliest reaper. There is no plot in the conventional sense of the term, merely a succession of incidents with only the significance they had in history.

SMITH, LABAN C. *No Better Land.* New York: Macmillan Co., 1946. Somewhat sentimental story about the Abel Elliot family, Wisconsin farm folk. Abel, in his sixties, blind, and partly paralyzed, and his wife Marie, twenty years younger, are both strong-willed people whose wills clash over their plans for their ten children. Eventually the two oldest children follow their own wishes, which largely coincide with Abel's, and the father dies at the end of the novel. The Elliots live in comparative isolation from the rest of the world. Attention is centered on the family squabbles, and there is little sense of participation in the world of the time, which is about 1907.

SOLES, GORDON H. *Cornbread and Milk: A Family Gathering.* Garden City, N.Y.: Doubleday & Co., 1959. A collection of sixteen stories about farm life in the 1920's and early 1930's, told in first person by a boy whose age ranges from seven to fourteen. Simple anecdotes for the most part, some contain elements of old southwestern humor—physical discomfiture, practical jokes, rustic hilarity. Included are tales about spring floods, threshing, a barn dance, snakes in the outhouse, a small boy's collection of rabbit pellets, and the devotion of a cat to a dying dog. Except for some profanity, this appears to be a book intended for children; a way of life is described, but there is no attempt to deal with psychological subtleties or economic problems.

STEGNER, WALLACE. *Remembering Laughter.* Boston: Little, Brown & Co., 1937. Domestic triangle involving Alec Stuart and his wife Margaret and her sister Elspeth, who has come over from Scotland to join them on their Iowa farm. Alec and Elspeth fall in love but bring their liaison to an abrupt end when they are discovered by Margaret. Elspeth is pregnant, but suspicion is publicly fastened on a hired man who is paid to leave for Norway. The child, Malcolm, does not learn of his birth until his father's death, when the boy is sixteen. Then he leaves for Chicago. Laughter ended for these people when Margaret came upon Alec and Elspeth. The whole incident seems melodramatic and not entirely convincing.

STEPHENSON, HOWARD. *Glass.* New York: Claude Kendall, 1934. Clumsily told account of George Rood's twenty-year struggle to keep on farming in the face of spreading industrialism in the form of gas wells and a glass factory. A widower with a small son at the beginning of the novel, George keeps right on farming through the alternate booms and busts in the glass plant across the road. The corrupting influence of the factory is personified by Jake Karcher, George's archenemy and the husband of the woman by whom George has a son and whom he finally marries after Jake's death. Poor characterization, an implausible plot, an over-dramatic, strained style, and other defects render this a rather ineffective treatment of a significant theme.

STONG, PHILIP DUFFIELD. *State Fair.* New York: Century Co., 1932. First and probably best of Stong's many novels about Iowa farm life. Mr. and Mrs. Abel Frake and their son and daughter, Wayne and Margy, take their prize hog, Blue Boy, to the state fair in Des Moines, where the parents win prizes for Blue Boy and other entries and the children (ages eighteen and nineteen respectively) meet young people of opposite sex and have brief affairs. Then they all go home happy over their experiences but unaffected in any deeper emotional sense. The attitude toward the young people's adventures is amoral. Good depiction of a well-adjusted farm family.

STONG, PHILIP DUFFIELD. *Stranger's Return.* New York: Harcourt, Brace & Co., 1933. Unconsummated domestic triangle. Louise Storr Dehart, who has left her husband, comes to her grandfather's farm near Pittsville (Keosauqua), Iowa, where her relatives, besides regarding her as a fallen woman, fear her as a threat to their prospects of inheriting Grandpa's fortune. Here she falls in love with a married man and becomes Grandpa's favorite, to whom he wills his fortune upon his death late in the novel. Guy Crane, the married neighbor, leaves with his family. Notable is the characterization of Simon, the hired man, reputedly the most sinful man in Van Buren County, the first and most successful of a series of such hired men in Stong's novels.

Stong, Philip Duffield. *The Long Lane*. New York: Farrar & Rinehart, 1939. Another domestic triangle, centered about Flora Brubaker, beautiful wife of Albert Brubaker, Iowa farmer and county treasurer, beloved by Albert's brother Merritt and a sort of hired man named Lea, who is in turn loved by the hired girl, Ariel. After Flora and Merritt run off to California, she gets a divorce from Albert and they marry. Albert then goes to Des Moines and becomes interested in Gilda, an actress. All this is seen through the eyes of Albert's son Kenneth, born about 1900. Again the author's attitude toward all this seems to be amoral. No serious issues are dealt with in seriousness or with penetration.

Stong, Philip Duffield. *The Princess*. New York: Farrar & Rinehart, 1941. Concerns chiefly Arnhold Edeson, orphaned at birth and brought up by a much older brother and a hired man of the kind frequently found in Stong's novels. After a promising beginning as a musician, she returns to the farm upon her brother's death and operates it until the end of the novel, when the prospect is that she will marry pianist Weldon Armbruster. Other characters, such as Epworth Drummond, an itinerant Methodist minister and farmer, appear on the scene. None are especially well characterized. The novel follows the Stong stereotype that first appeared in *State Fair*.

Stong, Philip Duffield. *Blizzard*. Garden City, N.Y.: Doubleday & Co., 1955. A group of people, some of whom had met before, are stranded by a blizzard in the farmhouse of Jim Mercer in Van Buren County, Iowa. Most of these are stock characters used by Stong before, but the juxtapositions are novel, and the whole thing provides pleasant reading with no ideological content to distract the reader. There is little about farm life, little use of distinctively rural speech or attitudes. Farm life is pretty idyllic, as it was in *State Fair*.

Stringer, Arthur John Arbuthnot. *The Prairie Wife*. Indianapolis: Bobbs-Merrill Co., 1915. Epistolary novel in which Chaddie McKail tells a friend how she came to marry Duncan Argyll McKail after having been engaged to a German diplomat (portrayed as one might expect in 1915) and went to live on a wheat ranch in Alberta. The needed domestic triangle is provided by a consumptive English nobleman whose actions are misinterpreted by Duncan, and an element of excitement is supplied by Chaddie's capture (with the aid of a Royal Canadian Mounted Policeman) of a dangerous murderer. The chief merit of the book, however, is its treatment of the setting, the prairies of the northwest, and of the life led by the inhabitants of that region.

STRINGER, ARTHUR JOHN ARBUTHNOT. *The Prairie Mother.* Indianapolis: Bobbs-Merrill Co., 1920. Sequel to *The Prairie Wife*, continues the adventures of Duncan and Chaddie. He has speculated and lost everything, except two ranches which are in her name, including money belonging to Lady Alicia Newland, his second cousin. They move to a primitive shack and turn Casa Grande, the main ranch, over to Lady Alicia. There follows a domestic quadrangle involving Lady Alicia, who seems to have entranced Duncan, and Peter Ketley, who falls in love with Chaddie. Everything turns out for the best in the end: Duncan regains his fortune, it is revealed that he was only pretending an interest in Lady Alicia in order to gain her financial help, Peter goes back to the oblivion whence he came, and domestic harmony is restored. Marred by an overabundance of literary allusions, amateur philosophizing on the man-woman relationship, and a plot that is clearly a concession to convention.

SUCKOW, RUTH. *Country People.* New York: Alfred A. Knopf, 1924. Plain, unvarnished account of the lives of August and Emma Kaetterhenry, German farmers in northeastern Iowa. They raise a family, suffer from anti-German feeling in World War I, endeavor to adapt themselves to changing conditions in agriculture, watch most of their children drift away from them, finally retire to town. Here August builds a new house, just in time to die and leave it and the responsibility of maintaining it to Emma. No purple passages, no striving for emotional effect. If anything, the book is under-written. Effective use of detail, both in characterizing individuals and in presenting convincing picture of the background. Painstaking accuracy of character portrayal produces effect of perhaps unconscious satire; the lives of these people impress the reader as barren and empty.

SUCKOW, RUTH. *The Odyssey of a Nice Girl.* New York: Alfred A. Knopf, 1925. Although listed by John T. Flanagan as a farm novel, the only treatment of farming is at the very beginning, where the heroine, Marjorie Schoessel, a small-town girl, is shown visiting her grandparents' farm. An exclusively feminine personality, she grows up in town, goes away to Boston after high school, to attend an "academy of expression," returns home for an unfruitful year, tries Chicago briefly, returns home again, finally goes to Colorado to marry a fruit rancher. Despite some talent, she is a rather negligible person, unsure of herself and her aims, inclined to go from one emotional extreme to another, dissatisfied wherever she is. The portrayal is skillful, but one may well question whether Marjorie deserves all the attention she receives from Miss Suckow.

SUCKOW, RUTH. *Iowa Interiors.* New York: Alfred A. Knopf, 1926. Collection of sixteen stories about Iowa life, some dealing with farmers, written in the same unemphatic style as the novels. Especially successful are stories treating retired men and women, especially men who find themselves with nothing to do. Other stories dealing with farm life are "Renters," "A Rural Community," and "A Start in Life." The effect of most stories is one of barrenness and futility, as in *Country People.* Author shows fine delicacy and understanding of her characters, uses straightforward style appropriate to her subject.

THOMAS, DOROTHY. *The Home Place.* New York: Alfred A. Knopf, 1936. Slightly more than a year in the life of the Arch Young family, Nebraska farmers in the 1920's. Arch's sons Tom and Ralph and their families are living on the home place, having lost their own farms. Early in the novel a third son, Harvey, and his city-bred wife descend upon the family—to stay—just after a letter has been sent to him requesting financial help. The rest of the book recounts the tensions and clashes caused by this crowded arrangement and their ultimate resolution. Competently written, with touches of humor, this novel succeeds within the narrow range it has set itself: exploration of the relationships among generally well-realized characters under unusually trying circumstances.

TURNGREN, ELLEN. *Listen, My Heart.* New York: Longmans, Green & Co., 1956. A novel for adolescent girls, centering about the Lars Almbeck family, impecunious Minnesota farmers of Swedish background, in the 1930's. Although beset by poverty, drought, and accident, they somehow survive and are looking forward to better times at the end of the book. Sigrid, the late teen-age daughter, who serves as the central intelligence, combines her father's expansiveness, optimism, and love of fun with her mother's caution and willingness to compromise. Although there is some oversimplification of characters and issues, the novel presumably conveys its message to the audience at which it is aimed. Surprisingly frank treatment (for such a novel) of a forced marriage and an attempted seduction.

TURNGREN, ELLEN. *Hearts Are the Fields.* New York: Longmans, Green & Co., 1961. Another light novel, designed for a teen-age audience, with a Minnesota farm setting early in the twentieth century. It concerns chiefly the attempt by Nils Enberg to control the lives of his children, an attempt which leads to the alienation of his oldest son, the unhappiness of his oldest daughter, and the flight from home of another son. This last break for freedom rather improbably shocks Nils into a realization of the futility of his effort, and this realization leads to a general reconciliation and a happy ending. Stereotyped characters and an overworked theme prevent this novel from being more than a modest success.

WAY, ISABEL STEWART. *Seed of the Land.* New York: D. Appleton-Century Co., 1935. Life story of Ruhamah Robbins, who comes to Michigan an orphan, marries stolid Dave Robbins, helps him establish himself in farming, and after his death continues to extend her farming operations and brings up their three sons. An exaggerated and idealized Alexandra Bergson, Ruhamah is a dominant type who molds others according to her wishes and directs affairs toward predetermined ends. Still her dream of establishing a dynasty of farmers remains unrealized at the end of the novel, when two of her sons have left her and the third has married the weak and self-indulgent daughter of a family of incompetents to whom Ruhamah has been inextricably bound throughout the story. Not a great novel, this is nonetheless a good one, employing effective symbolism in what is really an extended character sketch.

WEBBER, GORDON. *What End But Love.* Boston: Little, Brown & Co., 1959. Family chronicle, with overtones of the rural-urban clash. The action proper takes place on Memorial Day, 1934, at the Michigan farm home of the family patriarch, Holly Hobart, but most of the novel is devoted to recounting, by means of flashbacks, the careers of the various people assembled there for a family gathering. They range from an auto executive and a Methodist minister to a pig farmer and garbage collector. Thus on one level it is a study, in depth, of varying personality types within one extended family. On another level, and less effectively, it is a study of the gradual encroachment of industry and urban life on rural America. A strong novel technically, it misses making an important contribution to rural fiction only because it scarcely touches on farm life itself.

WELLMAN, PAUL ISELIN. *The Bowl of Brass.* Philadelphia: J. B. Lippincott Co., 1944. A tale of town building and county seat rivalry in southwestern Kansas late in the nineteenth century. The action is centered about the machinations of a group of disreputable promoters whose desire to obtain the county seat leads them to such devices as assigning names (from a Cincinnati telephone directory) to the inhabitants of a prairie-dog town and enrolling them as legal residents of the county. A love affair between a young farm hand and the youthful wife of a fanatically pious old farmer provides romantic interest. The style is undistinguished, but the author's sense of the comic redeems the novel from mediocrity.

WENDT, LLOYD. *Bright Tomorrow*. Indianapolis: Bobbs-Merrill Co., 1945. Story of anti-German feeling in a South Dakota community in the nine months preceding the United States entry into World War II. Mark Engles, a young farmer, suffers for his father's pro-German sentiments and is looked upon as a slacker by some local people, especially young men who have been drafted. Although Mark wants to enlist, he is saddled with the farm, and early in December 1941 he accidentally shoots himself in the foot, ending all likelihood of his serving in the army. Despite good description of farm life and accurate handling of speech, the novel lacks the authentic ring one might expect.

WESCOTT, GLENWAY. *The Apple of the Eye*. New York: Harper & Brothers, 1926. (Originally published in 1924.) Fictional study of the conflict in an adolescent boy's mind between the puritan and pagan attitudes toward sex. Dan Strane's mother teaches him that the body is a holy temple, not to be desecrated, but Mike Byron, a hired man with some university background, tells him that sex is harmful only if used to injure someone. When Mike gets a girl into trouble and deserts her and she goes insane and kills herself, Dan swings back to the puritan view. But the girl's father forgives Mike and takes a liberal position, so Dan's final position is closer to the pagan than to the puritan attitude. Background of farm life is skillfully depicted but definitely subordinated.

WESCOTT, GLENWAY. *The Grandmothers*. New York: Harper & Brothers, 1927. Subtitled "A Family Portrait," this novel is really a profound study of the emotionally blind, halt, and lame whose pictures appear in the family album that Alwyn Tower, an adolescent boy, examines at the beginning of the novel. Each person's life history is given, and fragments are included from the lives of minor characters who in some way influenced Alwyn's ancestors. A "heavy" book in the sense that it includes a relatively large amount of philosophical generalization and a small amount of dialogue and action, *The Grandmothers* attempts to analyze middle western civilization in terms of the deterioration of the high qualities of the pioneers through the baneful influence of the rural evangelical tradition. The conclusions are neither flattering nor hopeful. There is no condescension shown toward the farm people; all of the characters, rural and urban, are alike treated with something closer to pity than to disdain.

WILLIAMS, BEN AMES. *It's a Free Country*. Boston: Houghton Mifflin

Co., 1945. Eddie May, who has not finished high school, marries Lena Trump, who finished first in her class, and settles on his grandfather's farm, apparently in Iowa, about 1926. Twenty thousand dollars left by Grandpa dwindles rapidly under Eddie's mismanagement during the depression, the farm proves no good, and Eddie is unable to find work in town to support his growing family. Lena's only hope is that her daughter Lenora may achieve the goals of which marriage has deprived her. But when Lenora comes home pregnant and Lena sees the whole story repeating itself, she kills the girl with an axe. More sensational than searching, the novel suffers from poor characterization, improbabilities of plot, and undue brevity.

WILSON, MARGARET. *The Able McLaughlins.* New York: Harper & Brothers, 1923. Romantic, entertaining story of a Scottish colony in Iowa in the period during and after the Civil War. Wully McLaughlin, home on leave, falls in love with Chirstie McNair, and they reach an understanding. But when he comes back after the war, he finds her pregnant, as the result of being seduced by Peter Keith, on a promise of marriage. Wully marries Chirstie, and they pretend the child is their own. When Peter attempts to repeat his assault, Wully orders him out of the community. He later returns, and Wully sets out to kill him, but when he finds that Peter is dying and realizes his own happiness with Chirstie, he forgives Peter. Despite sentimentality and melodrama in the Wully-Chirstie-Peter triangle, the novel has distinct merits, chiefly the memorable portrayal of a distinct national group, the "Lairds of the Wapsipinicon."

WILSON, MARGARET. *The Law and the McLaughlins.* New York: Doubleday, Doran & Co., 1936. Inferior sequel to *The Able McLaughlins,* centered about a lynching and the unsuccessful attempt, prolonged over a period of time (1868–1876), to bring the criminals to justice. The main character is Willy (the "Wully" of the earlier novel), but he shares attention with his sister Jean, who develops a sympathy for the lynchers and even marries one of them, an unwilling accomplice in the act. Some space is given to the coming of the railroad and the development of a town on it, to which Willy and some of the other characters move. Little attention is given to farming, even in the earlier part of the book, when the characters are still ostensibly farmers.

WINTHER, SOPHUS KEITH. *Take All to Nebraska.* New York: Macmillan Co., 1936. A Danish family come to Nebraska after an unsuccessful attempt at farming in Massachusetts. Here they contend with a grasping landlord and an even more grasping private moneylender, indifference and hostility from the native Americans, and the usual quota of climatic and economic difficulties. A succession of misfortunes leaves them ready to return to Denmark in failure, when a sympathetic American takes pity on them and gives them encouragement and another chance to succeed. A bumbling style prevents this novel from being the major work of American fiction that its finely realized theme might otherwise make it. A half-hearted attempt at naturalistic frankness weakens rather than strengthens the total effect.

WINTHER, SOPHUS KEITH. *Mortgage Your Heart.* New York: Macmillan Co., 1937. Continuation of *Take All to Nebraska,* concerned mainly with the diverse careers of the Grimsen boys. Hans has a series of adolescent love affairs, goes away to the university, where he develops an interest in socialism and pacifism at the time of World War I. David and Alfred both marry, neither very wisely. Although Peter seems to be prospering, he is finally obliged to buy his rented farm at inflated prices to avoid being forced off. Despite the momentary lift caused by his ownership of land, the fear of a drop in prices leaves an ominous shadow over the Grimsen family as the novel ends.

WINTHER, SOPHUS KEITH. *This Passion Never Dies.* New York: Macmillan Co., 1938. In this final volume of the Grimsen trilogy, Hans leaves the university to help his father, hard-pressed by the postwar collapse of farm prices, has an affair with and marries Karla Marshall, who is later killed, later takes up with the daughter of the backer of local figures who are buying up farms at mortgage sales, and finally marries her. Meanwhile Alfred's wife dies, David and his wife break up, and Peter loses the farm but dies before he has to leave it. The trilogy ends in defeat for the older generation and with only a slight ray of hope for their children. The second and third novels are better written than the first but weakened (in the third) by melodrama.

WISE, EVELYN. *As the Pines Grow.* New York: D. Appleton-Century Co., 1939. A Southern gentleman straight out of nineteenth-century romantic fiction comes to Minnesota for his health and buys a large farm. Although he becomes the local patriarch, he never really comes to love the country and is profoundly displeased when his son gives indications of wishing to be a farmer. In spite of the father's efforts to make farming distasteful to the son, the latter persists in his affection for the soil and finally wins his father's consent to his wishes. A minor novel in nearly all respects.

ZIETLOW, E. R. *These Same Hills.* New York: Alfred A. Knopf, 1960. Sensitively told story of the maturation of eighteen-year-old Jim Heiss, whose father owns a ranch in western South Dakota. Torn between his parents' conflicting wishes concerning him, he gives up his trap line (approved by his father) in order to give more attention to school and preparation for college (approved by his mother). While running the trap line, he has been influenced by Rudolph Koenig, old bachelor who represents the past and a way of life admirable but no longer practicable. Koenig's death in a blizzard ends this relationship, and Jim turns toward the future. The characterization, dialogue, and setting are handled well, and serious issues are probed in a short novel.

BIBLIOGRAPHY

I. FICTION

The following list includes novels from regions other than the Middle West, pre-twentieth-century middle western fiction, two anthologies of middle western writing, and two collections of short fiction by twentieth-century authors who did some of their work in farm fiction. Works classified as "middle western farm fiction" will be found in the annotated bibliography.

CAREY [CARY], ALICE. *Clovernook, or Recollections of Our Neighborhood in the West.* [First Series.] New York: J. S. Redfield, 1852. A collection of thirty-six stories of rural life in southwestern Ohio.

———. *Clovernook, or Recollections of Our Neighborhood in the West: Second Series.* New York: A. C. Armstrong & Son, 1884. (Originally published in 1853.) Fourteen stories similar to those in the earlier volume.

CARROLL, GLADYS HASTY. *As the Earth Turns.* New York: Macmillan Co., 1936. A farm novel with a New England setting.

CATHER, WILLA. *Obscure Destinies.* New York: Alfred A. Knopf, 1932. Contains "Neighbour Rosicky" and two stories with a small-town setting.

EGGLESTON, EDWARD. *The Hoosier Schoolmaster.* New York: Orange, Judd & Co., 1871.

FISHER, VARDIS. *In Tragic Life.* Caldwell, Idaho: Caxton Printers, 1933. A harsh and brutal story of farm life in Idaho.

FLANAGAN, JOHN T., ed. *America Is West.* Minneapolis: University of Minnesota Press, 1945. An anthology of middle western writing.

FLINT, MARGARET. *The Old Ashburn Place.* New York: Dodd, Mead & Co., 1936. A New England farm novel, similar in style and setting to *As the Earth Turns.*

FREDERIC, HAROLD. *Seth's Brother's Wife.* New York: Charles Scribner's Sons, 1886.

FREDERICK, JOHN T., ed. *Out of the Midwest.* New York: McGraw-Hill

Book Co., 1944. An anthology comparable to *America Is West*, but confined to writings by authors whose work appeared after 1910.

GIBBONS, STELLA. *Cold Comfort Farm*. London: Longmans, Green & Co., 1932. A burlesque farm novel, apparently intended to satirize *Seth's Brother's Wife* or its British counterparts.

GLASGOW, ELLEN. *Barren Ground*. Garden City, N.Y.: Doubleday, Page & Co., 1925. A farm novel with a Virginia setting.

HOWE, EDGAR WATSON. *The Story of a Country Town*. New York: Albert & Charles Boni, 1926. (Originally published in 1883.)

——. *The Story of a Country Town*. New York: Dodd, Mead & Co., 1927. Contains an introduction by Howe, who also made substantial revisions in the text for this edition.

KIRKLAND, CAROLINE MATILDA. *A New Home, or Life in the Clearings*. New York: G. P. Putnam's Sons, 1953. (Originally published as *A New Home—Who'll Follow?* [New York: C. S. Francis, 1839].) Contains a useful introduction by John Nerber.

KIRKLAND, JOSEPH. *Zury: The Meanest Man in Spring County*. Boston and New York: Houghton Mifflin Co., 1887.

——. *Zury: The Meanest Man in Spring County*. Urbana: University of Illinois Press, 1956. A facsimile reprint containing a valuable introduction by John T. Flanagan.

MCCONNEL, JOHN LUDLOM. *Western Characters, or, Types of Border Life in the Western States*. New York: J. S. Redfield, 1853. Ten sketches, descriptive rather than narrative, of frontier types representative of various stages in the history of the Old Northwest. Only one, "The Pioneer," deals with farm life.

RILEY, HENRY H. *Puddleford, and Its People*. New York: Samuel Hueston, 1854. Series of twenty-two skecthes, unified by time, place, and a set of characters, dealing with small town life in the Old Northwest.

——. *The Puddleford Papers, or, Humors of the West*. New York: Derby and Jackson, 1857. A republication of the 1854 volume, with five additional chapters.

ROBERTS, ELIZABETH MADOX. *The Time of Man*. New York: Viking Press, 1926. A farm novel with a Kentucky setting.

STEINBECK, JOHN. *The Grapes of Wrath*. New York: Viking Press, 1939.

TAYLOR, BAYARD. *The Story of Kennett*. New York: G. P. Putnam's Sons, 1881. (Originally published in 1866.)

THOMPSON, MAURICE. *Hoosier Mosaics*. Gainesville, Fla.: Scholars' Facsimiles and Reprints, 1956. (Originally published in 1875.) Nine stories about rural life in Indiana, containing a mixture of romanticism and realism. Introduction by John T. Flanagan.

WESCOTT, GLENWAY. *Good-Bye Wisconsin.* New York: Harper & Brothers, 1928. A collection of short stories and other writings.

II. CRITICAL AND BIOGRAPHICAL BOOKS

AHNEBRINK, LARS. *The Beginnings of Naturalism in American Fiction.* Cambridge: Harvard University Press, 1950. Useful on Garland.

ATHERTON, LEWIS. *Main Street on the Middle Border.* Bloomington: Indiana University Press, 1954.

BENNETT, MILDRED R. *The World of Willa Cather.* New York: Dodd, Mead & Co., 1951.

BERNARD, HARRY. *Le Roman régionaliste aux Etats Unis.* Montreal: Fides, 1949.

BLEDSOE, THOMAS A., ed. *Hamlin Garland: Main-Travelled Roads.* New York: Rinehart & Co., 1954. Contains a valuable introduction which takes issue with Ahnebrink on the question of Garland's naturalism.

BRIGHAM, JOHNSON, ed. *A Book of Iowa Authors by Iowa Authors.* Des Moines: Iowa State Teachers Assoc., 1930.

BROWN, EDWARD K. *Willa Cather: A Critical Biography.* New York: Alfred A. Knopf, 1953.

BROWN, HERBERT ROSS. *The Sentimental Novel in America 1789–1860.* Durham: Duke University Press, 1940.

BROWN, MORRISON. *Louis Bromfield and His Books.* Fair Lawn, N.J.: Essential Books, 1957.

CARTER, EVERETT. *Howells and the Age of Realism.* Philadelphia: J. B. Lippincott Co., 1950.

COWIE, ALEXANDER. *The Rise of the American Novel.* New York: American Book Co., 1948.

DAICHES, DAVID. *Willa Cather: A Critical Introduction.* Ithaca: Cornell University Press, 1951.

DONDORE, DOROTHY. *The Prairie and the Making of Middle America.* Cedar Rapids. Torch Press, 1926.

GARLAND, HAMLIN. *Crumbling Idols.* Cambridge: Harvard University Press, 1960. (Originally published in 1894.)

———. *Roadside Meetings.* New York: Macmillan Co., 1930.

246   Bibliography

——. *A Son of the Middle Border.* New York: Macmillan Co., 1944. (Originally published in 1917.)

GARLAND, JOHN H., ed. *The North American Midwest.* New York: John Wiley & Sons, Inc., 1955.

GELFANT, BLANCHE HOUSMAN. *The American City Novel.* Norman: University of Oklahoma Press, 1954.

GROVE, FREDERICK PHILIP. *A Search for America.* New York, London, and Montreal: Louis Carrier & Co., 1928.

HAZARD, LUCY LOCKWOOD. *The Frontier in American Literature.* New York: Thomas Y. Crowell Co., 1927.

HENSON, CLYDE E. *Joseph Kirkland.* New York: Twayne Publishers, 1962.

HERRON, IMA HONAKER. *The Small Town in American Literature.* Durham: Duke University Press, 1939.

HUTTON, GRAHAM. *Midwest at Noon.* Chicago: University of Chicago Press, 1946.

JENSEN, MERRILL, ed. *Regionalism in America.* Madison: University of Wisconsin Press, 1951.

JORGENSON, THEODORE, and NORA O. SOLUM. *Ole Edvart Rölvaag: A Biography.* New York: Harper & Brothers, 1939.

KUNITZ, STANLEY J. *Twentieth Century Authors: First Supplement.* New York: H. W. Wilson Co., 1955.

KUNITZ, STANLEY J., and HOWARD HAYCRAFT. *Twentieth Century Authors.* New York: H. W. Wilson Co., 1942.

LEWIS, EDITH. *Willa Cather Living.* New York: Alfred A. Knopf, 1953.

LUCCOCK, HALFORD E. *Contemporary American Literature and Religion.* Chicago and New York: Willett, Clark & Co., 1934.

MCAVOY, THOMAS T., ed. *The Midwest: Myth or Reality?* Notre Dame, Ind.: University of Notre Dame Press, 1961. Includes contributions by John T. Flanagan, John T. Frederick, and others.

MILLETT, FRED B. *Contemporary American Authors.* New York: Harcourt, Brace & Co., 1940.

MORDELL, ALBERT, comp. *The World of Haldeman-Julius.* New York: Twayne Publishers, 1960. A collection of short pieces by Haldeman-Julius, most of them trivial. Contains "Foreword" by Harry Golden and "Profile" by Sue Haldeman-Julius.

MORLAN, ROBERT L. *Political Prairie Fires: The Nonpartisan League 1915–1922.* Minneapolis: University of Minnesota Press, 1955.

MURRAY, JOHN J., ed. *The Heritage of the Middle West*. Norman: University of Oklahoma Press, 1958.

PARRINGTON, VERNON LOUIS. *The Beginnings of Critical Realism in America*. New York: Harcourt, Brace & Co., 1930.

PATTEE, FRED LEWIS. *The New American Literature 1890–1930*. New York: Century Co., 1930.

QUICK, HERBERT. *One Man's Life*. Indianapolis: Bobbs-Merrill Co., 1925.

RAPIN, RENE. *Willa Cather*. New York: Robert M. McBride & Co., 1930.

RANDEL, WILLIAM PEIRCE. *Edward Eggleston*. Gloucester, Mass.: Peter Smith, 1962.

RICHARDS, CARMEN NELSON, and G. R. BREEN. *Minnesota Writes*. Minneapolis: Lund Press, 1945.

———. *Minnesota Writers*. Minneapolis: T. S. Denison, 1961.

RIDEOUT, WALTER B. *The Radical Novel in the United States, 1900–1954*. Cambridge: Harvard University Press, 1956.

RUSK, RALPH LESLIE. *The Literature of the Middle Western Frontier*. New York: Columbia University Press, 1925.

SALOUTOS, THEODORE, and JOHN D. HICKS. *Agricultural Discontent in the Middle West 1900–1939*. Madison: University of Wisconsin Press, 1951.

SMITH, HENRY NASH. *Virgin Land*. Cambridge: Harvard University Press, 1950.

SOROKIN, PITIRIM, and CARLE C. ZIMMERMAN. *Principles of Rural-Urban Sociology*. New York: Henry Holt and Co., 1929.

SUCKOW, RUTH. *Carry-Over*. New York: Farrar & Rinehart, 1936. Introduction by Miss Suckow contains interesting comments on her own work.

TAYLOR, CARL C., et al. *Rural Life in the United States*. New York: Alfred A. Knopf, 1949.

WARFEL, HARRY R. *American Novelists of Today*. New York: American Book Co., 1951.

WOOD, GRANT. *Revolt Against the City*. Iowa City: Clio Press, 1935.

III. ARTICLES

BAILEY, L. H. "Can Agriculture Function in Literature?" *The Midland*, IV (May–June 1918), 103–105.

BAKER, JOSEPH E. "Four Arguments for Regionalism," *Saturday Review of Literature*, XV (November 28, 1936), 3–4, 14.

————. "Regionalism in the Middle West," *American Review*, IV (March 1935), 604–614.

————. "Western Man Against Nature," *College English*, IV (October 1942), 19–26.

Boie, Mildred. "The Myth About the Middle West," *Spectator*, CXLV July 5, 1930), 9–10.

Boynton, Percy H. "O. E. Rölvaag and the Conquest of the Pioneer," *English Journal*, XVIII (September 1929), 535–542.

Bradford, Curtis. "Willa Cather's Uncollected Short Stories," *American Literature*, XXVI (January 1955), 537–551.

Brashear, Minnie M. "Missouri Literature Since the First World War: Part III—The Novel," *Missouri Historical Review*, XLI (April 1947), 241–265.

Bromley, Dorothy Dunbar. "A Prize-Winner's Adventures in Real Life," *Literary Digest International Book Review*, IV (August 1926), 557.

Buley, R. Carlyle. "Glimpses of Pioneer Mid-West Social and Cultural History," *Mississippi Valley Historical Review*, XXIII (March 1937), 481–510.

Caldwell, Erskine. "Brilliant and Tedious," *Nation*, CXXXVII (September 6, 1933), 277. Review of Bromfield's *The Farm*.

Carroll, Latrobe. "Willa Sibert Cather," *Bookman*, LIII (May 1921), 212–216.

"Chronicle and Comment," *Bookman*, LXX (January 1930), 529–544. Contains photograph of G. D. Eaton and Burton Rascoe, editors of *Plain Talk*, in their office.

Clark, John Abbot. "The Middle West—There It Lies," *Southern Review*, II (Winter 1937), 462–472.

Coblentz, Stanton A. "A Realist Portrays American Farm Life," *Literary Digest International Book Review*, III (April 1925), 331.

Commager, Henry Steele. "The Literature of the Pioneer West," *Minnesota History*, VIII (December 1927), 319–328.

Cordell, Richard A. "Limestone, Corn, and Literature: the Indiana Scene and Its Interpreters," *Saturday Review of Literature*, XIX (December 17, 1938), 3–4, 14–15.

Crawford, Nelson Antrim. "The American Farmer in Fact and Fiction," *Literary Digest International Book Review*, IV (December 1925), 25–26, 28; (January 1926), 100–101.

DiLeva, Frank D. "An Attempt to Hang an Iowa Judge," *Annals of Iowa*, XXXII (July 1954), 337–364.

——. "Frantic Farmers Fight Law," *Annals of Iowa*, XXXII (October 1953), 81–109.

——. "Iowa Farm Price Revolt," *Annals of Iowa*, XXXII (January 1954), 171–202.

Dondore, Dorothy. "Points of Contact Between History and Literature in the Mississippi Valley," *Mississippi Valley Historical Review*, XI (September 1924), 227–236.

Dougherty, Charles T. "Novels of the Middle Border: A Critical Bibliography for Historians," *Historical Bulletin*, XXV (May 1947), 77–78, 85–88.

Feld, Rose. "Iowa Town," *New York Times Book Review*, September 7, 1941, pp. 7, 22. Review of *County Seat*.

Fielding, William J. "Prince of Pamphleteers," *Nation*, CLXXIV (May 10, 1952), 452–453.

Flanagan, John T. "A Bibliography of Middle Western Farm Novels," *Minnesota History*, XXIII (June 1942), 156–158.

——. "Joseph Kirkland, Pioneer Realist," *American Literature*, XI (November 1939), 273–284.

——. "The Middle Western Farm Novel," *Minnesota History*, XXIII (June 1942), 113–147.

——. "A Note on Joseph Kirkland," *American Literature*, XII (March 1940), 107–108.

——. "Thirty Years of Minnesota Fiction," *Minnesota History*, XXXI (September 1950), 129–147.

Frederick, John T. "Early Iowa in Fiction," *Palimpsest*, XXXVI (October 1955), 389–420.

——. "The Farm in Iowa Fiction," *Palimpsest*, XXXII (March 1951), 121–152.

——. "The First Person Plural," *Midland*, I (January 1915), 1.

——. "New Techniques in the Novel," *Palimpsest*, XXX (June 1949), 169–172.

——. "Ruth Suckow and the Middle Western Literary Movement," *English Journal*, XX (January 1931), 1–8.

——. "The Writer's Iowa," *Palimpsest*, XI (February 1930), 57–60.

Gray, James. "The Minnesota Muse," *Saturday Review of Literature*, XVI (June 12, 1937), 3–4, 14.

HASS, VICTOR P. "No Chance of Victory," *New York Times Book Review*, August 5, 1962, p. 20.

HENSON, CLYDE E. "Joseph Kirkland's Influence on Hamlin Garland," *American Literature*, XXIII (January 1952), 458–463.

HERBST, JOSEPHINE. "Iowa Takes to Literature," *American Mercury*, VII (April 1926), 466–470.

HICKS, GRANVILLE. "The End of Mighty Thurs," *New York Times Book Review*, December 30, 1951, p. 5.

HOLADAY, CLAYTON A. "Kirkland's *Captain of Company K*: A Twice-Told Tale," *American Literature*, XXV (March 1953), 62–68.

HOLBROOK, WEARE. "The Corn Belt Renaissance," *Forum*, LXXII (July 1924), 118–120.

HOWELLS, WILLIAM DEAN. "Editor's Study," *Harper's New Monthly Magazine*, LXXXIII (September 1891), 639–640.

"An Iowa Farm," *New York Times Book Review*, October 5, 1930, p. 6.

KOHLER, DAYTON. "Glenway Wescott: Legend-Maker," *Bookman*, LXXIII (April 1931), 142–145.

KRUTCH, JOSEPH WOOD. "The Tragic Lift," *Nation*, CXIX (August 20, 1924), 194–195.

LABUDDE, KENNETH J. "A Note on the Text of Joseph Kirkland's *Zury*," *American Literature*, XX (January 1949), 452–455.

LEASE, BENJAMIN. "Realism and Joseph Kirkland's *Zury*," *American Literature*, XXIII (January 1952), 464–466.

"Leroy MacLeod," *Wilson Bulletin for Librarians*, VII (September 1932), 78, 88.

McDOWELL, TREMAINE. "Regionalism in the United States," *Minnesota History*, XX (June 1939), 105–118.

MATTHEWS, T. S. "Fiction vs. Blurbs," *New Republic*, LXXVI (September 20, 1935), 166.

MAY, GEORGE S. "Iowa's Consolidated Schools," *Palimpsest*, XXXVII (January 1956), 1–64.

MEYER, ROY W. "Naturalism in American Farm Fiction," *Journal of the Central Mississippi Valley American Studies Association*, II (Spring 1961), 27–37.

———. "The Scandinavian Immigrant in American Farm Fiction," *American Scandinavian Review*, XLVII (September 1959), 243–249.

"Minnesota Has a Writing Boom," *Life*, XXIV (March 8, 1948), 125–129.

MULDER, ARNOLD. "Authors and Wolverines," *Saturday Review of Literature*, XIX (March 4, 1939), 3–4, 16.

OLSON, JULIUS E. "Rölvaag's Novels of Norwegian Pioneer Life in the Dakotas," *Scandinavian Studies*, IX (August 1926), 45–55.

PAGE, EUGENE R. "I'm From Missouri," *Saturday Review of Literature*, XXII (April 27, 1940), 3–4, 19.

POWELL, DESMOND. "Sophus Winther: The Grimsen Trilogy," *American Scandinavian Review*, XXXVI (June 1948), 144–147.

SHERMAN, CAROLINE B. "The Development of American Rural Fiction," *Agricultural History*, XII (January 1938), 67–76.

———. "Rural Literature Faces Peace," *South Atlantic Quarterly*, XLII (January 1943), 59–71.

SMITH, HENRY NASH. "The Western Farmer in Imaginative Literature, 1818–1891," *Mississippi Valley Historical Review*, XXXVI (December 1949), 479–490.

"Social History of the Dakota Prairies," *New York Times Book Review*, May 17, 1925, p. 8.

STACE, FRANCIS. "Michigan's Contribution to Literature," *Michigan Historical Magazine*, XIV (Spring 1930), 226–232.

STEGNER, WALLACE. "The Trail of the Hawkeye: Literature Where the Tall Corn Grows," *Saturday Review of Literature*, XVIII (July 30, 1938), 3–4, 16–17.

SUCKOW, RUTH. "The Folk Idea in American Life," *Scribner's Magazine*, LXXXVIII (September 1930), 245–255.

———. "Iowa," *American Mercury*, IX (September 1926), 39–45.

———. "Mature Youth," *Nation*, CXIX (December 10, 1924), 654.

———. "Middle Western Literature," *English Journal*, XXI (March 1932), 175–181.

"Thomas Boyd Joins the Rush Back to the Farm," *New York Times Book Review*, August 30, 1925, p. 8.

IV. UNTITLED ARTICLES AND REVIEWS

Michigan Alumnus, XXXII (1926), 561; XXXVI (1930), 655. Contains biographical material on G. D. Eaton.

Midland, XX (March–April, May–June 1933), 56. Contains biographical material about Frederick and historical facts about the *Midland*.

Nation, CXX (May 6, 1925), 524. Review of *Backfurrow*.

New Yorker, XXII (January 18, 1947), 93. Review of *The Thresher*.

New Yorker, XXIII (March 29, 1947), 101. Review of *This Is the Year*.

New York Herald Tribune Books, September 2, 1962, p. 6. Review of *The Bones of Plenty*.

New York *Times*, January 11, 1939, p. 6; January 12, 1939, p. 5; January 13, 1939, p. 5; January 17, 1939, p. 12. Historical background on Missouri boot-heel demonstration described in Cook's *Boot-Heel Doctor*.

New York Times Book Review, February 15, 1925, p. 16. Review of *Backfurrow*.

New York Times Book Review, October 7, 1928, p. 20. Review of *Our Daily Bread*.

New York Times Book Review, September 7, 1941, p. 22. Review of *County Seat*.

Many other reviews have been consulted, but these are the only ones quoted in the text and notes of this book.

V. UNPUBLISHED MATERIALS

LEWISON, NORA V. "The Achievement of Willa Cather." Doctoral dissertation, State University of Iowa, 1944.

MEYER, ROY WILLARD. "The Middle Western Farm Novel in the Twentieth Century." Doctoral dissertation, State University of Iowa, 1957. This constitutes the basis for the present book, but additions and changes are sufficient to justify listing it separately.

ACKNOWLEDGMENTS

Among the many people who have contributed in various ways to the making of this book, the two to whom I owe the most are Professors Alexander Kern, chairman of the American Civilization program at the State University of Iowa, and Merrill F. Heiser, a member of the English Department at that university when the dissertation on which the book is based was in preparation. The suggestions of these two men, who served as co-chairmen of my committee, were helpful to a degree that even I am perhaps no longer fully able to appreciate, so thoroughly have the leads they offered been assimilated to my thinking. Of the other members of my committee, I owe a special debt to Professor Richard Wilmeth, of the Department of Sociology at the State University of Iowa. As one totally without formal training in sociology, I would have completely overlooked many of the implications of farm fiction as a reflection of rural life but for the helpful suggestions of Dr. Wilmeth.

The starting point for the original dissertation was a list of sixty middle western farm novels, compiled by John T. Flanagan in 1942. The overall organization of the dissertation and the judgments offered in the concluding chapter were in large part determined by my reading of the novels on this list.

Among the farm novelists themselves, I feel a special sense of gratitude to Herbert Krause, now at Augustana College, Sioux Falls, South Dakota, for his willingness to comment on my treatment of his works and to correct some misinterpretations which had crept into my observations.

In the task of tracking down many elusive, out-of-print novels and scraps of biographical information on some of the novelists, I have been aided by library personnel at several universities. Miss Ada Stoflet, reference librarian at the State University of Iowa libraries, deserves special mention, as do Mrs. Sue Heil, Mrs. Kay Skorr, and Mrs. Judith Lokensgard, who have successively handled interlibrary-loan duties at Mankato State College.

My wife Betty has followed this project since its inception and aided me in more ways than I can possibly enumerate. Her suggestions and criticisms, especially in regard to style, have been judicious, needed, and, I fear, largely ineffectual.

ROY W. MEYER

Index

The numbers in boldface indicate the pages in the Appendix on which a particular author or title is discussed.